Ian POPPLE Otto WAGNER Peter McDOUGALL

BONAIRE

SCUBA DIVE SNORKEL SURF

TURNER
PUBLISHING COMPANY

TURNER PUBLISHING COMPANY
Nashville, Tennessee
www.turnerpublishing.com

Reef Smart Guides Bonaire (Revised Edition)

www.reefsmartguides.com

Series concept and writer: Ian Popple
Art concept and illustrations: Otto Wagner
Writer/Editor: Peter McDougall

Front cover photo Nick Polanszky Photo/Shutterstock ©
Back cover photo Otto Wagner/Reef Smart ©

Library of Congress Control Number: 2025942189

Printed in the United States of America

REEF SMART GUIDES

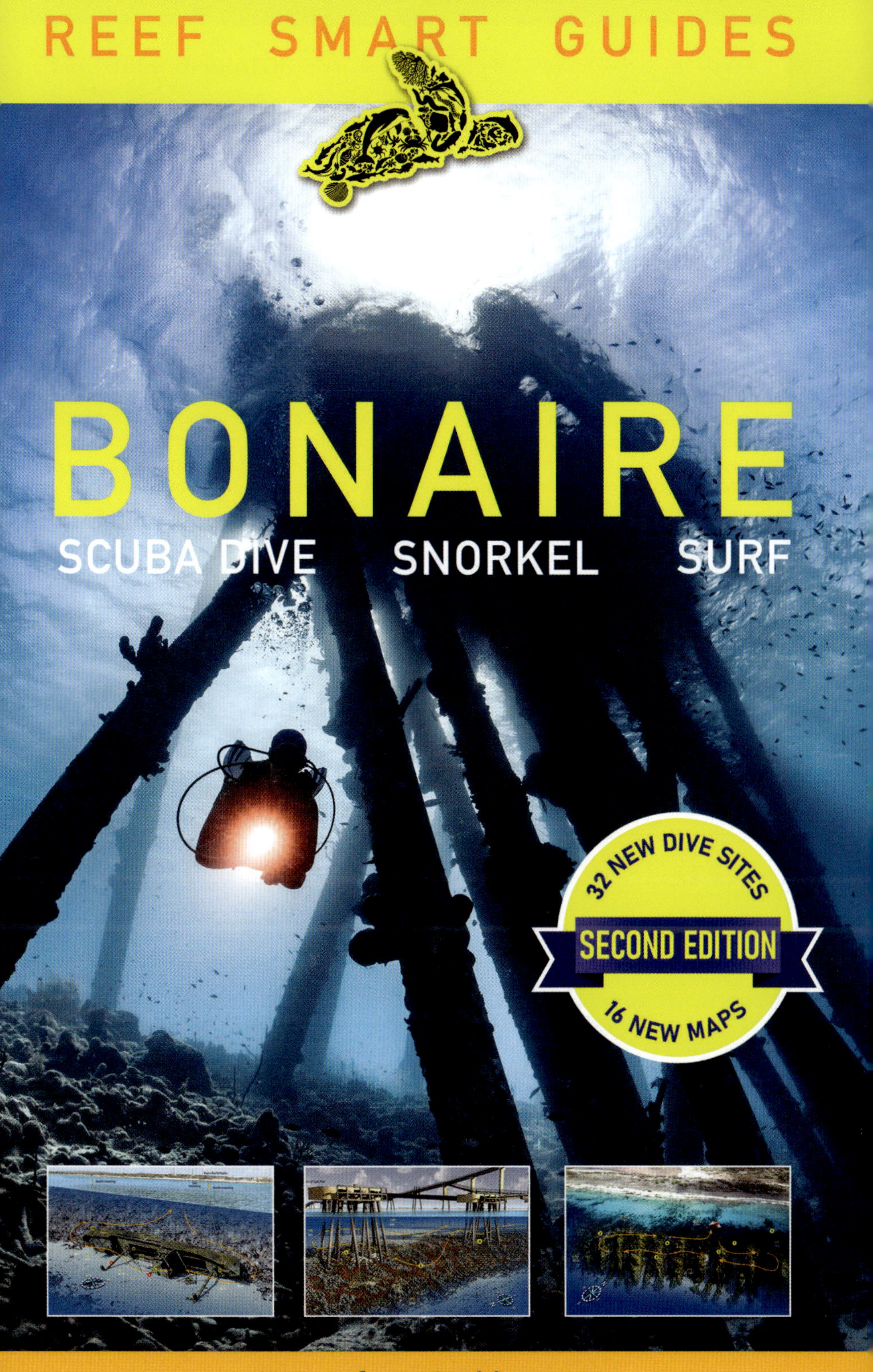

www.reefsmartguides.com

Acknowledgments

Reef Smart is indebted to numerous individuals and organizations who contributed their advice, knowledge, artwork, and support to the production of this guidebook. We would particularly like to thank Frederick Vloeberghs and Joyce Sonnevelt at Palm Trading and Paul Coolen at Buddy Dive Resort and Sapias Holding Ltd. Their support and valuable insight was crucial to the completion of this book. Augusto Montbrun, Martin Cicilia, and the professional and talented dive team at Buddy Dive Resort were always available to provide advice and frequently helped our mapping team reach dive sites during our data-collection trips. We would also like to thank Carmen Toanchina, who was an incredible source of support and knowledge for the second edition, and who assisted us in drafting the pages on stony coral tissue loss disease (SCTLD). We are also grateful to numerous recreational divers, too many to name, who happened to be visiting Bonaire during our fieldwork and were happy to share their experiences on all aspects of the island, from the dive sites to the Relax & Recharge options. We would like to mention Paul Kapsos in particular, as he accompanied us as we mapped a number of locations featured in this book. We would like to thank the representatives of STINAPA and the Reef Renewal Foundation Bonaire who responded to questions or reviewed text.

About Reef Smart:

Reef Smart creates detailed guides of the marine environment, particularly coral reefs and shipwrecks, for recreational divers, snorkelers and surfers. Our products are available as printed guidebooks, waterproof cards, wall posters, dive briefing charts and 3D interactive maps, which can be used on websites and as apps. Reef Smart also provides additional services to resorts that are dedicated to offering an environmentally aware experience for their guests. These include marine biology training for dive professionals and resort staff, implementation of coral reef monitoring and restoration programs, and the development of sustainable use practices that reduce the impact of operations on the natural environment.

www.reefsmartguides.com

How to use this book 6
Our "blue planet" 8
About Bonaire 9
Location and formation 9
The history of Bonaire 10
Bonaire today 11
Getting there and getting around 12
Environment 13
Ecosystems 15
Marine conservation and management 16
Reef Renewal Foundation Bonaire 18
Stony Coral Tissue Loss Disease (SCTLD) 20
Washington Slagbaai National Park 22
Bonaire beaches 24
In case of emergency 26
Emergency contacts 26
Kiteboarding 28
Diving and snorkeling 30
Diving and snorkeling services 32
Boka Bartól 38
Boka Katuna 40
Playa Bengé 42
Playa Funchi 44
Bisé Morto 46
Wayaká II 48
Boka Slagbaai 50
Playa Frans 54
Nukove (Doblet) 56
Carel's Vision 58
Tailor Made 60
Candyland 64
Windjammer 66
Karpata 68
La Dania's Leap 72
Rappel 74
Bloodlet 76
Tolo (Ol' Blue) 78
Country Garden 82
Bon Bini Na Kas 84
1000 Steps 86
Weber's Joy (Witches Hut) 90
Jeff Davis Memorial 92
Kalli's Reef 96
Oil Slick Leap 98
Barcadera 102
Andrea II 104
Andrea I 106
Petrie's Pillar 108
Small Wall 110
Coopers Barge 114
The Cliff 120
La Machaca 124
Reef Scientifico / Buddy's Reef 128
Bari 132
Front Porch 136
Something Special (Pali Grande) 142
Calabas Reef 146
18th Palm 148
Windsock 152
Corporal Meiss (North Belnem) 156
Bachelor's Beach (Fondu Di Kalki) 158
Chez Hines 162
Lighthouse Point 164
Punt Vierkant 168
The Lake 170
Hilma Hooker 174
Angel City 180
Alice in Wonderland 184
Aquarius 188
Larry's Lair 190
Jeannie's Glory 192
Salt Pier 194
Salt City 198
Invisibles 202
Tori's Reef 206
Pink Beach (Kabayé) 208
White Slave 210
Wanda 212
Margate Bay 214
Red Beryl 218
Atlantis 220
Fish Hut 222
Vista Blue 224
Sweet Dreams 228
Soft Coral Garden 230
Hidden Beach 232
Yellow Hut 234
Chogogo 236
Red Slave 238
Willemstoren Lighthouse 242
About Klein Bonaire 250
Jerry's Sponges 258
Keepsake 262
South Bay 266
Hands Off 270
Forest 274
Carl's Hill 278
Knife 282
Species 286
Index of Sites 318

How to use this book

Objective

The main objective of this guidebook is to provide a resource for people, particularly divers and snorkelers, who are interested in exploring the underwater environment of Bonaire. This guide is designed to be used alongside Reef Smart waterproof cards, which can be taken into the water. This book will be most useful for watersports enthusiasts, but it also includes information that any visitor to the area will find useful.

Mapping

We have attempted to catalog as many of the region's dive and snorkel sites as we can, from the northwest to the southeast and out to the island of Klein Bonaire. We have presented these sites using Reef Smart's unique 3D-mapping technology. These maps provide useful information such as depths, expected currents and waves, suggested routes, potential hazards and unique attributes.

Disclaimer

Reef Smart guides are for recreational use only—they are not navigational charts and should not be used as such. We have attempted to provide accurate and up-to-date information for each site, as well as activities to enjoy in the surrounding areas. However, businesses close and new ones open, prices are adjusted, and change is inevitable in the marine environment. The information contained in this guide is accurate only at the time of publication. The size and location of structures may vary. Depths and distances are approximated in both metric and imperial units, and the suggested route is optional. Every diver should dive to their certification and level of experience.

Reef Smart assumes no responsibility for inaccuracies and omissions and assumes no liability for the use of these maps. If you identify information that should be updated, please contact us at: info@reefsmartguides.com

ECO TIP

We hope this guide enhances your in-water experience. Share your passion for exploring the marine environment with others, because our oceans, and particularly coral reefs, need all the "likes" they can get. Coral reefs, as well as mangrove and seagrass ecosystems, are under serious pressure from a multitude of threats that include coastal development, pollution, over-fishing and global climate change. Some estimates put over half the world's remaining coral reefs at significant risk of being lost in the next 25 years; raising awareness can help protect them.

Information boxes

Additional information for the featured sites is provided in the form of special information boxes that appear throughout the book:

DID YOU KNOW?

Interesting facts about the site or the surrounding area.

SAFETY TIP

Advice that aims to improve safety.

ECO TIP

Information that will help limit damage to the ecosystem or improve environmental awareness.

RELAX & RECHARGE

Information on where refreshments can be purchased, or where to unwind on land. No compensation was received in exchange for featuring these establishments.

SCIENTIFIC INSIGHT

Information of a scientific nature that can help you understand what you see and experience.

Map icons

 Scuba dive

  Snorkel

 Wreck

 Access by boat

 Access by swim

 Access by car

 Access by walk

Surf

Kiteboard

 Wind surf

Species identification

The species listed for each location were chosen to represent the most unique or common organisms found at each site, as determined from personal observations, discussions with divers and snorkelers who have experienced these sites, and from scientific studies conducted in these areas. Many of the species described in this publication are mobile or cryptic (or both), and so may not always be found where indicated. However, we have attempted to place key species on each map in the locations where they are most commonly found.

Species description

The species letters and numbers on each map link to descriptions located at the back of the book (on pages 286-316). Reef Smart uses the most frequently cited common name for a species. As common names vary from place to place, we have also provided the scientific name for each species, which remains the same worldwide. Scientific names are usually of Latin or Greek origin and consist of two words: a genus name followed by a species name. By definition, a species is a group of organisms that can reproduce together such that it results in fertile offspring; a genus is a group of closely related species.

The descriptions of each species are based on the scientific literature as it existed at the time of publication. Scientific knowledge often advances, however, and the authors welcome any information that helps improve or correct future editions of this guidebook. In-depth species profiles, including images and videos, are available for free on our website—**Reefsmartguides.com.**

Our "blue planet"

Oceans

Water covers nearly three-quarters of our planet's surface and approximately 96 percent of this water is contained in the major oceans of the world. Together, the oceans drive our planet's weather, regulate its climate and provide us with breathable air, which ultimately supports every living creature on Earth.

The oceans are vital to our global economy. They produce the food that billions of people depend on for survival, while also being a source of resources, including valuable medicines that treat a wide range of ailments and diseases. The oceans also drive local and regional economies through tourism. Every year, millions of travelers are drawn to coastal regions to enjoy activities above the water and to explore what lies below the surface. Considering how important the oceans are to our way of life, it is incredible how little we know about what lies beneath the sea.

Coral reefs

The oceans include a wide range of different ecosystems, but perhaps the most frequently visited marine ecosystems of all are coral reefs. Coral reefs are known as the rainforests of the sea for good reason—they are one of the most diverse ecosystems on the planet, supporting nearly a quarter of all known ocean species. This figure is even more astounding when considering that coral reefs comprise just a fraction of one percent of the ocean floor. They are also particularly vulnerable to degradation, given they are only found in a narrow window of temperature, salinity and depth.

Humans have studied the biology and physiology of corals for decades, but the underwater environment remains largely foreign to most people. Fact is, we have more accurate maps of the surface of Mars than we do of the seafloor. And guides of the marine environment suitable for recreational users are almost non-existent.

Reef Smart aims to change this situation. Our detailed guides seek to educate snorkelers and divers alike. Our goal is to improve safety and enhance the marine experience by allowing users to discover the unique features and species that can be found at each site.

Preserve and protect

Hopefully our guidebooks and waterproof dive guides will help readers get to know the underwater environment in general, and reefs in particular. We feel that the more people can come to appreciate the beauty of the underwater world, the more they will be willing to take steps to protect and preserve it.

The world's oceans are experiencing incredible pressures from all sides. Rising temperatures, increasing acidification and an astonishing volume of plastics that end up in both the water and marine organisms are endangering these precious resources.

Yes there are some big problems to overcome. But we can do this. Each and every one of us can make a difference in the choices we make. And together we can help make sure the beauty of the coral reefs of this world are still around for future generations of snorkelers and divers to enjoy.

Sincerely, the Reef Smart team

A view of the water near downtown Kralendijk.

About Bonaire

Location and formation

Bonaire is located to the west of the Caribbean island chain known as the Lesser Antilles. It is 25 miles (40 kilometers) east of Curaçao and 50 miles (80 kilometers) north of the coast of Venezuela, and this small, remote island has established a reputation as an international dive destination. Bonaire is considered by many divers to have the best shore diving in the Caribbean, and possibly even the world, with something for everyone mere steps from the beach.

The island is flat, rocky, and dry. Its highest point tops out at just 784 feet (241 meters) above sea level, and it has a total area of 113 square miles (290 square kilometers). It measures 17 miles (27 kilometers) from north to south and varies in width from 3 to 7 miles (5 to 11 kilometers) with a shape that vaguely resembles a boot with its toes pointing south. Bonaire's rocks are volcanic in origin, dating back to the Cretaceous period that ended more than 65 million years ago. This mass of rock, known as the Washikemba formation, was pushed up toward the surface of the water after shifts in the underlying tectonic plates raised the surrounding continental shelf shortly after the Eocene epoch, a period that ended more than 33 million years ago.

Marine sediment settled on the volcanic rocks, eventually covering it in layers of limestone. Coral reefs formed during various parts of the Pleistocene era, which dates from 2.6 million years ago to just 11,700 years ago. As sea levels rose and fell during this time, the limestone and reef covering the island eroded away. Evidence of this process is visible today in the terraces (Lower, Middle, and Higher Terraces) that appear around the island, most notably in the northeastern regions of the national park. The original volcanic rock lies exposed in some parts of the island, while others still have their limestone covering. The corals shifted along with the changing sea level and are now restricted to the waters surrounding the island.

Paulo Miguel Costa/Shutterstock©

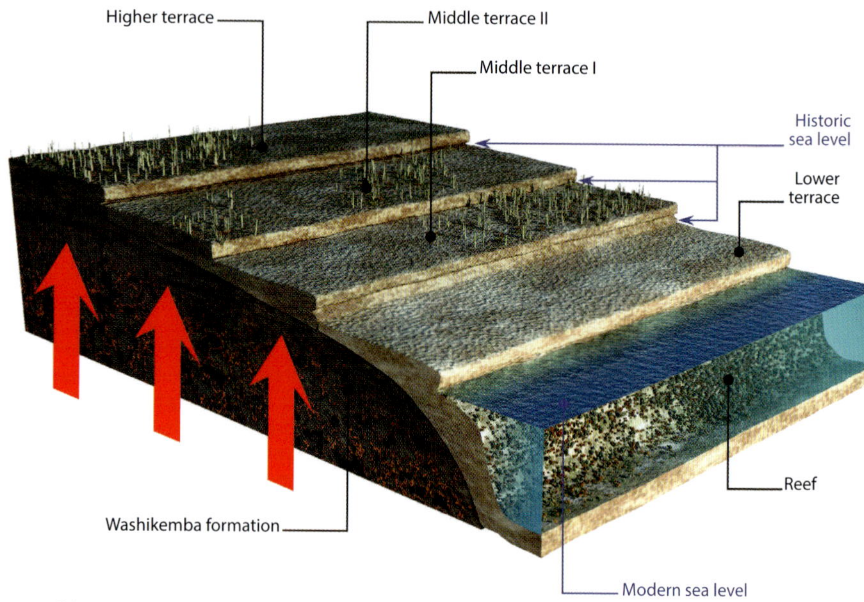

Diagram of the geology of Bonaire.

The history of Bonaire

Bonaire's recorded history began with the arrival of the Spanish in 1499, led by Spanish explorer Alonso de Ojeda and his Italian counterpart, Amerigo Vespucci. But the island's history began well before that year.

Early history

The first human presence on Bonaire dates back to 2,500 BC with the presence of the Arkaiko Indians. Later, the Caquetio Indians, a branch of the Arawak Indians who settled across much of the southern Caribbean, arrived in Bonaire between 800 AD and 1000 AD, traveling by canoe from the coast of what is now Venezuela. They left their mark in the form of petroglyphs and cave paintings at many sites around the island. When the Spanish conquered the three islands of Aruba, Curaçao, and Bonaire, they captured and enslaved the local indigenous population, and sent them to work the plantations and mines of Hispaniola.

Originally deemed useless by the Spaniards, Bonaire eventually became a cattle plantation, with the arrival of repatriated Caquetio Indians and domesticated animals. The few Spanish who remained on the island lived in the interior, in the village of Rincón. The island was eventually ceded to the Dutch in 1636 and was later resettled with African slaves.

Bonaire changed ownership multiple times due to the shifting European politics of the 18th century. In 1816, the island returned to Dutch control once and for all, and quickly developed into a major production center for salt. The economic growth did not last long, however, since the end of the slave trade just a few decades later shut the industry down for nearly a century.

Recent history

Bonaire's economy began to find its legs after the island's government built its first shipping pier in the harbor at the turn of the century. The new pier allowed cruise liners to disembark passengers directly to shore and ushered in a new commercial era for the island, along with making it easier to bring in supplies to the island's permanent residents. Construction of hotels and a modern airport helped establish Bonaire as a tourist destination in the years following the Second World War.

Salt production resumed in the 1960s and the tourism industry gradually increased over the past half century, particularly with the rise in popularity of recreational SCUBA diving and snorkeling.

Until recently, Bonaire has been part of the constituent country of the Netherlands Antilles. As of 2010, however, and after a referendum and a great many constitutional discussions, the Netherlands Antilles was dissolved. Bonaire, along with St. Eustatius and Saba, is now a municipality of the Netherlands. This means Bonaire residents have the same rights (and follow the same laws) as Dutch citizens living in continental Europe. By comparison, Curaçao, Aruba, and St. Maarten opted to become autonomous countries within the kingdom of the Netherlands, with their own separate governments.

Bonaire today

Population

Bonaire has a population of 24,000 people, which is experiencing a modest growth rate. The island's economy is largely dependent on tourism, thanks mainly to its mild, dry climate and stunning coral reefs. As a result, residents are outnumbered by annual visitors. The island's other major economic sectors include oil transference and salt production.

The basics

The official language of Bonaire is Dutch, although residents also speak their own local language of Papiamento, which is a mix of Dutch, Spanish, French, English, and Portuguese, among others. This language is shared with the residents of nearby Curaçao and Aruba. English is widely spoken in Bonaire, and Spanish speakers should have little trouble making themselves understood, given that Papiamento has strong Spanish roots.

The electricity supply in Bonaire is not quite a match for either North American or European standards: 127 volts / 50 hertz. The outlets are designed for both European and U.S. standard plugs, and most appliances should work well enough. But travelers may want to purchase (or rent) converters and surge protectors while on the island to help protect their more sensitive electronics due to any differences in voltage. The internet is widely available, with a number of free Wi-Fi zones established around the island. Tap water is safe to drink and is generated through desalination—a process where the salt and minerals in seawater are filtered out, leaving clean fresh water.

Visitors

Nearly two-thirds of the island's visitors arrive via cruise ship while the remainder primarily arrive by plane. Bonaire is also a popular destination for private yachts. Visitors originate from North America and other parts of the kingdom of the Netherlands for the most part, with the balance visiting from Latin America and Europe.

One of the famous yellow painted rocks that mark the dive sites of Bonaire.

The yellow facade of Rincón's St. Louis Bertrand Church.

Getting there and getting around

Getting there

The island is a popular cruise destination; visitors will often see a cruise ship towering over downtown Kralendijk, the island's capital and main city. Bonaire has one airport, Flamingo International Airport (BON), which is most frequently reached via connections through Curaçao or Aruba. Direct flights are

DID YOU KNOW?

For each dive and snorkel site in this guidebook, we describe how to get there by providing directions and time estimates from downtown Kralendijk. We selected the corner of Kaya Gobernador Nicolaas Debrot and Kaya L.D. Gerharts as the starting point. Please adjust drive times and directions based on the actual start point. We have also provided GPS locations for each site. Wherever possible, GPS for the shore-accessible sites are in the parking lot, while those sites only accessible by boat feature the location of the buoy.

Andy Troy/Shutterstock ©

possible from Amsterdam and from select North American cities, including Toronto, New York, Miami, Atlanta, and Houston.

Getting around

Bonaire has no public transit system. Visitors can use a taxi (call one by dialing +599-717-8100) or, more commonly, can rent a car or truck from one of the major rental agencies on the island. Renting a pickup truck is most popular among divers in Bonaire given the accessibility of shore diving sites and the ability to carry plenty of tanks and gear safely in the bed of the truck. Divers should reserve their choice ahead of time, particularly if they require one with an automatic transmission, as standard transmission cars far outnumber automatics on the island. North Americans will be comforted to learn that driving is on the right side of the road, although do not be surprised by the absence of traffic lights—Bonaire relies on traffic circles or roundabouts to manage traffic flow through intersections.

Scooters, quads (four-wheel all-terrain vehicles) and pedal bicycles of various formats are also available for rent. It does not often rain on the island outside of the rainy season (from December through March), but when it does rain, the roads can get very slippery. Be careful and obey the speed limits (which are posted in kilometers per hour). Roads are also narrow and not always in the best shape—particularly some of the dirt roads that service the sites in the northwest. Also, pay attention to road signage: In particular, the Queen's Highway converts from a two-way to a one-way road at the 1000 Steps dive site. Once past that point, visitors will have to continue along the highway to Karpata before heading north to Rincón and looping back to Kralendijk by way of the Kaminda Sabana Piedra Krus road, which briefly runs along the east coast.

Environment

Weather

Bonaire has a very dry and mild climate, with consistently warm temperatures no matter the time of year. Average highs range from 90°F (32°C) in August down to 86°F (30°C) in December and January. Average lows show little variation from month to month, ranging from 77°F (25°C) to 81°F (27°C) throughout the year. Bonaire's rainy season is from December through March, and though a regular daily shower might be expected during this time, the rain does not stick around for long. Bonaire lies outside the Caribbean hurricane belt.

Water temperatures in Bonaire are also quite stable throughout the year. They average around 79°F (26°C) in February and March, and 84°F (29°C) in September and October. Many divers wear only a rash-guard for protection, but for those who get cold easily, consider bringing a wetsuit or renting one from a local dive center.

Waves and visibility

Bonaire experiences a steady, easterly trade wind for most of the year. As a result, the protected west coast rarely experiences large waves or rough seas while the less-developed east coast has very strong surf. The latter is exposed to the full force of the wind except during late August and September, when the trade winds change direction and blow from the west. The corals of Bonaire thrive in the protected lee of the island. Another factor that contributes to the high quality of the reef is the crystal-clear waters. Visibility often exceeds 80 feet (25 meters) and great viz paired with steady sunshine and white coral sand turn the waters between the shore and the fringing reef a gorgeous azure-blue color that people have come to expect from a tropical paradise.

Currents and tides

The tidal cycle in Bonaire is mild, measuring a mere foot to a foot and a half (less than a meter). It is enough to make a difference in some of the entry points over shallow reefs, but nothing that will unduly impact a day of diving. Currents along the west coast are typically light, although there can be a strong long-shore current along the island's many reef walls. A few dive sites near the far south of the island and in the extreme north regularly experience strong currents, particularly where the east coast currents wrap around either end of the island and come into contact with the calmer waters of the west coast.

Natural mangroves line many of the coastal roads in southern Bonaire.

Andy Troy/Shutterstock ©

A view of the pink salt ponds from above the Cargill Salt Works.

Ecosystems

Coral reefs

All of Bonaire's reefs are fringing reefs, meaning they are situated close to shore—sometimes just 30 feet (10 meters) from the shoreline. Most reefs start relatively shallow and descend at a steep angle, and some of them form true walls that descend almost vertically down to depths of 130 feet (40 meters) or more.

The shallow back reef area between the reef line and the shore is often filled with soft corals and healthy stands of staghorn coral—a sign of the quality of Bonaire's reefs. Elkhorn coral replaces the staghorn in areas with stronger currents and wave action. This type of habitat offers protection to small juvenile reef fishes. And the proximity of this nursery habitat to the reef wall helps promote the diversity and abundance of reef species throughout the whole ecosystem.

Mangroves

Bonaire has small areas of mangrove habitat near the southern end of the island, along the stretch of coastal road to the south and around the saliñas in the north. A much larger mangrove system thrives on the east coast of the island in the shallow waters of Lac Bay. Mangroves help stabilize coastal shorelines and prevent erosion from damaging the nearby reef systems. Do not damage any mangrove trees when accessing dive sites from the shore and pay attention to the delicate aerial roots that may be underfoot when crossing a saliña to reach a shore dive. Park only in designated areas to avoid damaging the surrounding mangrove ecosystem.

The east coast mangrove ecosystem is located in Lac Bay. It is one of the best-preserved mangrove ecosystems in the Caribbean. The nearby Bonaire Mangrove Center (**Mangrovecenter.com**) offers guided kayak and boat tours throughout the day on every day of the week except Sunday, when the center is closed. Snorkeling tours are also provided through the mangrove channel and out across the adjacent seagrass beds. The Lac Bay mangroves are part of a system of marine protected areas and terrestrial parks that cover nearly 60 percent of Bonaire.

DID YOU KNOW?

One reason for the remarkable health and quality of Bonaire's fringing reefs is the fact that the island shelters the west coast from the high winds that almost exclusively come from the east. In the absence of high winds, the surf is rarely strong, which allows the corals to survive and thrive. Another reason: the low degree of development and lack of large-scale agriculture means there is little by way of nutrient-rich runoff to promote algal growth, which can outcompete corals for space on the reef. Last—but certainly not least—Bonaire has been very proactive in helping protect its reef resources and surrounding waters as far back as the 1960s, which helped sustain the country's coral reefs.

Marine conservation and management

Bonaire fringing reefs are home to more than 350 species of reef fishes and almost every species of hard and soft coral present in the Caribbean. The island is considered a biodiversity hotspot in the Caribbean and has earned an international reputation for not just the quality of its diving but its successful conservation programs as well—proof positive that tourism and conservation can be mutually beneficial forces. The Bonaire government takes their duty to manage these resources seriously, and the nation has undertaken many conservation and management initiatives to protect the environment. In fact, the Bonaire model is considered so successful that the United Nations Environment Program (UNEP) has designated it a demonstration site, and the model was the basis for a similar program in Indonesia.

STINAPA

Stichting Nationale Parken (STINAPA) Bonaire is a non-governmental organization tasked with managing the island's two main national parks: the Bonaire National Marine Park (Marine Park) and the Washington Slagbaai National Park (see page 22). Divers must pay a user fee (referred to as a Nature Fee by STINAPA) which can be paid online at **Stinapa.Bonairenaturefee.org**. All proceeds help support park management and services.

Isabelle Kuehn/Shutterstock ©

A stretch of the northwestern coast showcasing its lack of development.

Bonaire National Marine Park

The Marine Park encompasses the waters around Bonaire, including the harbor and the less developed east coast. The Marine Park was first established in 1979, but it quickly ran into financial challenges and was left without any day-to-day management. With the increase in dive-related tourism in the 1990s, efforts to finance the park and put it on a sustainable footing succeeded in revitalizing management and providing the island's reefs with a level of protection necessary to keep them healthy.

The management of Bonaire's coastal waters also includes two marine reserves. These stretches of coastline are off limits to divers even though they include a few well-known dives, such as the Windjammer wreck in the northwest part of the island just beyond Karpata. STINAPA occasionally issues permits to dive these sites for the purposes of research and monitoring, but they are not accessible to the general public and so are not described in detail in this guidebook.

Please respect the diving restrictions in these areas. The purpose of the marine reserves is to provide a control group should the reefs in Bonaire begin to show signs of degradation. The lack of diver pressure in these regions is an important part of maintaining a healthy reef system in Bonaire, so we strongly encourage divers to respect the rules regarding no diving in the reserves.

DID YOU KNOW?

Bonaire charges a tourism tax to visit the island. Most visitors opt to pay this online, prior to arrival, in order to avoid delays at the airport. After payment visitors receive a QR Code via the email address used to register, which must be shown to the authorities at the airport upon arrival.

Diving in Bonaire carries with it a few very important rules that all divers and snorkelers must follow. They include:

- All divers must attend an orientation at the dive center where they have their tanks filled, including information about the island and the rules regarding diving, as well as an in-water check out dive to demonstrate buoyancy control among other basic skills.
- Spear fishing is prohibited, and visitors must leave their gear with a customs official when they arrive.
- Collecting or removing anything, alive or dead, from the water is strictly prohibited. This includes dead coral found when walking across the beach.
- Divers must maintain control of their buoyancy to avoid touching or damaging the coral, or kicking up sediment from the bottom that might smother the coral or damage other marine habitats, such as seagrass beds.
- Divers and snorkelers are not permitted to wear gloves while in the water, with only a few medical exceptions that require a permit from the STINAPA headquarters near Oil Slick Leap.
- Chemical night sticks are not permitted in the waters of the Marine Park.
- Do not disturb or otherwise interfere with sea turtles either in the water or as they nest on land, including on the beaches of Klein Bonaire.
- Do not light campfires on the beach.
- Do not anchor anywhere in the Marine Park—mooring buoys are provided at all sites accessible by boat, and are available on a first-come, first-served basis for boats under 45 feet (15 meters) and for a maximum of 2 hours. No overnighting.
- Boats must navigate to the seaward side of the mooring buoys and remain in the dark water.

The rules and regulations for the Marine Park are in place to help protect the corals for future generations. Please respect the rules and contribute to keeping Bonaire one of the top shore-diving destinations in the world.

Reef Renewal Foundation Bonaire

Reef Renewal Foundation Bonaire (RRFB) is a non-profit organization focused on restoring Bonaire's biodiverse coral reefs as they face mounting threats and a rapidly changing environment. In collaboration with research partners and regional practitioners, RRFB uses science-backed techniques to enhance the abundance, genetic diversity, and overall resilience of vulnerable coral populations on Bonaire. Today, with the help of 16 partner dive operators around the island and a dedicated team of volunteers, RRFB has outplanted over 60,000 corals at sites around Bonaire, restoring a total reef area of over 140,000 square feet (13,000 square meters).

Reef Renewal Foundation Bonaire ©

Coral Nursery Network

RRFB grows thousands of coral fragments in their network of 15 nurseries around Bonaire and Klein Bonaire. Each nursery hosts a range of coral species and genotypes, which are monitored for tolerance to disease and heat stress. Fragments grow in these nurseries until they're ready to be outplanted on natural reefs, helping restore and strengthen Bonaire's coral populations.

Outplanting Efforts

When corals in the nursery grow large enough, RRFB divers transport them to restoration sites around Bonaire and Klein Bonaire. Their team uses species-specific outplanting methods, suited to local reef conditions, to securely attach the corals and support their survival. By monitoring coral growth and health over time, valuable data is gathered to refine restoration techniques and track progress.

Reef Renewal Foundation Bonaire ©

Reef Renewal Foundation Bonaire ©

Join the Movement

Volunteers are essential to RRFB's mission, driving coral restoration across the island. Any certified diver can become a Reef Renewal Diver by taking the Reef Renewal specialty course, offered exclusively through RRFB partner dive shops. Through this course, divers join a growing community of ocean stewards dedicated to actively restoring and protecting Bonaire's coral reefs. For more information on how to get involved, contact **info@reefrenewalbonaire.org.**

Courtesy of David J Fishman ©

Stony Coral Tissue Loss Disease (SCTLD)

Stony Coral Tissue Loss Disease (SCTLD) is one of the most devastating coral diseases known to impact marine ecosystems. First identified in 2014 off the coast of Miami, Florida, SCTLD quickly became known for its rapid spread and severe impact. It currently affects over 30 coral species, including those that form the structural foundation of Western Atlantic coral reefs.

The exact cause of SCTLD remains uncertain; however, researchers believe it is caused by a bacterial pathogen that spreads through waterborne transmission. Research shows that materials such as coral mucus, dead tissue or disturbed sediments may carry the pathogen, which can remain active in the water for extended periods.

The disease leads to tissue loss that exposes the coral skeleton, often resulting in complete colony mortality in a matter of weeks. Unlike many other coral diseases, SCTLD's ability to infect a wide range of coral species and its aggressive progression make it particularly devastating. To date, outbreaks of SCTLD have been reported in 33 countries and territories across the Caribbean.

Some of the coral species most affected by SCTLD include

- Boulder brain coral *(Colpophyllia natans)*
- Pillar coral *(Dendrogyra cylindrus)*
- Elliptical star coral *(Dichocoenia stokesii)*
- Grooved brain coral *(Diploria labyrinthiformis)*
- Smooth flower coral *(Eusmilia fastigiata)*
- Maze coral *(Meandrina meandrites)*
- Symmetrical brain coral *(Pseudodiploria strigosa)*

Timeline of SCTLD progression

- **2014-2017** The disease was first detected near Miami and spread rapidly through Florida's coral reef system, including the Florida Keys, causing significant coral mortality.
- **2018** SCTLD was confirmed in Jamaica, the Mexican Caribbean, and St. Maarten, marking its spread beyond U.S. waters.
- **2019** The disease reached Belize, the Dominican Republic, Turks and Caicos, Puerto Rico, and the U.S. Virgin Islands.
- **2020-2021** SCTLD was confirmed in over 22 countries across the Caribbean, including the Bahamas, St. Lucia, and additional regions in Central America.
- **2022** SCTLD was detected on Bonaire's reefs, threatening one of the Caribbean's most renowned marine ecosystems. Authorities responded swiftly with measures such as closing infected dive sites, implementing strict dive gear decontamination protocols, and using antibiotic treatments to slow the disease's progression.

Bonaire's Response to SCTLD

1. Rapid detection and monitoring: Dive operators, scientists and volunteers have been trained to identify SCTLD and report new cases. Regular reef monitoring ensures early detection and targeted interventions.
2. Treatment with antibiotics: A special antibiotic paste (such as amoxicillin mixed with a coral-safe base) is applied to infected corals to slow the progression of the disease. While this treatment is labor-intensive, it has shown promise in saving individual coral colonies.
3. Education, outreach and gear disinfection protocols: Bonaire has launched public awareness campaigns to educate visitors and residents about SCTLD, its impacts, and how they can help. This has included gear disinfection protocols that can help prevent the spread of the disease between dive sites.
4. Research and collaboration: Bonaire's conservation teams are working closely with international scientists and regional organizations to better understand SCTLD and develop more effective treatment strategies.

A brain coral affected by stony coral tissue loss disease (SCTLD).

Liz Grogan/Shutterstock©

Washington Slagbaai National Park

Bonaire's National Park covers just under 14,000 acres (more than 56 square kilometers) of the island's northwestern region—an area just smaller than the size of Manhattan Island in New York. Originally known as Washington National Park, it was founded on May 9, 1969, when the owner of the Washington plantation donated the land for use as a nature preserve.

The park's name changed to the Washington Slagbaai National Park in 1979 when the Slagbaai plantation gained protected status, leading to the successful preservation of an area equivalent to a fifth of the island of Bonaire. The park is accessible through a single entrance located about 2.5 miles (4 kilometers) north of Rincón. There is a visitor center and museum at the entrance. The park itself contains multiple hiking trails, cultural sites, two protected wetland areas—Saliña Slagbaai and Saliña Goto—and seven dive and snorkel sites located on the park's more sheltered west coast.

STINAPA manages the park and charges an access fee to all visitors. Divers can enter the park for free by bringing their STINAPA Nature Fee tag or receipt, as well as identification. Visitors are not allowed to spend the night in the park unless they have reserved a stay in the Boka Slagbaai plantation house ahead of time.

When visiting the park, divers should consider getting there early; the gates are open from 8:00am to 5:00pm but the rangers will not permit anyone to enter past 2:30pm. Divers should begin their final dive by 2:30pm to ensure there is enough time to exit the park. The round-trip drive through the park can take two hours or more, depending on conditions, and rangers recommend visitors depart Wayaká II by 3:30pm,

The Suplado Blow Hole on the northeast coast of the island.

RELAX & RECHARGE

Visitors to the park should not miss **The Rose Inn**. This chilled out restaurant located in downtown Rincón serves hearty and delicious Caribbean stews—often chicken, fish, beef or goat—accompanied by local sides such as plantain, polenta and moro, which is a flavorful mix of rice and beans. Do not be in a hurry when you visit this place—the food is served in their shaded outdoor courtyard at the relaxed pace of Rincón life, often with a soundtrack of old-school reggae or calypso. So, sit back, unwind, soak up the atmosphere and enjoy a traditional taste of Bonaire. **The Rose Inn** is closed on Wednesdays.

and Boka Slagbaai by 4:00pm, to ensure there is enough time to exit the park before the gates close. Rangers do a sweep of the park starting from the north at 3:30pm to make sure everyone is respecting these deadlines.

The roads in the park are unpaved and can be deeply rutted at times, so a vehicle with relatively high clearance, such as a four-wheel drive, is recommended. In the rainy season (December through March) some dive sites may become inaccessible because of the condition of the road. Consider calling ahead after a heavy rain to check on the status of the road before driving all the way up to the park: +599-788-9015.

In addition to the dive sites, there are several other notable features, such as Playa Chikitu, which is one of Bonaire's only true sand beaches, the Suplado Blow Hole, which is most impressive during periods of high surf, and the 190-foot-tall (58-meter) limestone cliffs at Seru Grandi. The massive boulders in the nearby area are remnants of powerful tsunamis that lifted these rocks out of the ocean and deposited them on the flats.

SAFETY TIP

Washington Slagbaai National Park covers a massive area of beautiful and unspoiled habitat. It is also a remote and unpopulated region with little to no access to water. When venturing into the park, divers should make sure to have at least a half tank of gas and a spare tire. They should bring plenty of water along with sunscreen and proper attire, including a hat for sun protection. For visitors planning on a hike, check in at the park entrance to learn about possible routes, and remember to stick to the path.

Bonaire beaches

Due to the forces that formed Bonaire, the island is not ringed with continuous, sandy beaches like those found on other Caribbean islands. But hidden away among the nooks and crannies of an otherwise rocky coastline are nearly two dozen gorgeous beaches that offer a great place to unwind. Described below are some of the best beaches on Bonaire. Others, such as **Wayaká II**, **Boka Slagbaai**, and **Atlantis Beach**, are associated with individual dive sites, and are discussed in more detail in the dive section of the book.

Kokolishi Beach (Playa Kokolishi)
Kokolishi Beach is a secluded, 80-foot-wide (25-meter) stretch of dark-sand beach tucked away at the back of a long, narrow cove. It is found near the northern tip of the island, and while it may not be worth a whole day, it is worth a visit while passing through the park.

Chikitu Beach (Playa Chikitu)
Located a ways off of the National Park's long road and less than a half mile (0.7 kilometers) southeast of Kokolishi Beach, Chikitu Beach is a picturesque cove looking out on the rough waters of the Atlantic. There is no swimming here due to dangerous currents and rip tides, but this is one of the only places on Bonaire that has real sand dunes.

Coco Beach (Playa Lechi, Eden, Harbour Village)
This stretch of beach is actually a few beaches adjacent to the Bari and Front Porch sites. This is not a secluded beach, but there is plenty to enjoy here, including beach volleyball and refreshments.

The turquoise waters of Bachelor's Beach.

Reef Smart ©

Te Amo Beach
Located just north of Playa Palu di Mangel (Donkey Beach, next to Windsock), Te Amo Beach is a white-sand beach that looks out on the calm waters between Klein Bonaire and downtown Kralendijk. The beach is crowded on weekends, but less so during the week.

Bachelor's Beach
Bachelor's Beach is a must-visit beach south of the airport. The beach is a small stretch of white sand at the base of the cliff, and it offers a memorable experience with the perfect turquoise waters that signal a Caribbean paradise.

Lac Cai
Located on the northern edge of Lac Bay on the east coast, Lac Cai beach is a gorgeous sandy beach next to the shallow, clear blue waters of the bay, and with a photo-worthy backdrop of healthy mangrove stands. This beach is popular with locals on the weekend but is a little off the beaten path for many visitors.

Sorobon Beach
Located at the southern edge of Lac Bay on the east coast, Sorobon Beach is a long stretch of sand where a small community has built up as a mecca for wind surfing. There are plenty of spots to relax along the waterfront, and even a beach bar called, appropriately enough, the Hang Out Beach Bar.

No Name Beach
This sandy beach is the drop-off point for the water taxi on the northeastern corner of Klein Bonaire, the uninhabited island that sits just 0.5 miles (0.8 kilometers) off the west coast of Bonaire. The beach has two shelters that provide shade and a few BBQ grills available but little else (charcoal is not provided). There is plenty of sand, sun, and warm water, however. This is a great way to spend a day away from the hustle and bustle of the main island, just bring plenty of water and sunscreen.

In case of emergency

There are many marine organisms that can put a damper on a visit to Bonaire, from jellyfish to fire corals and moray eels. Many of these potentially dangerous marine creatures are listed in a special section at the end of the book (pages 292–295) with information on the harm these species can cause and some of the common treatments.

Crime does exist on Bonaire, although the island is considered one of the safer places in the Caribbean for visitors. Visitors should approach their trip with an appropriate level of caution and safety-conscious behavior. Divers and snorkelers should not leave anything of value in a car while they go out into the water. In fact, many rental companies suggest leaving vehicle doors unlocked to demonstrate the absence of anything of value inside.

In the unlikely event of an injury, there are several places to seek quality medical care on the island. Bonaire's only hospital is the San Francisco Hospital located in downtown Kralendijk. The hospital has 60 beds, and patients who need to spend the night must bring their own overnight supplies, such as pillow, blankets, and toiletries. There are also a few clinics on the island, including some that cater to the diving community. Bonaire also has its own decompression chamber located just across the road from the hospital, which is available with a referral from the doctor on duty or the hospital. It also has an air ambulance service.

The healthcare system in Bonaire is adequate for most needs, but if the injury or illness is beyond the ability of the island's medical expertise, patients may need to be transported to Curaçao or elsewhere for treatment. Visitors should consider purchasing travel and dive-related health insurance prior to their trip. Without coverage, an accident could be costly.

In case of an emergency, here are some important numbers and places to seek help:

Emergency contacts

Police:	911
Hospital and Ambulance:	912
Fire department:	911

Headquarters of the Dutch Caribbean Police Force - Bonaire
4 Kaya Libertado Simon Bolivar, Kralendijk
Tel: +599-715-8000 (non-emergency)
Tel: +599-717-8000 (non-emergency)
Email: politie@politiecn.com
Politiecn.com/en/locations/

San Francisco Hospital (Fundashon Mariadal)
Kaya Soeur Bartola, Kralendijk
Tel: +599-715-8900 (non-emergency)
Email: info@fundashonmariadal.org
Fundashonmariadal.com

The Foundation Recompression Chamber Bonaire (located in the San Francisco Hospital)
Kaya Soeur Bartola, Kralendijk
Tel: +599-717-8187
Email: info@o2bonaire.com
O2bonaire.com

An exercise during diver safety training.

Roy Pedersen/Shutterstock ©

Kiteboarding

Bonaire offers visitors and locals near-perfect conditions for kiteboarding. Consistent winds, flat water and accessible beaches will appeal to kiteboarders of all experience levels. The kiteboarding schools and rental locations are concentrated near the southeastern coast, operating out of a small stretch of coastline known as Atlantis Beach—just over 3 miles (5 kilometers) south of the Salt Pier along the coastal road. The beach has become such a focal point for kiteboarding on the island that visitors are more likely to hear people refer to it by its unofficial name, Kite Beach.

The site is easy to spot from the road thanks to the small improvised village that springs up on the site during the day; the dozens of kiteboarders that can be seen out on the water at any given moment are another useful reference. The location includes two large school buses operated by the kiteboarding outfits. Food trucks, tents, lounge areas and even Wi-Fi hotspots offer kiteboarders a level of convenience and luxury they may not recognize in between trips out on the water.

The two big outfits operating out of Kite Beach are FX Bonaire Kiteschool and Kiteboarding Bonaire, details bottom right. Both companies offer gear rentals and lessons for all experience levels from IKO-certified (International Kiteboarding Organization) instructors. A third operator, Chogogo Kite, operates from Coco Beach just north of Kralendijk.

Wind surfing

If kiteboarding is not appealing, head to the east coast and visit Sorobon Beach at Lac Bay. The shallow waters of the bay and steady winds from the east offer the opportunity for an afternoon of incredible wind surfing. Rentals are available on site as well as lessons for those interested.

A wind surfer cruises over the reef.

Maria Nelasova/Shutterstock ©

A kiteboarder catches some air.

FX Bonaire Kiteschool
Atlantis Beach (Kite Beach)
Kralendijk, Bonaire
Tel: +599-701-7873
Email: info@bonairekiteschool.com
Bonairekiteschool.com

Kiteboarding Bonaire
Atlantis Beach (Kite Beach)
Kralendijk, Bonaire
Tel: +599-701-5483, +599-786-4987
Email: info@kiteboardingbonaire.com
Kiteboardingbonaire.com

Windsurf Place
Sorobon, at Lac Bay
Kralendijk, Bonaire
Tel: +599-717-2288
Email: info@bonairewindsurfplace.com
Bonairewindsurfplace.com

Jibe City
Sorobon, at Lac Bay
Kralendijk, Bonaire
Tel: +599-717-5233
Email: info@jibecity.com
Jibecity.com

Diving and snorkeling

Bonaire has some of the best shore diving and snorkeling in the world. Its fringing reefs start just steps from the beach and offer a mix of shallow, soft coral forests, steep reef walls covered in sponges and hard corals, and a diverse assemblage of reef creatures that are sure to amaze even the most experienced of divers. The quality of the coral reefs is in part due to the steps taken by governmental and non-governmental organizations to preserve and protect the natural environment. The result: a paradise for divers and snorkelers.

The island takes its role as a steward of its marine resources seriously, from the government down to the many dive professionals who call Bonaire home. Everyone involved in the dive industry understands the importance of preserving the coral reefs for future generations and they all help uphold the rules. We have outlined some of the most important rules on page 17, so please follow them.

Bonaire's sites

One of the great things about diving and snorkeling in Bonaire is the ability to explore the marine environment with incredible freedom. To get the most out of their experience, divers will need either local knowledge or this guidebook and its accompanying waterproof cards. This guidebook includes information for every official dive site on Bonaire—and even some of the unofficial ones—including how to get to each site, how best to access the reef and a brief description of what divers can expect once they are in the water. Our three-star rating system

Reef Smart ©

Shore diving in Bonaire often means setting up gear on the ground.

SAFETY TIP

One popular dive site that has long been on the official list of Marine Park dive sites is no longer open. Located in downtown Kralendijk, #33 Town Pier was closed by STINAPA due to the risks associated with increased boat traffic.

STINAPA also does not recognize many east coast dive sites due to the inherent risks of diving those waters. The east coast offers some spectacular diving but these sites feature very strong currents and large waves. There are many stories of divers choosing to dive these challenging sites without a guide, only to end up being swept out to sea and needing to be rescued by boat.

Bonaire offers the opportunity to enjoy incredible shore diving at a leisurely pace and schedule. Divers and snorkelers should be smart about how and where they explore.

Snorkelers can enjoy easy access and calm waters at many of Bonaire's reefs. Gail Johnson/Shutterstock ©

provides information about the difficulty level, current strength, depth, and the quality of the reef and fauna likely to be encountered at a specific site.

For 37 of the most popular dive sites, this guidebook goes into greater detail, including 3D underwater maps of the sites and recommended routes. We also point out what species to look for and what key features to observe. Collectively, these site profiles provide a great idea of what is in store before entering the water.

Snorkeling

Bonaire has plenty for divers, but many of the dive sites also include fantastic snorkeling opportunities. Many of Bonaire's sites feature nearshore shallow plateaus that are filled with soft and hard corals, all of which support a variety of reef creatures—and are accessible to snorkelers at the surface. We use a snorkel icon to help highlight sites that offer the best snorkeling experience.

Diving and snorkeling services

Businesses are listed in alphabetical order. The information is accurate as of the publication.

4Wheel Diving Bonaire
Kaya Rotterdam 22, Kralendijk
Tel: +599-777-0440
Email: info@4wheeldiving.com
4wheeldiving.com

AB-Dive
Kaya Industria 31, Kralendijk
Tel: +599-717-8980
Email: info@ab-dive.com
Ab-dive.com

Area9 Mastery Diving Research Center
Barcadera 2, Kralendijk
Tel: +599-700-7808
Email: info@masterydiving.com
Masterydiving.com

Beyond the Corals
@ Bloozz Resort Bonaire
EEG Boulevard 37, Kralendijk
Tel: +599-795-3949
Email: info@beyondthecorals.com
Beyondthecorals.com

BIOdiversE
Kralendijk
Tel: +599-795-2436
Email: info@diveinbonaire.com
Diveinbonaire.com

Bonaire East Coast Diving
Kaminda Sorobon, Sorobon Beach
Tel: +599-717-5211
Email: info@bonaireeastcoastdiving.com
Bonaireeastcoastdiving.com

Bonaire Scuba
Kaya Uranus 2, Kralendijk
Tel: +599-777-3483
Email: info@bonairescuba.com
Bonairescuba.com

Buddy Dive
@ Belmar Oceanfront Apartments
EEG Boulevard 88, Kralendijk
Tel: +599-717-7878
Email: dive@belmar-bonaire.com
Belmar-bonaire.com

Buddy Dive
@ Buddy Dive Resort
Kaya Gobernador N. Debrot 85, Kralendijk
Tel: +599-717-5080
Email: info@buddydive.com
Buddydive.com

Buddy Dive
@ Buddy Dive Watersports
Kaya Libertador Simon Bolivar 6, Kralendijk
Tel: +599-717-5085
Email: watersports@buddydive.com
Buddydive.com

Captain Don's Habitat
Kaya Gobernador N. Debrot 103, Kralendijk
Tel: +599-717-8290
Email: roger@habitatbonaire.com
Habitatbonaire.com

Carib Inn
Julio A. Abraham Blvd 46, Kralendijk
Tel: +599-717-8819
Email: info@caribinn.com
Caribinn.com

Dive Center Scuba Do Bonaire @ Chogogo Resort
Kaya Gobernador N Debrot 75B, Kralendijk
Tel: +599-777-3200
Email: info@scubadobonaire.com
Scubadobonaire.com

Dive Diva Bonaire
Kralendijk
Tel: +599-785-8358
Email: info@divedivabonaire.com
Divedivabonaire.com

Dive Experience Bonaire
Kaya Virgo 16 A, Kralendijk
Tel: +599-787-2620
Email: info@dive-experience-bonaire.com
Dive-experience-bonaire.com

Dive Factory
Kaya Sirena, Kralendijk
Tel: +599-700-9819
Email: info@divefactorybonaire.com
Divefactorybonaire.com

Dive Friends Bonaire @ Retail & Dive
Kaya Gob. N. Debrot 52, Kralendijk
Tel: +599-780-2572
Email: info@divefriendsbonaire.com
Divefriendsbonaire.com

Shore dives are popular, but some sites can only be reached by dive boat. Reef Smart ©

Dive Friends Bonaire @ Delfins Beach Resort
Punt Vierkant 44, Kralendijk
Tel: +599-780-2572
Email: info@divefriendsbonaire.com
Divefriendsbonaire.com

Dive Friends Bonaire @ Dive Inn
EEG Boulevard 97, Kralendijk
Tel: +599-780-2572
Email: info@divefriendsbonaire.com
Divefriendsbonaire.com

Dive Friends Bonaire @ Hamlet Oasis
Kaya Gobernador N. Debrot 123, Kralendijk
Tel: +599-780-2572
Email: info@divefriendsbonaire.com
Divefriendsbonaire.com

Dive Friends Bonaire @ Port Bonaire
Kaya International 1, Kralendijk
Tel: +599-780-2572
Email: info@divefriendsbonaire.com
Divefriendsbonaire.com

Dive Friends @ Sand Dollar/Den Laman
Kaya Gobernador N. Debrot 77, Kralendijk
Tel: +599-780-2572
Email: info@divefriendsbonaire.com
Divefriendsbonaire.com

Dive Friends @ Yellow Submarine
Kaya Playa Lechi 24, Kralendijk
Tel: +599-780-2572
Email: info@divefriendsbonaire.com
Divefriendsbonaire.com

Setting up the boats for a day of diving at Buddy Dive Resort.

Divemaster Life
Bona Bista A36, Kralendijk
Tel: +599-796-2907
Email: info@divemasterlife.com
Divemasterlife.com

Divi Dive
@ Divi Flamingo Beach Resort
Julio A. Abraham Blvd 40, Kralendijk
Tel: +599-717-8285
Email: dive@diviflamingo.com
Diviresorts.com/bonaire

Div'ocean
Julio A. Abraham Blvd 82 #301, Kralendijk
Tel: +599-717-4944
Email: info@divoceanbonaire.com
Divoceanbonaire.com

Flamingo Diving
EEG Boulevard 260, Kralendijk
Tel: +599-786-8123
Email: info@flamingodiving.com
Flamingodiving.com

Gone Diving
Kaya Felipi G. Clarinda 8c, Kralendijk
Tel: +31-62-428-2659
Email: gonedivingbonaire@gmail.com
Gonedivingbonaire.com

Great Adventures Bonaire
@ Harbour Village
Kaya Gobernador N. Debrot 71, Kralendijk
Tel: +599-717-7500
Email: divemanager@harbourvillage.com
Harbourvillage.com

Private Divers Bonaire
Kaya Grandi 65, Kralendijk
Tel: +599-786-6763
Email: info@privatediversbonaire.com
Privatediversbonaire.com

Reef Divers Bonaire
Kaya Solo 3, Belnem
Tel: +599-785-1238
Email: reefdiversbonaire@gmail.com
Reefdiversbonaire.com

Scuba Elite
Kaya Antonio Neuman 7, Kralendijk
Tel: +599-795-6341
Email: info@scuba-elite.com
Scuba-elite.com

Technical Diving Services (TDS)
@ Capt. Don's Habitat
Kaya Gobernador N. Debrot 103, Kralendijk
Tel: +599-786-4782
Email: info@tdsbonaire.com
Tdsbonaire.com

Toucan Diving
@ Plaza Beach & Dive Resort
J.A. Abraham Blvd 80, Kralendijk
Tel: +599-717-2500
Email: diveshop@bonaire.valk.com
Toucandiving.com

Tropical Divers
J.A Abraham Blvd. 87, Kralendijk
Tel: +599-717-5111
Email: info@tropical-divers.com
Tropicaldiversbonaire.com

VIP Diving
Julio A. Abraham Blvd 77, Kralendijk
Tel: +599-701-7701
Email: info@vipdiving.com
Vipdiving.com

VIP TEC Diving
Julio A. Abraham Blvd 75, Kralendijk
Tel: +599-701-7701
Email: tec@vipdiving.com
Vipdiving.com

Wanderlust Dive Center
Kaya Perenales 3, Kralendijk
Tel: +599-786-9918
Email: info@wanderlustdivecenter.com
Wanderlustdivecenter.com

Wannadive
@ Eden Beach Resort
Kaya Gobernador N. Debrot 73, Kralendijk
Tel: +599-717-8884
Email: info@wannadive.com
Wannadive.com/eden-beach

Wannadive
@ Grand Windsock
EEG Boulevard 3, Kralendijk
Tel: +599-717-8884
Email: info@wannadive.com
Wannadive.com/grand-windsock

Xprodiver Bonaire
Kaya Grandi 54, Kralendijk
Tel: +599-777-7333
Email: bonaire@xprodiver.com
Xprodiver.com

Dive and snorkel sites — Access

1 Boka Bartól
1A Boka Katuna
2 Playa Bengé
3 Playa Funchi
4 Bisé Morto
5 Wayaká II
6 Boka Slagbaai

6A Playa Frans
7 Nukove (Doblet)
8 Carel's Vision
8A Tailor Made
8B Candyland
8C Windjammer
9 Karpata
10 La Dania's Leap
11 Rappel
12 Bloodlet
13 Tolo (Ol'Blue)
14 Country Garden
15 Bon Bini Na Cas
16 1000 Steps
17 Weber's Joy (Witch's Hut)
18 Jeff Davis Memorial
19 Kalli's Reef
20 Oil Slick Leap
21 Barcadera
22 Andrea II
23 Andrea I
24 Petrie's Pillar
25 Small Wall
25A *Coopers Barge*
26 The Cliff
27 *La Machaca*
28 Reef Scientifico
29 Buddy's Reef
30 Bari Reef
31 Front Porch
32 Something Special (Pali Grande)
33 Town Pier — CLOSED
34 Calabas Reef
35 18th Palm
36 Windsock
37 Corporal Meiss (North Belnem)
38 Bachelor's Beach (Fondu Di Kalki)
39 Chez Hines
40 Lighthouse Point
41 Punt Vierkant
42 The Lake
43 *Hilma Hooker*
44 Angel City
45 Alice In Wonderland
46 Aquarius
47 Larry's Lair
48 Jeannie's Glory
49 Salt Pier
50 Salt City
51 Invisibles
52 Tori's Reef
53 Pink Beach (Kabayé)
54 White Slave
54A Wanda
55 Margate Bay
56 Red Beryl
57 Atlantis
57A Fish Hut
58 Vista Blue
59 Sweet Dreams
59A Soft Coral Garden
59B Hidden Beach
59C Yellow Hut
59D Chogogo
60 Red Slave
61 Willemstoren Lighthouse

Dive and snorkel sites East Coast Bonaire — Access

61A Baby Beach
61B Shrimp Factory
61C Turtle City
62 White Hole
62A Funchi's Reef
63 Cai
63A Boca Onima

Dive and snorkel sites Klein Bonaire — Access

A No Name (Playita)
B Ebo's Reef
C Jerry's Sponges
D Just a Nice Dive
E Nearest Point
F Keepsake
G Bonaventure
H Monte's Divi
I Rock Pile
J Joanne's Sunchi
K Captain Don's Reef
L South Bay
M Hands Off
N Forest
O Southwest Corner
P Munk's Haven
Q Twixt
R Sharon's Serenity
S Valerie's Hills
T Mi Dushi
U Yellow Man
V Carl's Hill
W Ebo's Special
X Leonora's Reef
Y Knife
Z Sampler

N
W
E
S
Boca
PLAYA MAKOSHI
BOKA CHIKITU
PARK ENTRANCE
BOKA PAMPER
BOKA ONIMA
RINCON
PIEDRA KRUS
BOKA OLIBA
Karpata
COLOMBIA
TOLO
SUPLADO
BOKA SPELONK
Caves
BOKA KANOA
BOCA RINCON
BOKA DI TOLO
Barkadera Caves
Spelonk Lighthouse
BARKADERA
123m
Seru Largu
BOLIVIA
BOKA CHIKITU
LONT
Caves
SANTA BARBARA
117m
Seru Grandi
LAGUN
Noord Salina
GUATEMALA
WASHIKEMBA
BOCA WASHIKEMBA
KLEIN BONAIRE
KRALENDIJK
PIEDRA DOS STENCHI
West Punt Lighthouse
DAM GRANDI
Bachelor's Beach
FLAMINGO INTERNATIONAL AIRPORT
BAKUNA
Mangrove
BOKA PRETU
PUNT VIERKANT
Cai
SUPLADO
LIMA
Punt Vierkant Lighthouse
Lac Bay
Salt Pans
Sorobon Beach
Salt Pier
PLAYA MANTEKA
Plenchi
Pink Beach
Punto Kabayero
Solar Salt Works
Piedra Pretu
TRES KURA
Condenser Basins
Atlantis Beach
Pekelmeer Flamingo Sanctuary
DOS KURA
KURA RONDO
LACRE PUNT
Willemstoren Lighthouse

Boka Bartól

Difficulty ●●●
Current ●●●
Depth ●●○
Reef ★☆☆
Fauna ★★☆

Access about 45 mins from the park entrance
about 120 mins from Kralendijk

Level Advanced Open Water

Location

Washington plantation
GPS: 12°18′10.5″N, 68°23′54.6″W

Getting there

Head north out of Rincón on Kaya G.R.E. Herrera toward Washington Slagbaai National Park. Boka Bartól is the northernmost dive site in the park and can only be reached via the long (yellow) route shown on page 23. Continue past the Suplado Blow Hole and Boka Kokolishi on the east coast and follow the road inland. At Boka Bartól, the road returns to the coast and runs southwest between the sea and Saliña Bartól. The overall drive from the park entrance is just over 6 miles (10 kilometers), or about 45 minutes of driving without stopping. There is a parking lot with space for several cars just before a small yellow concrete structure and adjacent to a picnic bench with a tiki-style parasol.

Access

Descend the relatively steep beach composed of large coral rocks. The ground transitions to a rutted reef plateau at the shoreline, which is more stable but can be slippery, so divers should watch their step.

Waves generally approach from the north and can break across the entire bay. However, the sandy area between the two large rocks at the southwestern end of the beach is slightly deeper—waves break less often here, making this the safest place to access the dive site. The buoy is located about 330 feet (100 meters) off the beach. The site can also be reached by boat.

Description

Boka Bartól is exposed to the open ocean, so the current can be incredibly strong, generally moving from south to north. The site is relatively pristine because its remote location means it is infrequently visited.

The site is known for its large fish, including barracuda, stingrays and eagle rays. The sand bottom shelters garden eels and peacock flounders and sea turtles may be found among the soft corals. The coral cover is better to the north of the buoy, but for safety reasons, most divers start their dive by heading south, into the prevailing current.

1A BONAIRE

Boka Katuna

Difficulty ●●●
Current ●●●
Depth ●●○
Reef ★☆☆
Fauna ★★☆

Access about 47 mins from the park entrance

Level Advanced Open Water

Location

Washington plantation
GPS: 12°17′58.7″N, 68°24′08.2″W

Getting there

Head north out of Rincón on Kaya G.R.E. Herrera toward Washington Slagbaai National Park. Boka Katuna is less than half a mile south of Boka Bartól and can only be reached via the long (yellow) route shown on page 23. Follow the directions for Boka Bartól then continue along the road.

The site is not an official dive site in the numbered list released by STINAPA, but a small sign on the side of the road marks the site where a short track leads off to the right ending at the cliff edge after about 100 feet (30 meters). There is room to park several cars here. The dive site is in a small bay that measures about 480 feet (146 meters) across and is protected from wave action, although some swells from the north do bend around the point and enter the bay.

Access

To reach the dive site, descend the 40-foot (12-meter) cliff to the rocky beach below. There is a rough path down to the water built out of rocks, located 90 feet (27.5 meters) along the cliff from the parking lot. Accessing this site can be very challenging for most divers, especially when carrying heavy dive gear. Exercise extreme caution when descending to the beach.

Once on the beach, enter the water and swim out between the two large rocks located on either side of the beach. There is no mooring buoy at this site, so access by boat is only possible if someone remains in the boat to hold its position, since anchoring is prohibited anywhere in the Marine Park.

Description

Boka Katuna is known for its strong currents and dangerous undertow, particularly when the surf is up. These characteristics make this site better suited to experienced divers. This site is not recommended for snorkelers.

The exposed nature of the site has its benefits, however, since it also means Boka Katuna is relatively pristine and offers a good chance of seeing triggerfish, stingrays, eagle rays and barracuda.

Playa Bengé

Access about 51 mins from the park entrance
about 105 mins from Kralendijk

Level Advanced Open Water

Location
Washington plantation
GPS: 12°17’24.5″N, 68°24’41.3″W

Getting there

Head north out of Rincón on Kaya G.R.E. Herrera toward Washington Slagbaai National Park. Playa Bengé is the last dive site before the park’s long route intersects with the short route. About a half mile (0.8 kilometers) from Boka Katuna is an intersection with a road that heads to the right with a sign indicating Playa Bengé. Take this road and pass through the barrier. Follow the winding road for a half mile to a parking lot with enough space for several cars.

Access

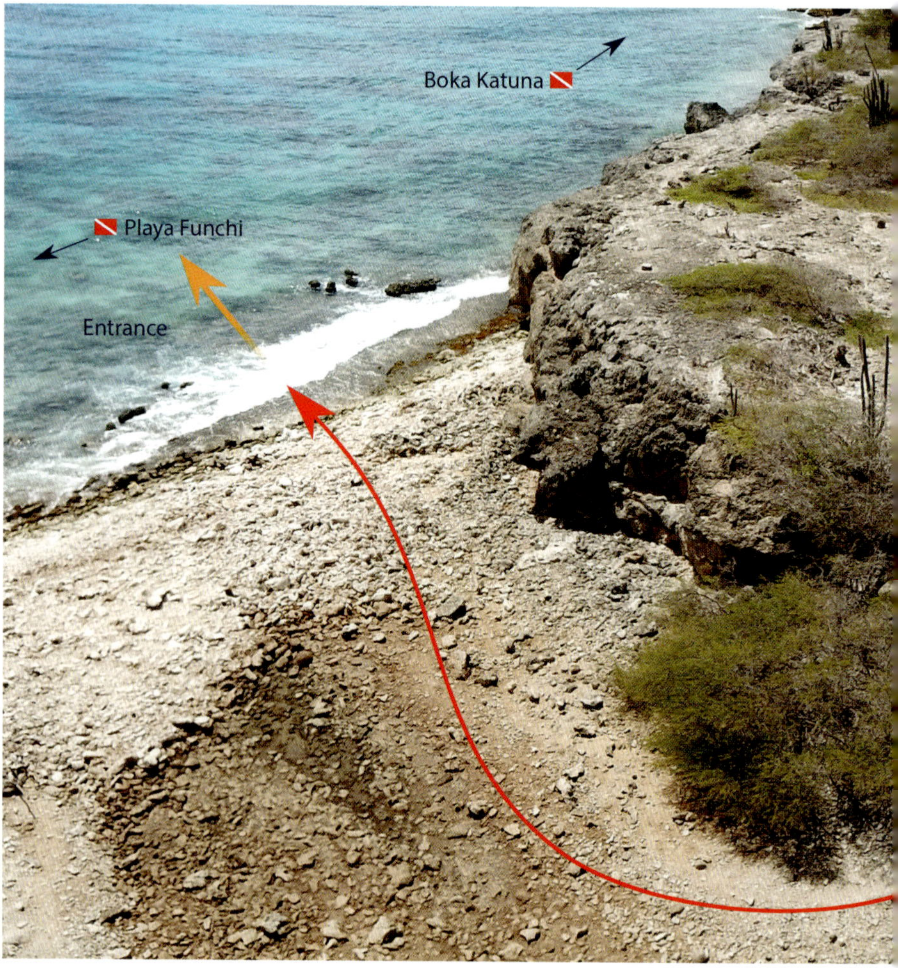

A path adjacent to a green and yellow barrier leads down to a dry river bed and onto the beach. There are lots of large rocks and rubble on the beach, which can be challenging to navigate with dive gear. Large swells enter the bay from the north and tend to break about 60 feet (18 meters) from shore. Once clear of the surf zone, kick out to the buoy located 450 feet (137 meters) from the shore.

Description

Sea turtles are known to nest on this beach, so do not disturb any nests that are present. This site is also known for particularly strong rip currents, so scope out the conditions before entering the water. Snorkelers will enjoy the shallow spur and groove formations, and the variety of marine life including staghorn coral, squid and nudibranchs. Divers may see schools of parrotfish, snapper and grouper along the deeper reef wall to the east, along with the occasional shark or manta ray.

SAFETY TIP !

Rip currents flow from the shore to the open sea and can be incredibly strong, particularly in stormy weather and at low tide. They can be extremely dangerous for swimmers, particularly weak or inexperienced swimmers. They can be difficult to spot, but there are several tips that can improve safety:

- Scan the water for signs of a rip current before entering. Areas without breaking waves, or with cloudy or choppy water, often indicate rip currents.
- Observe any floating objects, such as bits of wood or seaweed. Areas where floating objects are washed out to sea are often rip currents.
- If caught in a rip current, always swim perpendicular to the current to get free, rather than against it.

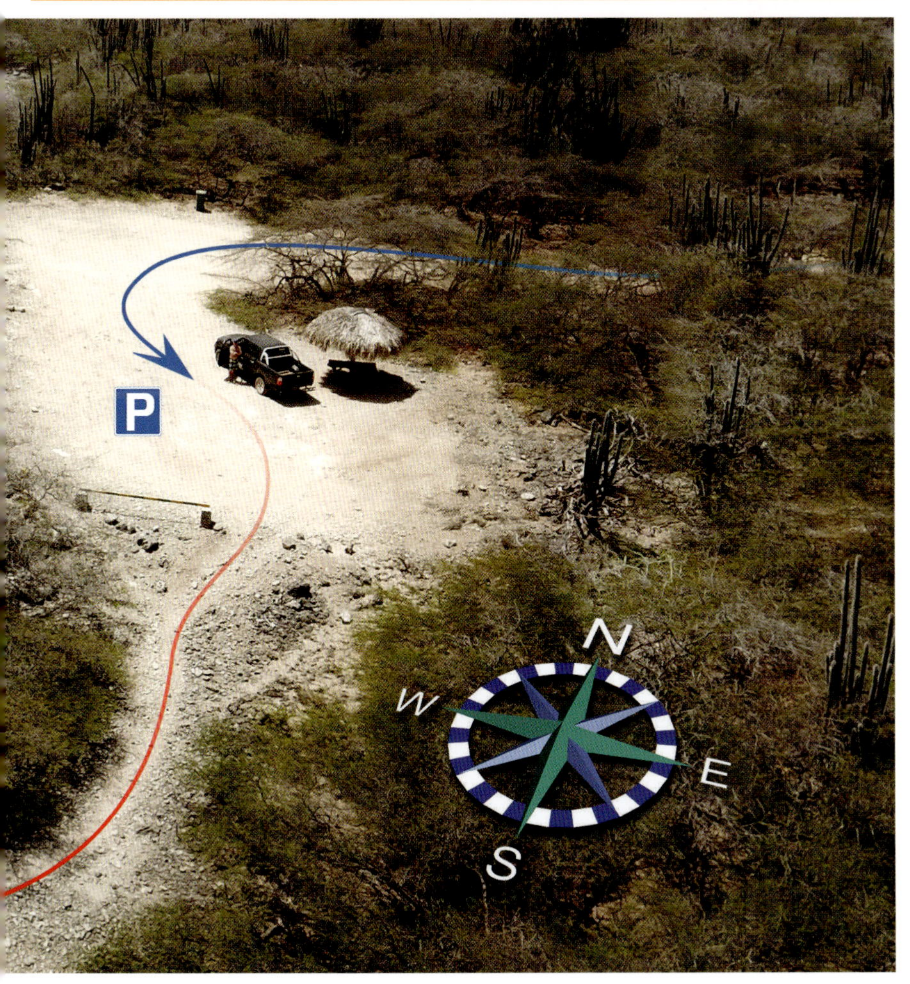

Playa Funchi

Access about 25 mins from the park entrance
about 103 mins from Kralendijk

Level Open Water

Location
Slagbaai plantation
GPS: 12°16′56.6″N, 68°24′49.6″W

Getting there

Playa Funchi can be reached via either the long or short routes through the National Park. It is a 5.5-mile (9-kilometer) drive from the park entrance on the short route, and about 2.2 miles (3.5 kilometers) south from Playa Bengé on the long route. Playa Funchi is also the westernmost beach on the island.

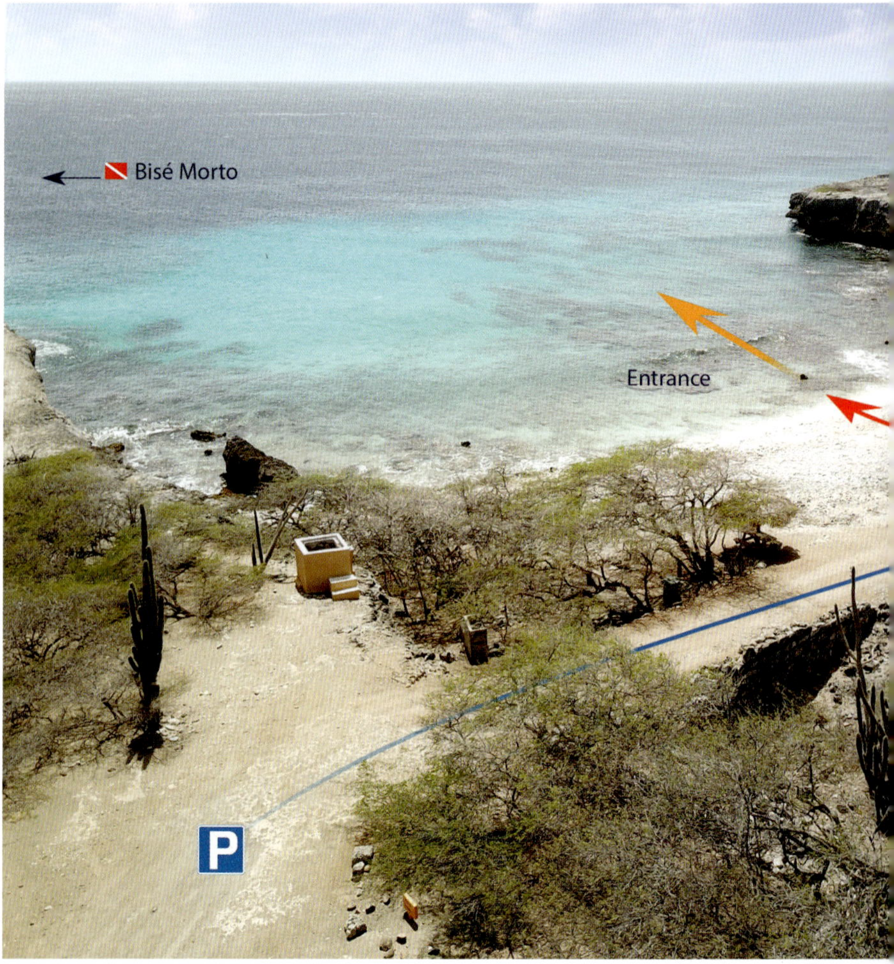

Head north out of Rincón on Kaya G.R.E. Herrera toward Washington Slagbaai National Park. Enter the park taking either the long or short route and continue until the two intersect on the west coast. Drive southwest from the intersection of the long and short routes; the road forks after a third of a mile (0.5 kilometers). Follow the sign to take the right fork toward Playa Funchi. The road continues straight for a while and then bends to the right just before a large parking lot situated on the cliff above the beach. Park here or drive down the steep slope to the smaller parking lot between the beach and Saliña Funchi. Iguanas, geckos and blue whiptail lizards (known locally as blau-blau) are often found on the beach here. Flamingos are common in Saliña Funchi.

Access

Playa Funchi is in a sheltered bay about 300 feet (92 meters) across with seating and some shade. The mooring buoy is anchored a ways from shore in a large sandy area. The beach consists of rounded, flat rocks, which makes accessing the water easier than at other sites in the park. Be aware that the rocks can move underfoot, so tread with care. Waves may break close to the beach here, but they tend to be smaller than those at Playa Bengé.

Description

Currents at Playa Funchi can be strong, particularly rip currents, so be sure to check the conditions before venturing into the water. The site is known for its great snorkeling, with the wide, relatively shallow waters playing host to a variety of marine life, including trunkfish, chubs, razorfish and staghorn corals. Divers may see midnight parrotfish, anemones, schools of horse-eye jacks and plenty of soft corals and sea fans on the reef.

Bisé Morto

Difficulty ●●●
Current ●●●
Depth ●●●
Reef ★★☆
Fauna ★★☆

Access about 27 mins from the park entrance
about 100 mins from Kralendijk

Level Open Water

Location

Slagbaai plantation
GPS: 12°16′36.4″N, 68°24′51.8″W

Getting there

Bisé Morto is just a half mile (0.8 kilometers) down the road from Playa Funchi—a 27-minute drive from the entrance of the National Park along the short route. Head north out of Rincón on Kaya G.R.E. Herrera toward Washington Slagbaai National Park. From there, follow the directions to Playa Funchi but continue past the parking lot toward the ocean. The road heads directly toward the coast before turning left and running parallel to the shoreline. Cross the cattle grid and continue driving until the Bisé Morto inlet on the right. There is a small parking lot on the right immediately after the site.

Access

Access to Bisé Morto is challenging, even compared to the other sites in the park. A 25-foot (7.5-meter) sheer cliff stands between the parking lot and the water below. Ropes are required to lower dive gear to the beach and to climb down safely (as well as exit the site).

Once on the small rocky beach divers must be careful to avoid the shallow reef areas on either side of the narrow bay, which is only about 45 feet (14 meters) across. Wave action can be strong at this site, so divers should surface swim through the swells and into deeper water as quickly as possible. The small beach may not actually be visible at high tide, so dives must be timed according to the tides. There is a yellow mooring buoy located in the sand directly off the beach.

Description

As with most other sites in the park, the waves and current at Bisé Morto can be strong, particularly rip currents. The name of the site means "dead deer," supposedly in reference to the fields of staghorn coral found here. Divers may see French angelfish, scrawled filefish, triggerfish and large grouper at this site. Some divers have also reported seeing larger pelagic organisms here, such as whale sharks and humpback whales. The shallower areas are known to offer better diving than the deeper reef at this site.

Wayaká II

Difficulty ●○○
Current ●○○
Depth ●●○
Reef ★★☆
Fauna ★★★

Access about 30 mins from the park entrance
about 95 mins from Kralendijk

Level Open Water

Location

Slagbaai plantation
GPS: 12°16′10.9″N, 68°24′49.0″W

Getting there

Wayaká II is just over half a mile (1 kilometer) south of Bisé Morto. Head north out of Rincón on Kaya G.R.E. Herrera toward Washington Slagbaai National Park. Once in the park, follow the directions to Playa Funchi and Bisé Morto. After Bisé Morto, the road hugs the shore for about 0.4 miles (0.6 kilometers) before turning inland. Immediately after this bend is a right turn with a sign pointing toward the three beaches, Wayaká I, II and III. Wayaká II is the most visited beach of the three. There is plenty of room for parking on the right-hand side of the road.

Access

From the parking lot follow the short, winding path that leads to the cliff edge. A set of uneven stairs leads down to a small, sheltered beach, which is protected by several reef areas that are exposed at low tide. The bay has virtually no breaking waves and offers incredible visibility, which makes this an excellent place to snorkel and dive. In fact, the Wayaká sites are widely regarded as the best places to snorkel in the National Park.

The beach largely disappears at high tide, so divers should time their visits accordingly. There is some shade available and a small cave in the cliff to explore. To access the snorkeling area, walk off the beach and follow the sand channel that cuts through the shallow reef areas on either side of the beach. There is a yellow mooring buoy located in the sand about 300 feet (92 meters) from shore.

Description

The Wayaká sites are in a sheltered bay with plenty of fish, particularly French angelfish, parrotfish, including both midnight and rainbow, as well as puddingwives, surgeonfish, blue tangs, Bermuda chub, sergeant majors, rock beauties and trunkfish. Small grouper, such as coneys and graysbies, are also very common.

6 BONAIRE

Boka Slagbaai

Difficulty ●●○
Current ●●○
Depth ●●○
Reef ★☆☆
Fauna ★★☆

Access: about 40 mins from the park entrance; about 95 mins from Kralendijk

Level Open Water

Location
Slagbaai plantation
GPS: 12°15′52.8″N, 68°24′48.3″W

Getting there

Boka Slagbaai is the southernmost dive site in Washington Slagbaai National Park and can be reached via either the long or short route through the park—it is a 75-minute drive along the long route but just 40 minutes via the short route. Boka Slagbaai is located just a third of a mile (0.5 kilometers) south of the Wayaká sites, but the drive requires 10 minutes because the road detours around Saliña Wayaká—a distance of 2 miles (3 kilometers). When the road returns to the coast, a small parking area can be seen on the right, just before the road drops sharply into the sheltered bay where several yellow historical buildings are located. There is plenty of parking on either side of these buildings.

Access

The beach consists mainly of sand with some rocks. Waves do not generally break here, which means entering and exiting the water is relatively easy. There are two mooring buoys at this site, located about 400 feet (122 meters) from the beach and close to the edge of the drop-off. Currents can be strong this far from shore, so divers and snorkelers must watch for changes in the conditions and monitor their air supply to avoid a lengthy surface swim back to shore.

Description

Boka Slagbaai boasts a beautiful beach that separates a long, shallow saliña from what was once a commercially important harbor. The Slagbaai plantation began operation in this area in the late 1600s after the Dutch West India Company took over the island. In the 1860s, the government sold the plantation to private owners who built housing and a warehouse just off the beach. The original buildings were recently restored and now offer a colorful backdrop as divers and snorkelers enter and exit the water.

Flamingos are an iconic species in Bonaire.

The buildings are not the only remnants of this site's past as a working harbor. Rounded ballast stones litter the middle section of the sand-bottomed back reef area. Sailing ships dropped these stones as they took on shipments of goat meat, charcoal, salt, chalk, and wood that were

the staples of the Slagbaai plantation. The site is also scattered with other historical artifacts, including anchors and cannons. Two cannons dating from the eighteenth century, which are now heavily encrusted with marine life, can be found at the base of the cliff in the southern part of the bay at a depth of about 7 feet (2 meters). These cannons were once part of a fort that was constructed on top of the cliff to protect the port from pirates. Replica cannons are also located in the northern part of the bay.

Mary K Schmidt/Shutterstock ©

In the back reef, corals can be found along the left and right sides of the bay, at the base of the northern and southern bluffs. The northern side is dominated by blade fire coral while the southern side has large brain and star coral mounds that provide habitat for many reef fish, such as filefish, boxfish, and parrotfish, including large rainbow parrotfish.

The middle section of the wide bay is dominated by coral rubble, sand, and some patch reef. Razorfish and sand tilefish are particularly common here. The reef starts to slope gradually toward the drop-off, which forms a gentle arc from north to south, mirroring the shape of the bay.

The drop-off contains a number of sand channels that run vertically from the top of the reef to the bottom. The slope is shallower at the northern end of the site and gradually becomes steeper, almost wall-like, toward the south. Large coral mounds can be found at the top of the southern section of reef, with plate-form corals found at depth. Schools of creole wrasses and rainbow runners flow along the reef slope while large cubera snapper patrol the deeper areas.

Route

Boka Slagbaai offers plenty of reef for snorkelers to explore; the shallow bay is nearly 3.5 acres in size, and though the back reef does not have dense coral cover, it has plenty of reef fish to watch. The water gets deeper out past the mooring buoys and is more interesting for those snorkelers able to dive below the surface.

Divers have a choice of swimming out to the reef along the north or south edges of the bay. Divers typically head out to the drop-off, keeping a look out for the cannons. The drop-off starts about 60 feet (18 meters) past the yellow mooring buoys, which are anchored in the sand at a depth of about 16 feet (5 meters). The top of the drop-off is about 30 feet (9 meters) in depth. The reef stops at around 150 feet (46 meters) depth. The route divers take along the reef slope should depend on the direction of the current.

DID YOU KNOW?

The road from Wayaká I, II and III to Boka Slagbaai passes between Saliña Wayaká and Brandaris, which at 784 feet (241 meters) is the highest point on the island of Bonaire. A hike to the top of Brandaris takes between 30 minutes and one hour, depending on the pace the group sets, and offers spectacular views of Washington Slagbaai National Park and beyond. On a clear day, visitors can even see the neighboring island of Curaçao. Park authorities advise hikers to begin climbing Brandaris by noon at the latest.

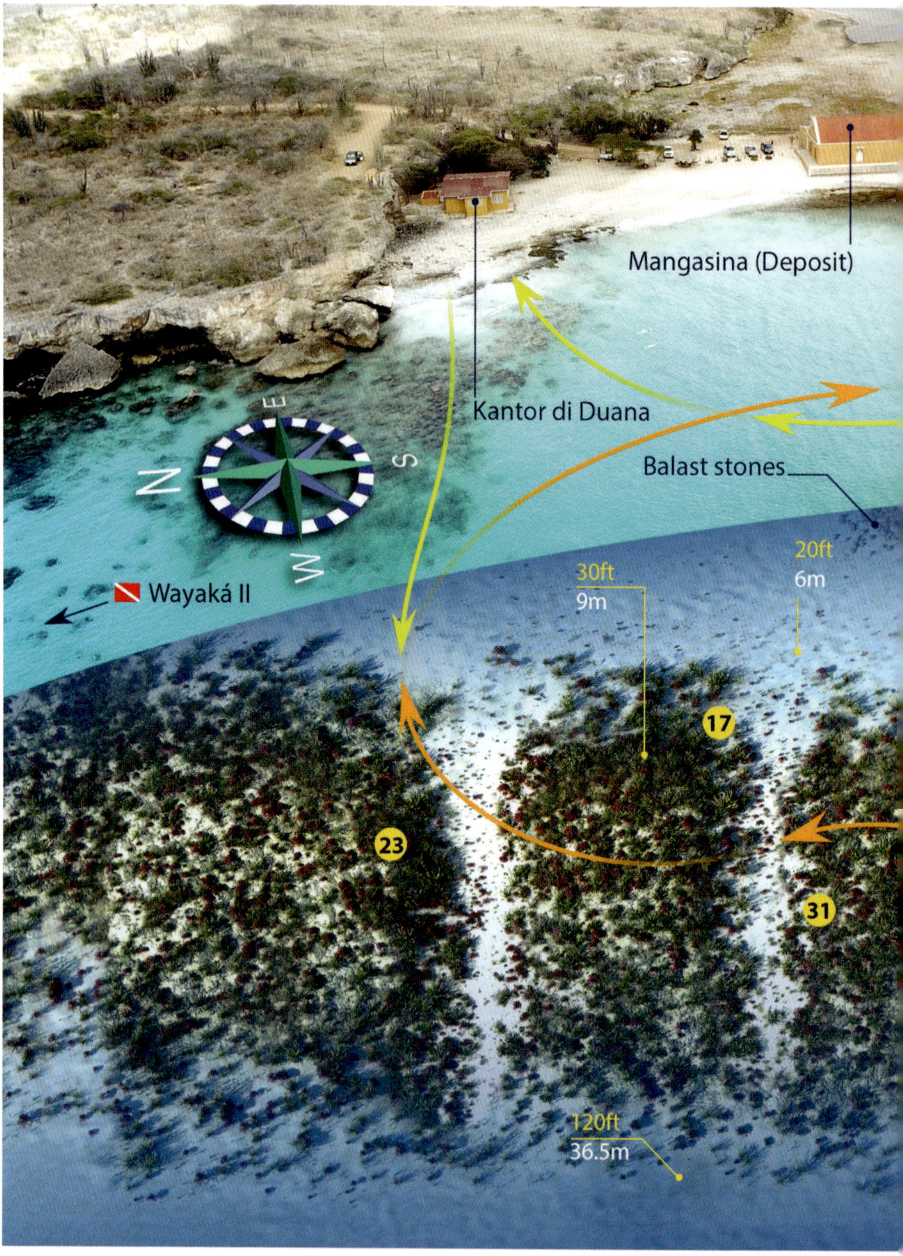

BOKA SLAGBAAI

Mangasina (Deposit)

Kantor di Duana

Balast stones

Wayaká II

30ft
9m

20ft
6m

17

23

31

120ft
36.5m

DID YOU KNOW?

Some believe the name Boka Slagbaai derives from the Dutch word "Slachtbaai," meaning slaughter, which provides some insight into the historical activities that took place in the bay. For centuries, the plantation was used for the slaughter of livestock, particularly goats and sheep. The salted meat, known locally as jorki, was stored here before being shipped to Curaçao every two weeks. Many historians contend that the term originates from the Papiamento "salu" or salt, instead. If so, the current name would be an evolution of the original name sla baai, or salt bay.

Kas di Vito
Tienda
Cliff jump
24
42
Site buoys
Playa Frans
13
16ft
5m
16ft
5m
30ft
9m
32
67
120ft
36.5m

6A

BONAIRE

Playa Frans

Difficulty	●●○
Current	●●●
Depth	●●○
Reef	★★☆
Fauna	★★☆

Access about 47 mins from Kralendijk (by car)
about 83 mins from Kralendijk (by boat)

Level Open Water

Location
Brasil plantation, Bonaire
GPS: 12°14′46.1″N, 68°24′49.2″W

Getting there

Playa Frans is the northernmost site outside of the Washington Slagbaai National Park. It is one of a handful of sites located west of the BOPEC (Bonaire Petroleum Corporation) facility. This site is remote and getting there requires a four-wheel-drive vehicle, a full tank of gas and plenty of water. Plan for the drive to take in excess of 45 minutes.

Head north out of downtown Kralendijk, taking the Queen's Highway out to the Karpata dive site. Once at Karpata, turn left onto Kaminoa Karpata. The road hugs the coast until it reaches the narrow saliña that heads to Goto Meer. Head toward the gates of BOPEC, but do not enter them; instead, turn right and take the dirt road north, which runs along the fence line of the facility. When the fence turns a corner, continue straight toward the paved section of road—a left turn leads to the washed out remains of the old road.

Drive up and around the BOPEC facility before rejoining the coast about 1.5 miles (2.5 kilometers) later. The road forks soon thereafter; take the right fork. After 1.3 miles (2 kilometers) there is a house on the left just before the road heads inland, immediately followed by a sharp left turn up a hill. Continue to the end of this road—another 0.7 miles (1.1 kilometers) or a total of 2.1 miles (3.5 kilometers) from the fork in the road. There is a small yellow rock near the entrance to the area that holds a few cottages and older buildings. Saliña Frans is located to the right of the road and the beach and dive and snorkel site of Playa Frans is located on the left. Park just beyond the final building on the left, adjacent to the water.

Access

Most divers and snorkelers enter the water by descending the concrete boat ramp at this site. Be careful as the ramp can be slick underfoot. The water in this area is sheltered by the shallow corals located just off shore from the beach. Divers should put their fins on and surface swim out through the narrow channel between the corals to the main reef, which is located about 300 feet (92 meters) off shore. The site is marked by a buoy, which is a good place for divers to surface at the end of their dive to locate the access channel for a safe return to the beach.

Description

Playa Frans is one of Bonaire's more remote and secluded beaches. Sea turtles use this stony beach for nesting, so be careful not to disturb them or their nests, which may be indicated by sea turtle tracks on the beach. The back reef is full of shallow, algae-covered coral that attracts large parrotfish and schools of blue tangs and surgeonfish. The deeper reef is known for its large brain and pillar corals, as well as some massive purple tube sponges. The reef drop-off starts just over 330 feet (100 meters) from shore and descends to a maximum depth of 130 feet (40 meters). The most interesting sections of this reef are in the shallower areas, however, so there is no need to descend that deep.

Nukove (Doblet)

Difficulty ●●○
Current ●●○
Depth ●●●
Reef ★★☆
Fauna ★★☆

Access about 45 mins from Kralendijk
about 80 mins from Kralendijk

Level Advanced Open Water

Location

Brasil plantation, Bonaire
GPS: 12°14′26.6″N, 68°24′44.1″W

Getting there

Nukove is one of a handful of sites located west of the BOPEC (Bonaire Petroleum Corporation) facility in the southwestern corner of Washington Slagbaai National Park. This site is remote and getting there requires a four-wheel-drive vehicle, a full tank of gas and plenty of water. Plan for the drive to take about 45 minutes.

Head north out of downtown Kralendijk, taking the Queen's Highway out to the Karpata dive site. Once there, turn left onto Kaminoa Karpata. The road hugs the coast until it reaches the narrow saliña that heads to Goto Meer. Head toward the gates of BOPEC but do not enter them; instead,

Entrance
Playa Frans

turn right and take the dirt road north that runs along the fence line of the facility. When the fence turns a corner, continue straight toward the paved section of road—a left turn leads to the washed out remains of the old road. Drive up and around the BOPEC facility before rejoining the coast about 1.5 miles (2.5 kilometers) later. The road forks soon thereafter; take the right fork.

After 1.3 miles (2 kilometers) there is a house on the left located just before the road heads inland, followed by a sharp left turn up a hill. A yellow rock by the side of the road with Nukove written on it is located just 0.25 miles (0.4 kilometers) later—a total of 1.7 miles (2.8 kilometers) from the fork in the road. Turn left onto that smaller road and park when by the cliff near the ocean.

Access

To access the beach from the parking lot, turn right and take the rough stone stairs that lead down to the coral beach. The steps are uneven and the rocks on the beach have a tendency to move underfoot, so consider carrying dive gear down the steps in stages and donning it once on the beach. Enter the water carefully, as the surface of the coral rubble in the surf zone can be slippery. The site is also accessible to snorkelers, although the potential for strong currents means only experienced snorkelers should consider exploring this site.

Description

Nukove is known for its multiple fish cleaning stations, and a variety of sponges and black corals. Divers and snorkelers may encounter parrotfish, filefish, black durgons, and a variety of basslets, as well as large pelagic species like tarpon and jacks. The currents can be strong at this site, particularly at the drop-off, which starts at around 30 feet (9 meters) and descends to a depth of more than 130 feet (40 meters). When surfacing, use the cliff and any parked vehicle as a reference point for navigating back to the beach. The beach itself can be hard to see from the water depending on the wave action.

8 BONAIRE

Carel's Vision

Difficulty ●●○
Current ●●○
Depth ●●○
Reef ★★☆
Fauna ★☆☆

Access about 74 mins from Kralendijk

Level Open Water

Location

Brasil plantation, Bonaire
GPS: 12°13'50.6"N, 68°24'46.2"W

Getting there

Carel's Vision is one of a handful of sites located west of the BOPEC (Bonaire Petroleum Corporation) facility just south of the Washington Slagbaai National Park. This site is remote and while it is possible to drive to the site and view the mooring buoy from a cliff, it is only accessible by boat. Ask at one of the local dive centers to find out when they are next heading out to this site. Because of the distance from Kralendijk, Carel's Vision is not on the regular schedule of most dive centers, so special arrangements may be required.

Access

The relatively weak currents and shallowness of this section of reef make it accessible to divers of all levels.

Description

Carel's Vision is named after Carel Steensma, a Dutchman who played an instrumental role in establishing the Marine Park in 1979. This site is known for its many corals, including star corals, brain corals, and black corals, along with its large elephant ear sponges. Parrotfish and triggerfish are also common, while stingrays and eagle rays are often spotted in the deeper parts of the reef.

SCIENTIFIC INSIGHT

Black corals belong in the order Antipatharia. They do not have a calcium carbonate skeleton like the stony corals found on most reefs, but instead grow a shell of proteins and chitin. They also do not have a symbiotic relationship with photosynthetic algae, which means they can grow in waters without significant amounts of sunlight. This allows them to grow at much greater depths than stony corals. Despite their name, black corals can be a wide range of colors, including red, white, green or yellow. They can be tall or short, bushy or thin, and scientists have recently shown that some individuals, found in the deeper waters of the Caribbean and in the Gulf of Mexico, are more than 2,000 years old.

Tailor Made →

Access by boat only

Site buoy

8A

Tailor Made

BONAIRE

Difficulty ●●●
Current ●●●
Depth ●●●
Reef ★★★
Fauna ★★☆

Tailor Made
Kralendijk

Access about 40 mins from Kralendijk

Level Advanced Open Water

Location
Brasil plantation, Bonaire
GPS: 12°13'23.9"N, 68°24'12.8"W

Getting there

Tailor Made is not on the official list of STINAPA sites. It is located just west of the BOPEC (Bonaire Petroleum Corporation) facility, right before the coastline turns to the north. This part of the island is remote and getting there requires a four-wheel-drive vehicle, a full tank of gas and plenty of water. Plan for the drive to take about 40 minutes.

Head north out of downtown Kralendijk, taking the Queen's Highway to the Karpata dive site. Once there, turn left onto Kaminoa Karpata. The road hugs the coast until it reaches the narrow saliña that heads to Goto Meer. Head toward the gates of BOPEC but do not enter them; instead, turn right and take the dirt road north, which runs along the fence line of the facility. When the fence turns a corner, continue straight toward the paved section of road—a left turn leads to the washed out remains of the old road. Drive up and around the BOPEC facility before rejoining the coast about 1.5 miles (2.5 kilometers) later. The road hugs the coast for 0.25 miles (0.4 kilometers), with the ocean on the left and Saliña Tam on the right. When the road forks, take the left fork toward the rocky, coral beach. There is a turnaround spot located after 400 feet (120 meters) with a small grove of bushes next to a pile of boulders and car tires (referred to as dive totems by local guides). Park here, leaving the trail clear for other divers.

Access

From the pile of boulders and tires located next to the road, a small path runs down to the shoreline. Enter the water carefully as the rocks can move underfoot. Divers will need to zigzag through the coral heads in the shallow part of the reef. Start out heading right for around 20 feet, before turning left and heading out through the gap in the reef. There are many live corals here, so divers must be careful not to touch them. The surf is often rough here, so divers should consider waiting to put on their fins until they are in water that rises above waist level. As larger waves approach, divers may need to brace themselves or use their dive buddy for support to avoid getting knocked over by the surf.

Description

Tailor Made is one of the more remote dive sites in Bonaire and requires some additional planning and precautions compared to some of the sites closer to Kralendijk. A visit to Tailor Made is well worth the extra effort, however, as the reef has spectacular topography and high biodiversity.

The first section of reef is present right in the surf zone, which can make accessing the site a little challenging, particularly as the waves and current can be quite strong here. The reef is shallow enough to break the surface in places, so divers should make their way carefully through the gap in the corals. Marine life is found even in these shallow areas, such as large rainbow parrotfish that forage in the waters all the way into the surf zone.

As divers move into deeper water, they may notice multiple stands of elkhorn coral rising above the reef, along with a handful of large coral heads. The slope descends gradually, starting at a depth of 15 feet (5 meters) down to 20 feet (6 meters) by the reef line, which sits nearly 100 feet (30 meters) out.

Approaching the reef, divers will see a profusion of star corals interspersed with stands of gorgonians. The slope steepens here, descending toward the drop-off, and is slightly scalloped. There is a large coral mound that tops out at a depth of 24 feet (7.5 meters), which is a handy reference to use when returning to the entry/exit point.

Tailor Made's wall includes plate-form corals, large sponges and a variety of reef fishes. It is marked by a half dozen ridges and their associated valleys, making this an interesting site

SAFETY TIP

The dive sites in the northwestern part of the island are remote. It is important to plan ahead and bring additional supplies that might not otherwise be required for some of the more frequently-visited sites to the south.

Packing plenty of water is important. Also consider bringing a small first aid kit to treat the types of small cuts and scrapes that are common when accessing dive sites with high surf and shallow corals.

Many of the reef walls in this part of the island bottom out at 130 feet or more (40 meters). Given the time it would take to seek medical attention, it is advisable to avoid decompression dives in this area. These more remote locations offer healthy reefs that are not often visited by other divers. But it is important to take precautions while exploring these sites in order to do so safely.

Large rainbow parrotfish can be seen on the reef as well as in the surf zone at Tailor Made.

Brian Lasenby/Shutterstock ©

from the point of view of its terrain. Small sand channels are sprinkled throughout the site in valleys. To the west, the transition area between reef and drop-off widens and deepens. It forms a slight plateau with sand basins stocked full of gorgonians and yellow pencil coral, separated by elevated ridges of coral. The eastern edge of the site is marked by two coral pillars standing about 59 feet (18 meters) apart at the top of the drop-off. A wide sand channel descends the wall between them. The best diving at this site is in a 33-foot (10-meter) band that runs along the edge of the reef drop-off. This section is filled with dense stands of gorgonians and a maze of star coral mounds, offering ideal habitat for an incredibly diverse assemblage of reef fishes, including angelfish, snapper, parrotfish, graysbies, coneys and grunts.

Route

Divers should start by threading their way through the shallow corals in the surf zone, following the path laid out in the access section above. From there, they typically swim in a southerly heading toward the drop-off zone. The currents tend to come from the east at this site, so divers often begin their dive by heading into the current. They then descend the wall or cruise along the top section of the drop-off zone as they advance to the east. There is plenty to see on the

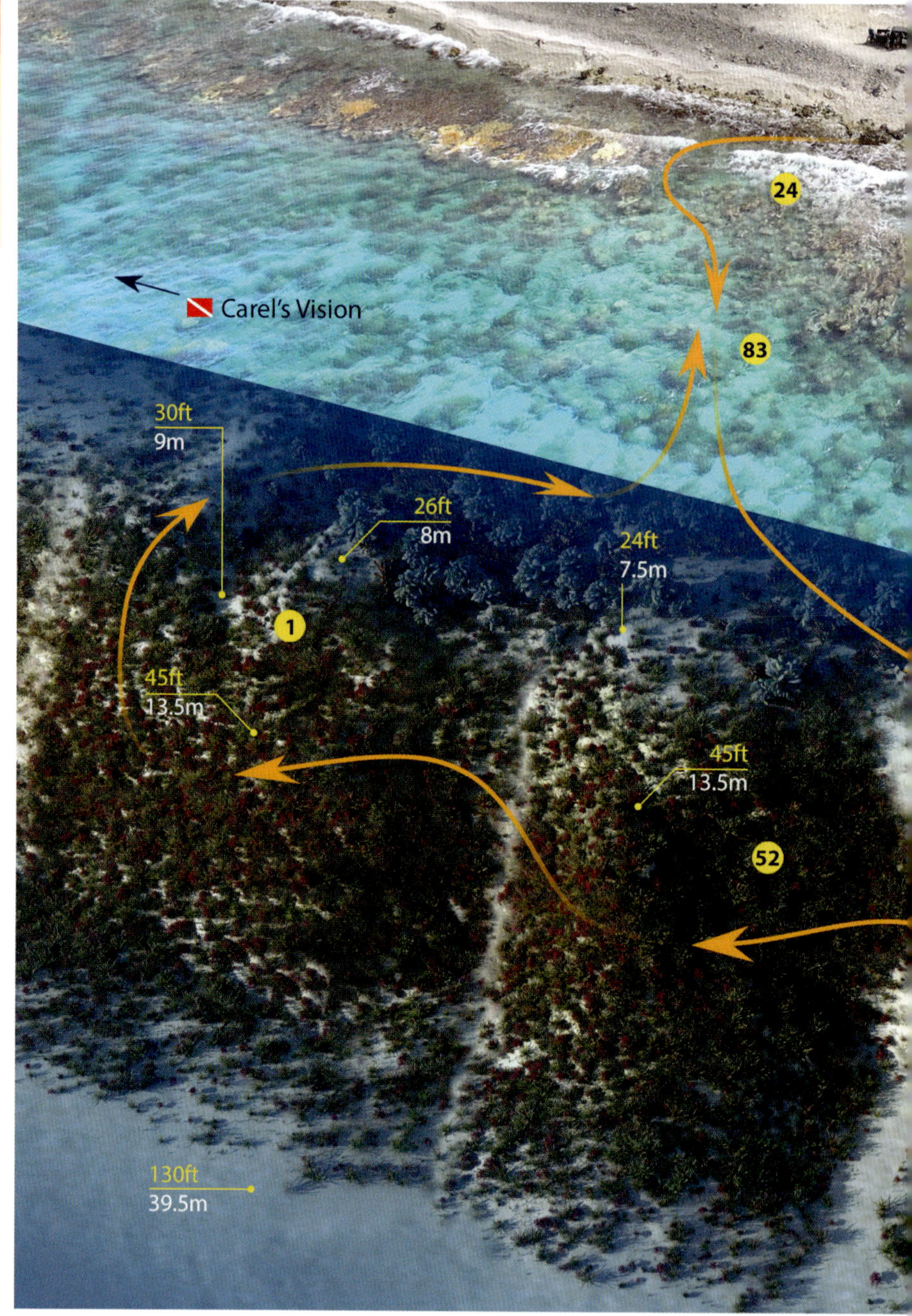

wall, but the upper edge of the drop-off offers some of the best views of the site.

A slightly wider sand channel provides a good reference point to turn around and return toward the west. At the western edge of the site, divers ascend to the plateau section of the reef and start heading back toward the buoy. Divers should consider taking their time on their return route so they can look for species hiding under the forest of gorgonians and soft corals, and within the maze of star coral mounds. Once they have

returned to their starting point on the drop-off zone, divers typically make their way back on a northerly heading, aiming for the gap in the reef through which they entered.

Candyland

Access about 39 mins from Kralendijk

Level Advanced Open Water

Location
Brasil plantation, Bonaire
GPS: 12°13'22.0"N, 68°24'3.5"W

Getting there

Candyland is not on the STINAPA list of official sites. It is located just west of the BOPEC (Bonaire Petroleum Corporation) facility right before the coastline turns to head north. This part of the island is remote and getting there requires a four-wheel-drive vehicle, a full tank of gas and plenty of water. Plan for the drive to take about 39 minutes.

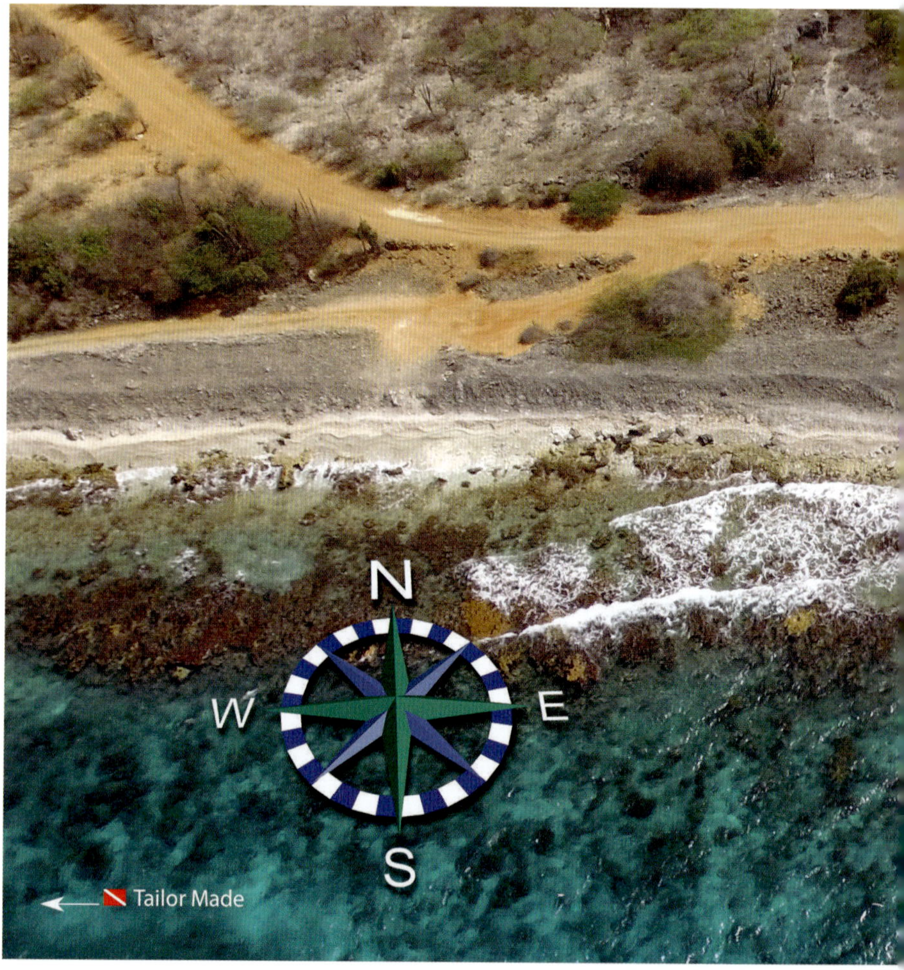

Head north out of downtown Kralendijk, taking the Queen's Highway out to the Karpata dive site. Once at Karpata, turn left onto Kaminoa Karpata. The road hugs the coast until it reaches the narrow saliña that heads to Goto Meer. Head toward the gates of BOPEC but do not enter them; instead, turn right and take the dirt road north, which runs along the fence line of the facility. When the fence turns a corner, continue straight toward the paved section of road—a left turn leads to the washed out remains of the old road. Drive up and around the BOPEC facility before rejoining the coast about 1.5 miles (2.5 kilometers) later. The road hugs the coast for 0.25 miles (0.4 kilometers), with the ocean on the left and Saliña Tam on the right.

The small path down to the shore at Candyland is marked on either side with large rocks, just 200 feet (60 meters) before the road forks. Pull off to the right-hand side of the road to park.

Access

A short path of crushed coral wends its way from the road down to the water's edge at Candyland. Like nearby Tailor Made, the entry into the water is challenging, with high surf that can easily knock a diver over. Divers should put on their fins only after they enter the water, and then should kick quickly out through the waves into deeper water. There is a channel through the reef directly in front of the path on shore, that will take divers safely to the outer reef.

Description

The reef at Candyland is relatively pristine and the shallow back reef is known to be great for snorkeling; there are plenty of healthy brain and plate corals that snorkelers can observe from the surface. As with most sites in this part of the island, the surf can be high, so it is only suitable for strong swimmers. The reef slope here is known for its large coral pillars. Fish biodiversity is high, including large parrotfish, grunts, snapper and small grouper.

Windjammer

Access about 60 mins from Kralendijk

Level Technical

Location

Wecua Punt, Bonaire
GPS: 12°13′10.4″N 68°22′41.8″W

Getting there

Windjammer is located adjacent to the BOPEC (Bonaire Petroleum Corporation) oil terminal in northwestern Bonaire, about 500 feet (152 meters) off the eastern side of BOPEC's east ship dock. Shore access is currently restricted by BOPEC, so divers can only visit this site by boat. The 9.3-mile (15-kilometer) boat ride takes approximately one hour from Kralendijk.

Access

Currents in the area around *Windjammer* can be strong at times, even at depth. The currents, coupled with the significant depth, make this site only accessible to experienced technical divers with the appropriate equipment and gases. A certified guide is also required to visit this site. Visibility is usually good.

A tech diver explores the partially inverted deck of *Windjammer.* Rich Synowiec ©

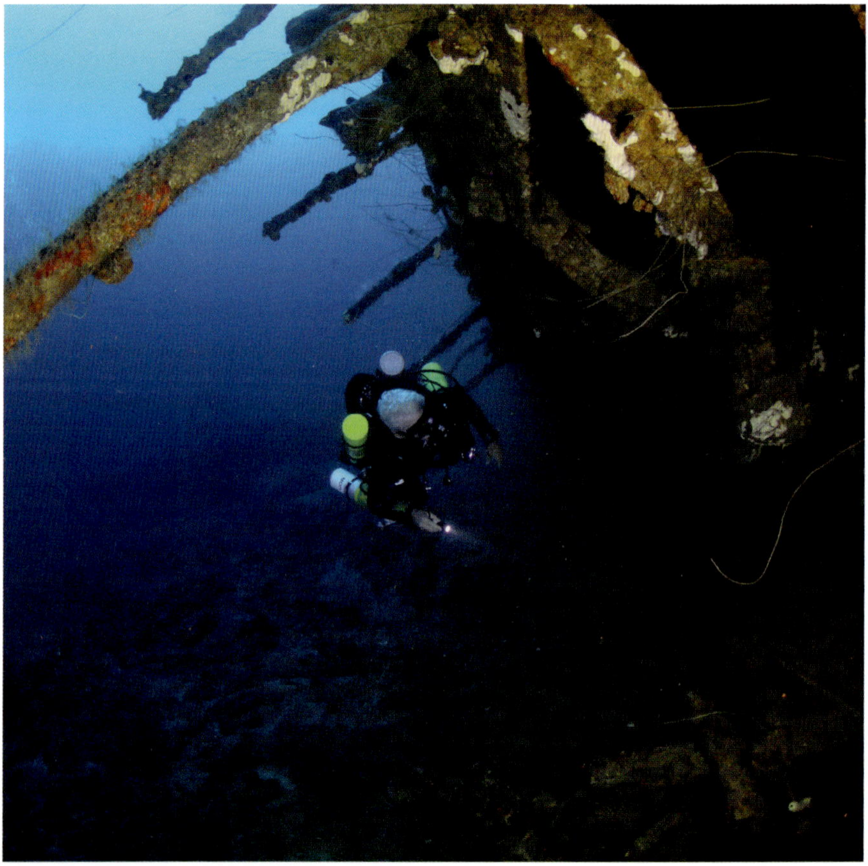

FEATURED OPERATOR 

VIP TEC Diving is a premier PADI Tec Diving Center in Bonaire and a member of the respected VIP Diving organization. VIP TEC Diving offers courses from entry level to full Trimix, as well as CCR training. They also offer custom gas blends and have tanks in various sizes for CCR, backmount, and sidemount configurations. Their highly experienced instructors lead dives to numerous stunning sites across Bonaire that lie beyond recreational depths. They will even create tailored experiences so divers can explore Bonaire's hidden depths the VIP way.

Tel: +599-701-7701
Email: info@vipdiving.com
Visit: **Vipdiving.com**

Description

Windjammer was originally an iron-hulled, three-masted sailing ship called *SV Mairi Bhan* (Gaelic for Bonnie Mary) built in Glasgow, Scotland, in 1874 for P. Henderson & Company. This Scottish company owned and managed multiple sailing ships that carried immigrants and Royal Mail cargo from the United Kingdom to Australia, New Zealand and Burma (now Myanmar). *Mairi Bhan* was one of the finest and fastest sailing ships in the Henderson fleet, capable of completing the Scotland to New Zealand voyage in as little as 75 days. As the Henderson fleet switched over to more economical and reliable steam-powered ships, however, the *Mairi Bhan* was sold to an Italian company called Denegri & Mortola, based in Genoa. She carried Italian leather goods, olive oil, fabrics and marble from Italy to Trinidad. These goods were often traded for asphalt, which was then brought back to Europe via Marseilles, France.

During a return voyage to Europe on December 7th, 1912, a storm pushed the ship onto a nearshore reef in northwest Bonaire. During the grounding, a kerosene lamp ignited several barrels of asphalt, which forced the crew to abandon ship—four crewmembers died in the incident. The ship remained stuck on the reef for several weeks before dislodging and sinking into deeper water.

For many years, the wreck was simply known as the *Deep Schooner,* the *Ghost Ship* or the *Windjammer*—the latter is commonly used in Bonaire today. The ship's foremast rests on the seabed at a depth of just 35 feet (10.5 meters) but the rest of the ship lies on her starboard side at a depth of approximately 200 feet (61 meters). The shallowest part of the main wreckage is the port side of the hull, which has a depth of approximately 160 feet (49 meters). The deepest part of the wreck is the main mast and crow's nest, which extend downward to approximately 210 feet (63 meters).

The wreck is covered in various soft and hard corals, including black corals, wire corals and deep-sea fans. The wreck also contains multiple sponge species and offers penetration opportunities for those with the necessary training and experience. Divers have been known to see tarpon, barracuda, jacks, black grouper, green moray eels, lobster, angelfish and lionfish on the *Windjammer.*

Route

Given the technical nature of the wreck dive, divers should choose a route that works for their experience and technical limitations, including planned gas mix and bottom time.

Name:	*Windjammer*
Type:	Barque
Previous names:	*SV Mairi Bhan*
Length:	139ft (72.9m)
Tonnage:	1,386 grt
	Barclay, Curle & Co. Ltd.,

Construction:	Whiteinch (Glasgow), Scotland, 1874
	Denegri & Mortola, Genoa
Last owner:	December 7, 1912
Sunk:	

Karpata

Difficulty ●●○
Current ●○○
Depth ●●●
Reef ★★★
Fauna ★★☆

Access about 20 mins from Kralendijk (car)
about 45 mins from Kralendijk (boat)

Level Open Water

Location
Karpata, Bonaire
GPS: 12°13′10.4″N, 68°21′06.7″W

Getting there

Karpata is located 8 miles (13 kilometers) north of Kralendijk by car—a 20-minute drive. Head north on Kaya Gob. N. Debrot past the Harbour Village Marina and Hato, where the road becomes Bulevar Gob. N. Debrot. The road moves inland at Sabadeco, also known as Santa Barbara Crowns, and returns to the coast at Oil Slick Leap, where it becomes the Queen's Highway. Just past the Tolo dive site, the road cuts inland for about 0.4 miles (0.7 kilometers) before returning to the coast. About 2 minutes later, the road passes through a stone wall with the derelict Landhuis Karpata field station on the right; the site is marked with yellow rocks. There is plenty of parking on the left-hand side of the road, as well as picnic benches for a post-dive snack and rest. In total, Karpata is about 1.1 miles (1.8 kilometers) past the Tolo dive and snorkel site. It is the farthest dive site north that can be accessed easily without a four-wheel-drive vehicle. When they leave, visitors to Karpata by car must continue north and inland via the town of Rincón.

Karpata is one of the best dive sites to run into juvenile and sub-adult sea turtles.

Isabelle Kuehn/Shutterstock ©

FEATURED OPERATOR 

Buddy Dive Watersports professional and friendly dive staff have extensive knowledge of every dive and snorkel site in Bonaire, whether it's a boat dive along the shores of Klein Bonaire or a shore dive at one of the island's more spectacular but challenging sites, like Karpata. Buddy Dive Resort, located just north of Kralendijk, is a PADI 5-star resort with a Drive-Thru air and Nitrox fill station, which makes accessing sites like Karpata a breeze. The resort's friendly and approachable dive staff ensure every in-water experience is relaxed and enjoyable, while maintaining a reputation for safety and personalized care.

Tel: +599-717-5080
Email: info@buddydive.com
Visit: **Buddydive.com**

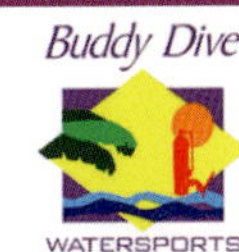

Access

Steps lead down from the parking lot to a small rocky beach. A concrete platform extends into the water; the safest place to enter and exit the water is to the right of this structure. Divers often use this platform for support as the rocky seabed and wave action can easily knock them down. Divers should not place cameras, masks or fins on the concrete platform because waves break over the top and often wash items into the water. The mooring buoy is located about 150 feet (46 meters) out from the beach and slightly to the north. Surface swim out toward the buoy and descend as rapidly as possible to avoid being pushed around by the waves.

Description

Karpata is one of the best-known dive sites in Bonaire and is one of the most northerly sites to receive a steady stream of visitors. It offers an amazing experience for both divers and snorkelers. The shallow back reef is full of gorgonians and hard corals, including star coral mounds and stands of elkhorn and staghorn coral. Green sea turtles regularly visit this site and are frequently seen in the shallow back reef, as are schools of squid and large rainbow parrotfish.

The drop-off starts at a depth of about 25 feet (7.5 meters), although it can be partly obscured by the soft corals that cover the upper section of the reef wall. The reef drops sharply down to a depth of 150 feet (46 meters), with deep vertical grooves breaking the wall into distinct sections. The wall is covered in a combination of hard corals, sponges, and gorgonians; sea whips abound, as do large elephant ear sponges. Some of the best diving can be done above a depth of 80 feet (24.5 meters).

As divers work their way along the wall, they should look into the deep clefts in the reef for lobsters and moray eels. A few old anchors are scattered around the site as well—remnants of when boats once anchored here.

Route

After entering the water, divers typically swim out toward the buoy. They then descend to the reef wall and head east (left), as the King Willem-Alexander Marine Reserve is to the west, where diving is not permitted. About halfway through their dive, divers often ascend the wall and head

DID YOU KNOW? 

The yellow building that sits across the road from the Karpata dive and snorkel site carries the name of Landhuis Karpata, although the locals refer to it as Kas Grandi, which means big house in Papiamento. It was constructed in 1870 on the grounds of a fort that was originally established to protect the section of coast between the Kralendijk and Slagbaai ports from marauding pirates.

The property, originally known as the Borneo plantation, functioned for many years as an aloe and castor bean oil plantation. It was completely renovated and refurbished in the early 1980s and converted into a marine ecology center run by STINAPA. The building has now fallen into disrepair, but it is still possible to wander through the ruins and see the painted lettering on the walls indicating the roles played by different rooms and buildings, including Lodging, Office and a room for Dive Gear. The remnants of a wet lab used to study species in saltwater tanks are also evident in one of the rooms.

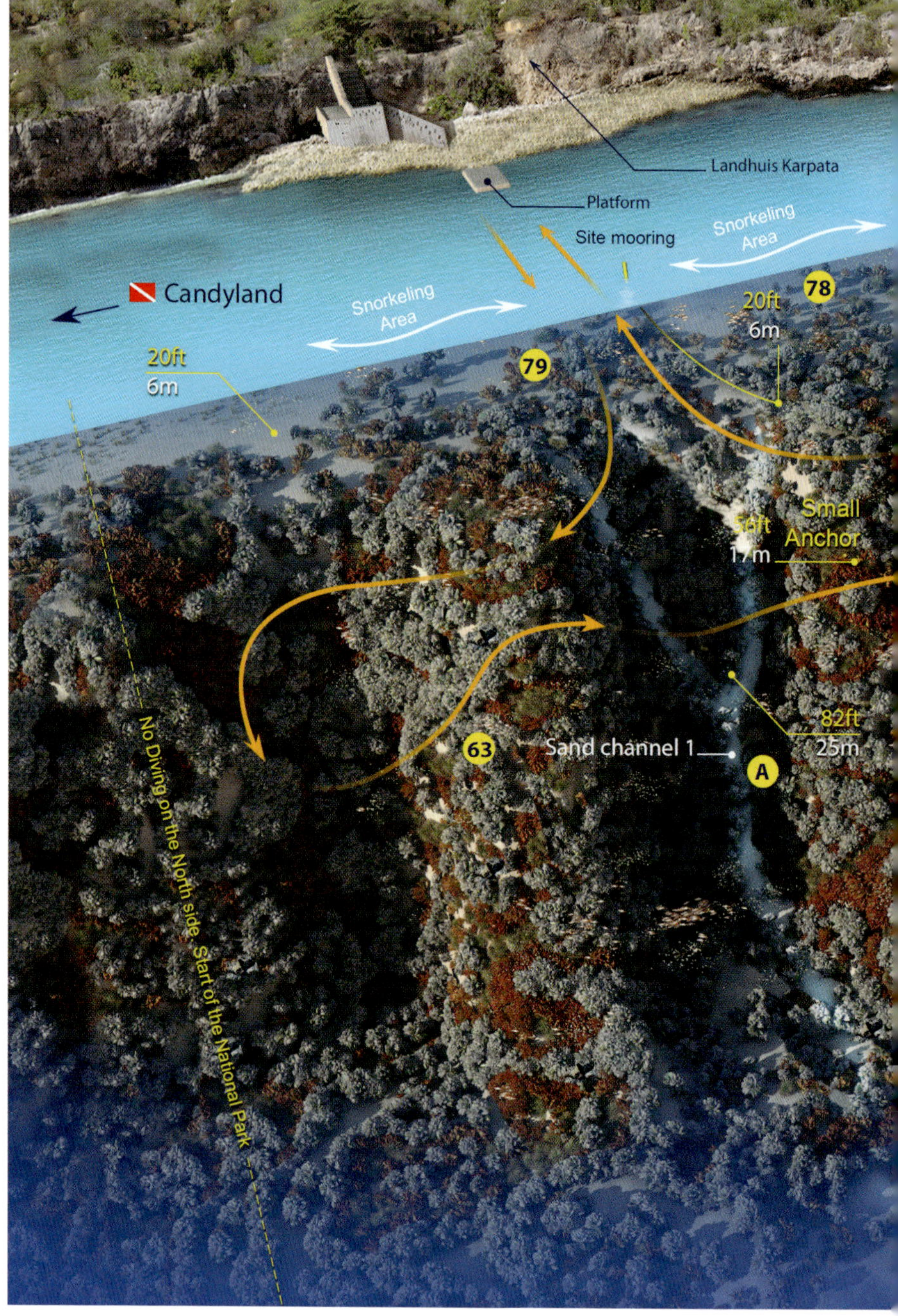

back toward the buoy making their way along the top of the reef wall or through the shallower back reef. Divers typically exit where they entered, to the left (facing the shore) of the concrete wharf, using it for support as they climb out on the slippery rocks.

There is much to see on this dive, so divers should not try to rush the experience. Karpata is one of those dive sites that divers can return to time and time again.

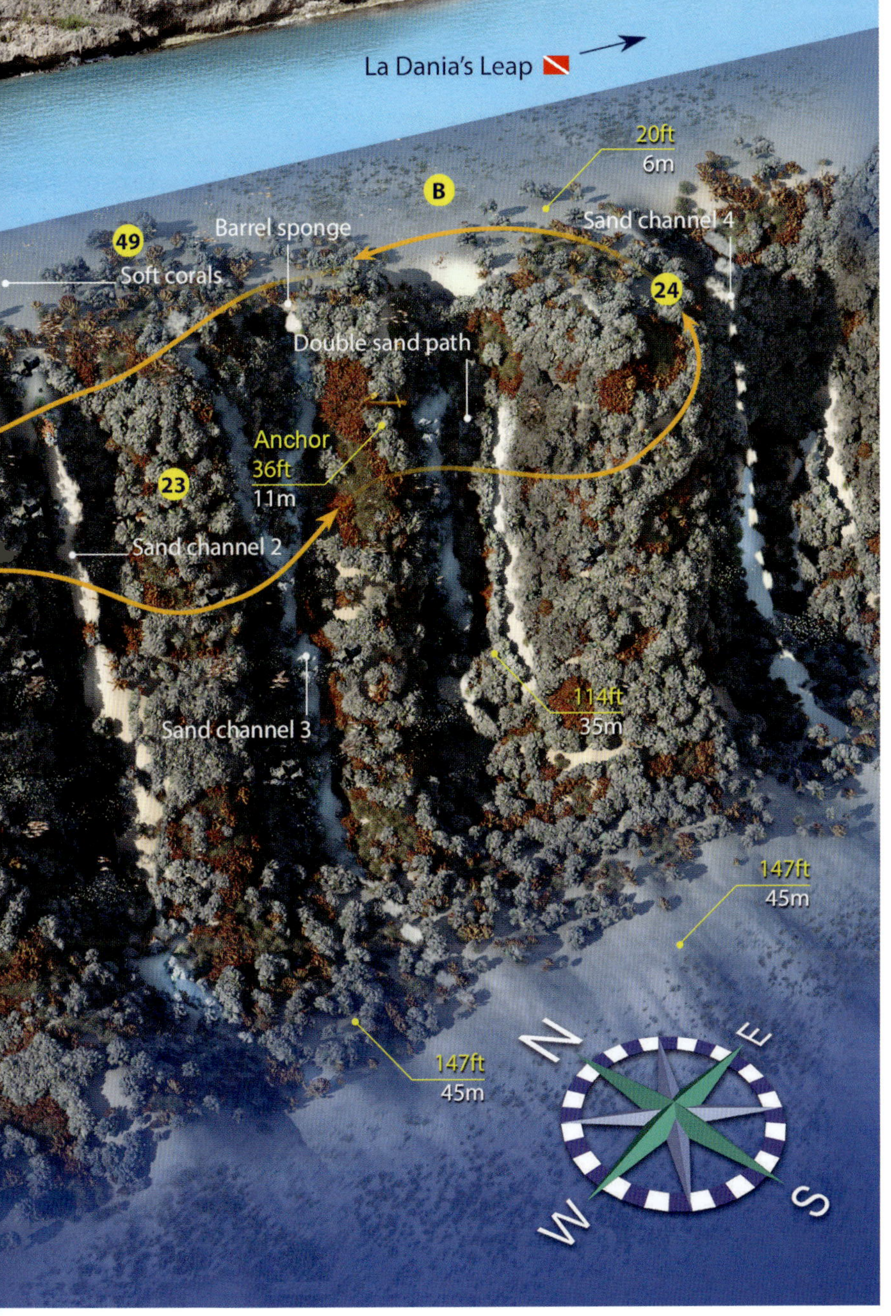
La Dania's Leap
20ft
6m
B
Barrel sponge
Sand channel 4
49
Soft corals
24
Double sand path
Anchor
36ft
11m
23
Sand channel 2
114ft
35m
Sand channel 3
147ft
45m
147ft
45m
N
E
W
S

La Dania's Leap

Difficulty ●●●
Current ●●○
Depth ●●●
Reef ★★★
Fauna ★★☆

Access about 18 mins from Kralendijk
about 43 mins from Kralendijk

Level Advanced Open Water

Location

Karpata, Bonaire
GPS: 12°13′7.2″N, 068°20′53.0″W

Getting there

La Dania's Leap is just under 8 miles (13 kilometers) north of Kralendijk by car and a mere 0.3 miles (0.5 kilometers) south of the famous Karpata dive site. Drive north on Kaya Gob. N. Debrot past the Harbour Village Marina and Hato, where the road becomes Bulevar Gob. N. Debrot. The road moves inland at Sabadeco, also known as Santa Barbara Crowns, and returns to the coast at Oil Slick Leap, where it becomes known as Queen's Highway.

Continue past the 1000 Steps and Tolo dive sites to where the road briefly cuts inland before returning to the coast a half mile later. Just 0.9 miles (1.4 kilometers) past the Tolo site the road takes a downhill grade and starts turning to the right. There is a yin-yang symbol on the road and a pathway

FEATURED OPERATOR

VIP Diving runs dive trips to some of the most unique shore-accessible sites on Bonaire, including the island's rugged east coast and famous northern sites such as La Dania's Leap and Karpata. Their talented dive professionals lead divers safely off the cliffs at La Dania's Leap to explore both sites during the same dive. VIP Diving is proud to be the only 5-Star Blue Destination Dive Center in Bonaire, underscoring their commitment to preserving Bonaire's marine environment and supporting the local community. VIP Diving is about more than just diving.

Tel: +599-701-7701
Email: info@vipdiving.com
Visit: **Vipdiving.com**

on the left heading down toward the rocky shore. Parking at La Dania's Leap is limited at best, so divers usually unload gear on the roadside here, before parking at Karpata and walking back along the road. When they leave, visitors to Karpata by car must continue north and inland via the town of Rincón.

Access

Follow the path that leads from the road to the short cliff edge at La Dania's Leap—a distance of about 200 feet (65 meters). The path starts out as a dirt track but switches to dead, fossilized coral when it approaches the shore. There is plenty of space down by the water's edge, so divers might want to consider carrying their gear down and putting it on once near the water.

There is a yellow rock at the entry point on the edge of the cliff that marks the short drop into the water, which is about 4 feet (1.2 meters) and can only be done one diver at a time. Once in the water, divers should swim away from the cliff and toward the yellow marker buoy as quickly as possible, to not get caught in a wave surge.

It is not possible to exit the water at this site, so divers typically head west, exiting the water at the adjacent Karpata dive site—which is another reason to park at Karpata. The dive takes approximately 30 minutes depending on the current. La Dania's Leap is an incredible experience, but definitely not one for the faint-hearted.

Description

La Dania's Leap is very similar to nearby Karpata. The reef is known as a fantastic vertical wall dive, offering divers the opportunity to see large grouper, snapper, parrotfish, angelfish, and trumpetfish. The coral cover is dense and the reef wall is broken up by distinct sand channels. Many divers report that it is worth exploring the deeper reef areas of La Dania's Leap, even though it means skipping the deeper sites at Karpata near the end of their dive. Fortunately, there is plenty to check out in Karpata's shallower waters.

Rappel

Difficulty
Current
Depth
Reef
Fauna

Access about 42 mins from Kralendijk

Level Advanced Open Water

Location

Tolo, Bonaire
GPS: 12°13'03.1"N, 068°20'39.2"W

Getting there

Rappel is a boat-only dive site located at the base of a cliff located between the Bloodlet and La Dania's Leap dive sites. It is approximately 6.5 miles (10.5 kilometers) north of Kralendijk by boat. This stretch of the Bonaire coastline adjacent to the Queen's Highway does not provide any opportunity for divers to exit the water until they reach Karpata, which is just over 0.5 miles (0.8 kilometers) northwest of Rappel. Divers should reach out to their nearest dive center to find out when Rappel next appears on their schedule.

Access

The currents at Rappel can be quite strong. When that happens, this site is best suited to those with drift diving experience.

Description

Rappel is a popular dive site that got its name after the first divers to access this site did so by rappelling down the cliff face, back before there were established mooring buoys. We do not recommend this method of entry, and it is much safer to access the site by boat. Rappel is sometimes referred to as Boka di Tota, and it is known for its incredible corals, including massive sea fans and other gorgonians, which cover the shallow shelf area and steep drop-off. Divers will likely come across lobsters, nudibranchs and flamingo tongues, as well as tiger grouper and barracuda. French angelfish and bar jacks are also common here, as are cleaning stations. The cliff is undercut by a shallow cavern just below the waterline that can be very dangerous to explore given that currents are usually fairly strong at Rappel.

Bloodlet

Difficulty
Current
Depth
Reef
Fauna

Access about 41 mins from Kralendijk

Level Open Water

Location

Tolo, Bonaire
GPS: 12°12'56.6"N, 68°20'31.0"W

Getting there

Bloodlet is a boat-only dive located between Tolo and Karpata. It is approximately 6.2 miles (10 kilometers) north of Kralendijk by boat. The stretch of the Bonaire coastline adjacent to the Queen's Highway has high, inaccessible cliffs. It is possible for divers to pick their way through the dense and thorny underbrush to reach the rocky shoreline at Bloodlet, but we strongly recommend against this approach. Divers should instead start their dive off on a positive note by accessing Bloodlet via boat. Divers can contact their nearest dive center to find out when they are next visiting this site.

Access

The currents at Bloodlet tend to be less strong than those at nearby Rappel because of the way the coastline projects into the ocean just east of the dive site. Bloodlet is more suitable for less-experienced divers relative to its neighboring site, but divers should pay attention to conditions and modify their dive plan accordingly.

Description

Bloodlet gets its name from the price exacted from divers who are determined to access this site from shore dive. Much of Bonaire's natural foliage is covered in thorns. And aside from the potential damage to skin and gear, it is simply not a fun way to reach the dive site. As such, Bloodlet is best accessed by boat.

The site is known for its wide sandy plateau that shelters elkhorn coral and a dense reef structure that supports hard corals as well as sponges, including plenty of tube sponges and large elephant ear sponges. Sea turtles are known to frequent this site, as do schools of surgeonfish and tangs, and the occasional barracuda.

13

BONAIRE

Tolo (Ol' Blue)

Difficulty ●●○
Current ●●○
Depth ●●○
Reef ★★★
Fauna ★★★

Access about 17 mins from Kralendijk
about 40 mins from Kralendijk

Level Open Water

Location
Tolo, Bonaire
GPS: 12°12'55.4"N, 68°20'14.0"W

Getting there

Tolo is located 7 miles (11.2 kilometers) north of Kralendijk by car—a 17-minute journey. Drive north on Kaya Gob. N. Debrot past the Harbour Village Marina and Hato, where the road becomes Bulevar Gob. N. Debrot. The road moves inland at Sabadeco, also known as Santa Barbara Crowns, and returns to the coast at Oil Slick Leap, where it becomes known as Queen's Highway. Continue north past 1000 Steps.

Just under one mile (1.5 kilometers) after the road becomes one way in a northerly direction, divers will see a green sign marked Tolo. There is a lay-by on the left-hand side of the road. Immediately after the lay-by is a small track on the left that leads to the Tolo parking area, which is marked with a yellow rock. The parking area consists of a flat plateau adjacent to a small cliff overlooking the dive and snorkel site. When they leave, visitors to Karpata by car must continue north and inland via the town of Rincón.

Access

Several stone steps cut into the short cliff provide access to the beach. The steps are uneven and include rocks that are positioned to provide better footing, but divers may find it challenging to traverse wearing full dive gear. They should take their time and tread carefully.

The beach itself consists largely of coral rock that transitions into a flat, sometimes slippery, coral plateau at the water's edge. There is a mooring buoy at this site, anchored in the sandy back reef. It is placed close to the drop-off, around 65 feet (20 meters) from shore.

Description

Tolo, sometimes referred to as Ol' Blue, is one of only a few shore dives in the northern section of sites that has easy entry and exit points. It is also a spectacular dive site with an incredible reef and plenty of reef species. The site is protected from easterly winds because it sits in a bay carved out of the cliffs that run along much of this stretch of coastline. The limited current in the bay and the shallowness of the water between the shore and the reef line makes this a great site for snorkelers as well. And given the lack of development in the surrounding landscape, the corals and reef fish have thrived in the relatively pristine environment.

Staghorn corals thrive in the clear waters of Bonaire.

The flat back reef section of the site is stunning, with plenty of soft coral, as well as large yellow pencil coral—all on a backdrop of white coral sand. Patches of this sand occur throughout the area, creating mixed habitat that acts as a nursery for juvenile fish. Yellow pencil coral, in particular, offers excellent habitat for juveniles, and the presence of such high-quality nursery habitat so close to the reef slope helps support the adult population living on the primary reef.

The flat back reef transitions quite abruptly to the drop-off zone. This section of the reef wall is dominated by plate-form corals, which give the reef the appearance of a cheese grater. Toward the west, the reef transition is much more gradual, creating a more rounded section before it drops down as a wall, starting at around 40 feet (12 meters). Boulder star corals and soft corals dominate this part of the reef. Massive sponges appear throughout the site

David Fishman ©

along the wall, particularly a huge orange elephant ear sponge found at 60 feet (18 meters) in the eastern section of the reef wall. Tolo boasts its share of gorgonians along the flat upper section and on the face of the wall—particularly sea whips along the latter section. A myriad of reef fish, such as porcupinefish, rock beauties, fairy basslets, snapper, and parrotfish, round out the assemblage.

Route

A preferred route is to head out directly from the steps out toward the reef line—divers should not bother to swim out to the buoy. The coral rubble will soon give way to star coral, gorgonians and sea fans at a depth of 16 feet (5 meters) and the start of the reef slope. From there, divers typically drop down the wall to their target depth. The wall bottoms out at around 140 feet (43 meters) with plenty to see all the way down. Divers should pay attention to their depth profile, as it is easy to be distracted by the pristine surroundings.

Once they have reached their target depth, divers generally turn toward the west. Note how this part of the reef is dominated by plate-form corals—a form that corals often take at depth and on walls, where a flatter surface helps them

collect more sunlight. Divers often continue along the wall, ascending slowly as they go, passing purple sponges and porcupinefish, rock beauties, snapper, and black margates. Lobsters are often spotted in reef crevices while jacks feed above the reef.

Near the western side of the reef, the plate-form coral starts to give way to high densities of boulder-form star corals. The reef wall eventually bends around slightly to the north, signaling that it is time to head up to the top of the reef. A tall column of coral that tops out at a depth of 35 feet (10.5 meters) is a useful landmark to watch out

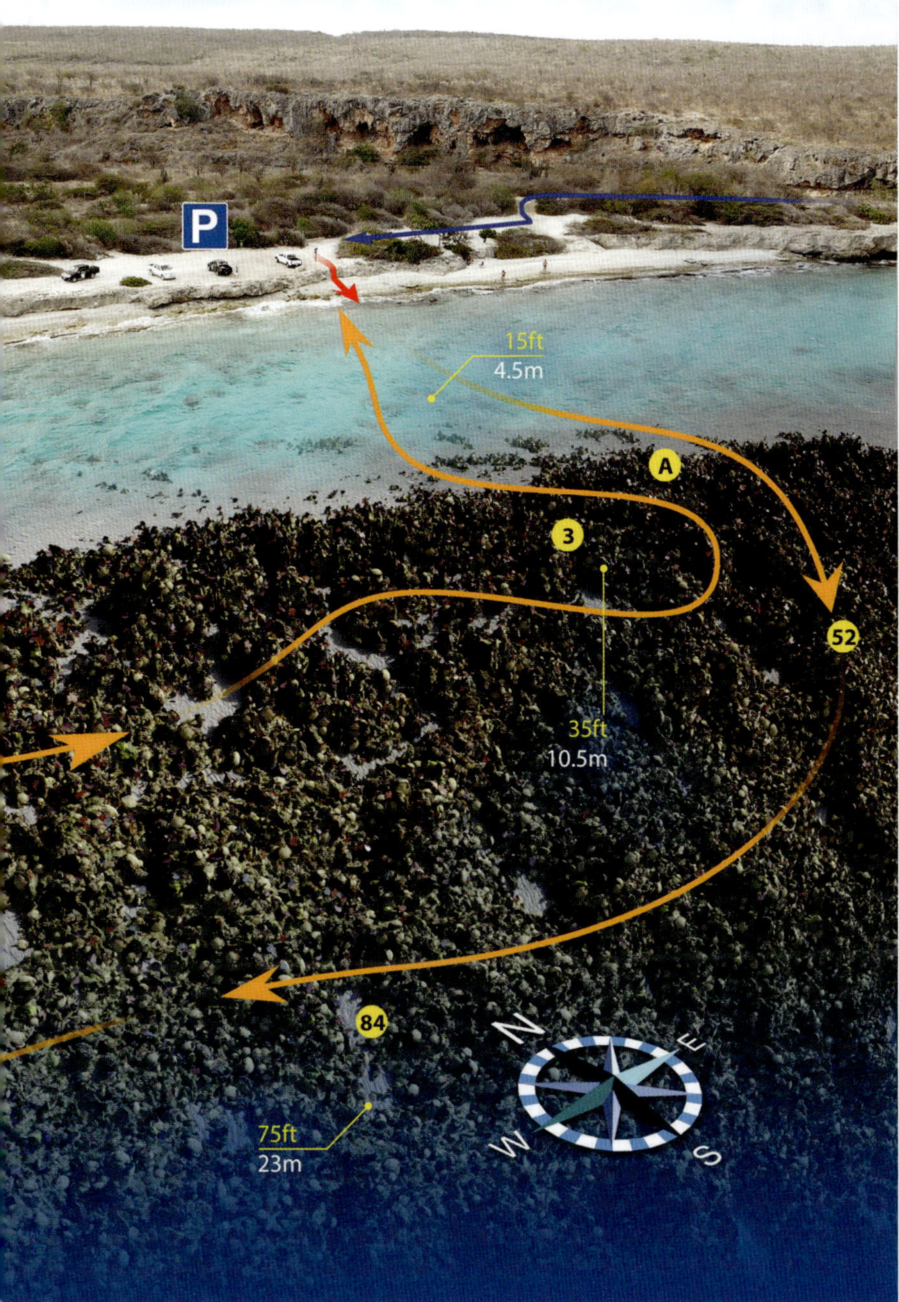

for near the top of the wall. But the dive is far from over. The buoy is anchored at a depth of 16 feet (5 meters) right next to a massive stand of what was once healthy staghorn coral. The staghorn is about 65 feet (20 meters) from the reef line. As divers pass the staghorn, they will swim through forests of gorgonians interspersed with small coral heads, where they may spot plenty of parrotfish, even the relatively rare midnight parrotfish. The reef will eventually give way to rubble once again on the way back toward shore and the exit point.

Country Garden

Difficulty ●●○
Current ●●○
Depth ●●○
Reef ★★☆
Fauna ★★☆

Access about 38 mins from Kralendijk

Level Open Water

Location

Tolo plantation
GPS: 12°12'48.6"N, 68°20'02.2"W

Getting there

Country Garden is a boat dive located between Tolo and Bon Bini Na Kas. It is almost 6 miles (10 kilometers) north of Kralendijk by boat. The Bonaire coastline that runs adjacent to this section of the Queen's Highway has high, inaccessible cliffs. The sites in this region are therefore only suitable for boat diving. Divers should check with their local dive center to find out the next scheduled visit to the site.

Access

The currents at Country Garden are generally modest. Divers of all experience levels will be able to access this site from a boat.

Description

Country Garden has also been called Country Gardens as well as Mushroom City. The site is known for large limestone pillars that have separated from the cliff wall and become encrusted with corals. These pillars now host a variety of reef fish, including chromis, soldierfish, squirrelfish, grunts and snapper. Cleaner fish, butterflyfish and goatfish are also common at this site, along with honeycomb cowfish and graysbies. There are many holes along the reef where spotted morays and green morays can also be found.

RELAX & RECHARGE

On your return trip through Rincón, consider stopping in at **Posada Para Mira.** Located just west of the town along Kaya Para Mira, the restaurant has a large covered terrace with exceptional views across the surrounding hills. Its elevated position provides a gentle breeze while you dine on local cuisine at its best. Their specialties include traditionally made stoba di kabritu (goat stew) and sopi di yuana (iguana soup), served with a range of local sides. Posada Para Mira is open from 11:00am to 6:00pm, Monday, Wednesday, Friday and the weekend.

Bon Bini Na Kas →

Access by boat only

Site buoy

Bon Bini Na Kas

Access about 36 mins from Kralendijk

Level Open Water

Location

Tolo plantation
GPS: 12°12’43.8”N, 68°19’46.2”W

Getting there

Bon Bini Na Kas is a boat-only dive site located just north of 1000 Steps, and close to 5.5 miles (9 kilometers) north of Kralendijk by boat. The Bonaire coastline that runs adjacent to the

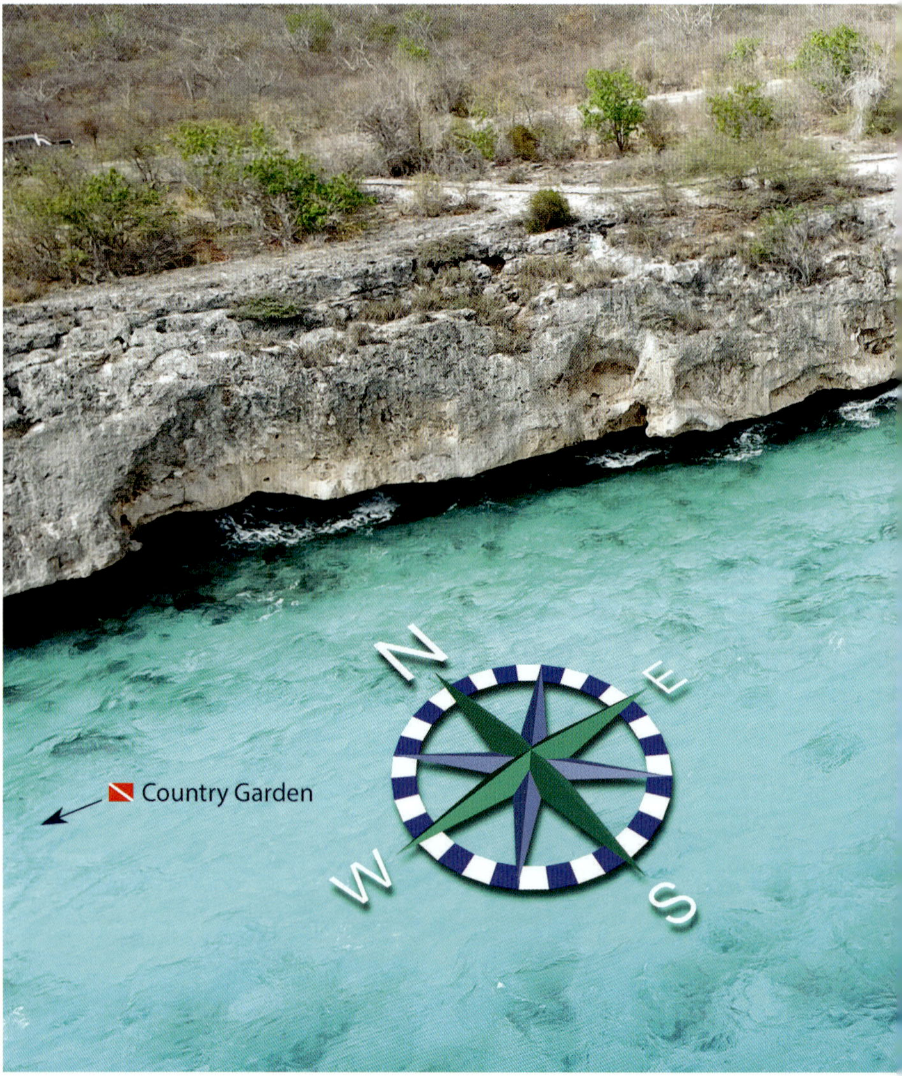

Queen's Highway has high, inaccessible cliffs. The sites in this region are therefore only suitable for boat diving. Divers should check with their local dive center to find out when they are next scheduled to visit Bon Bini Na Kas.

Access

The currents at Bon Bini Na Kas are generally moderate, making this dive site accessible by boat to divers of all experience levels.

Description

Bon Bini Na Kas means "welcome home" in Papiamento. Visitors are likely to hear "Bon Bini" echoed throughout Bonaire in a variety of contexts throughout their stay on the island.

This site is known for its sea plumes and sea rods, as well as stands of staghorn corals and large sponges. Divers also regularly see the many reef fish species associated with these various types of corals and sponges. These include trumpetfish, sharpnose puffers, filefish and parrotfish, particularly stoplight, Queen and princess. Sea turtles are also frequently seen at this site, and lobsters and green moray eels can be found in cracks and crevices in the reef.

1000 Steps

Difficulty ●●○
Current ●○○
Depth ●●○
Reef ★★★
Fauna ★★☆

Access about 15 mins from Kralendijk
about 34 mins from Kralendijk

Level Open Water

Location
Tolo, Bonaire
GPS: 12°12'38.8"N, 68°19'16.9"W

Getting there

1000 Steps is located 6 miles (9.5 kilometers) north of Kralendijk by car. Drive north on Kaya Gob. N. Debrot past the Harbour Village Marina and Hato, where the road becomes Bulevar Gob. N. Debrot. The road moves inland at Sabadeco, also known as Santa Barbara Crowns, and returns to the coast at Oil Slick Leap, where it becomes known as Queen's Highway. About 0.9 miles (1.4 kilometers) down this road—a 3-minute drive—the road bends right as it ascends a small hill before turning back to the left. 1000 Steps is located 0.28 miles (0.45 kilometers) after this bend.

There is ample parking on the right-hand side of the road just after the entrance to Radio Nederland Wereldomroep (Radio Netherlands International Foundation). The steps down to the beach are on the opposite side of the road to the parking lot and are marked with yellow rocks.

Access

1000 Steps is a very popular dive and snorkel site and can get busy at times. The cliff edge, where the stairs to the beach begin, offers incredible views of the bay and is a favorite photo spot. Divers must take great care as they climb and descend the steps between the parking lot and the beach; they are uneven in places and can become slippery when wet. The beach is rocky, but access to the water is relatively easy. The mooring buoy is visible at the edge of the sandy back reef. Most divers surface swim toward the buoy, descend on the edge of the reef and head north.

Description

1000 Steps is one of the most famous dive and snorkel sites in Bonaire. The name comes from the long coral-stone staircase built in the late 1960s that divers must climb down (and back up again) with their heavy dive gear to access the site. It is a misnomer, however, in that there are only 72 steps, although it can feel like 1000 when carrying wet gear. This location is another one of the Bonaire sites that offers spectacular, high-quality corals and an abundance of reef creatures.

The steps leading down to the water at 1000 Steps.

The shallow back reef has plenty of hard and soft corals set against a backdrop of white sand, which gives the bay its beautiful turquoise color when viewed from the top of the cliff. Large stands of

DID YOU KNOW?

1000 Steps is the last dive site along the Queen's Highway where it is possible to turn around and head back into Kralendijk directly. After 1000 Steps, the road becomes one-way only, which means visitors will have to continue north along the coast toward Karpata before returning to Kralendijk via the town of Rincón and the interior of the island. This was done in part for safety, given the narrow roads, but also to help ensure visitors pass through the more remote Rincón. Fortunately, the town has plenty to offer hungry divers looking for a bite to eat and a drink after a day of diving. Some of the Relax & Recharge boxes in this guidebook are dedicated to Rincón-based eateries. Enjoy!

ReefSmart ©

delicate staghorn coral provide valuable habitat for a range of species, particularly grunts and damselfish, along with the juveniles of species that frequent the deeper water, such as snapper and parrotfish.

The reef transitions from a gradual slope to a steeper drop-off at around 30 feet (9 meters), just seaward of the yellow mooring buoy. Here, the reef becomes a steep wall with vertical grooves and accompanying sand channels. The grooves are not as pronounced as they are at the nearby Karpata dive site, but they still provide plenty of complexity, with large pillar-like coral mounds along the upper edge of the reef, some as large as 15 feet (4.5 meters).

The reef wall has plenty of sponges and sea whips, along with a dense mix of both coral heads and plate-form corals. Sea turtles frequent this site, as do barracuda, jacks, parrotfish, and a diverse array of other species, including morays, wrasses, and a variety of boxfish. Lobsters are also often spotted in overhanging areas.

Route

Most divers head out toward the mooring buoy before descending the reef wall. From there,

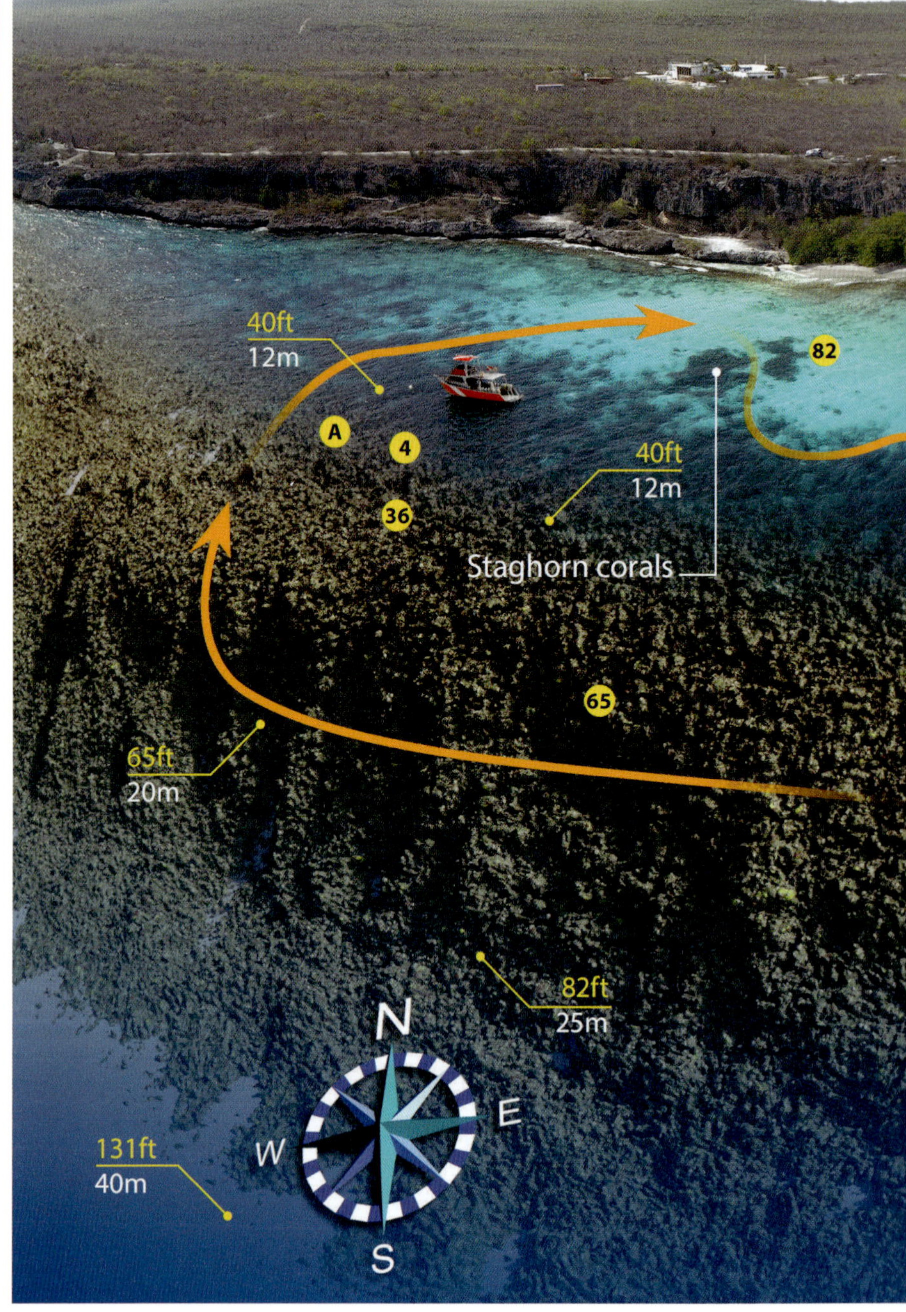

they often head north along the wall, keeping an eye open for the many cleaning stations found at this site. After about 20 to 30 minutes, divers typically make their way back toward the shore. Most conduct an extended safety stop as they zigzag through the shallow back reef area, which offers complex and wonderful habitat to explore.

Snorkelers may venture out to the drop-off, but most choose to focus their attention on the shallower back reef. This area is the ideal depth

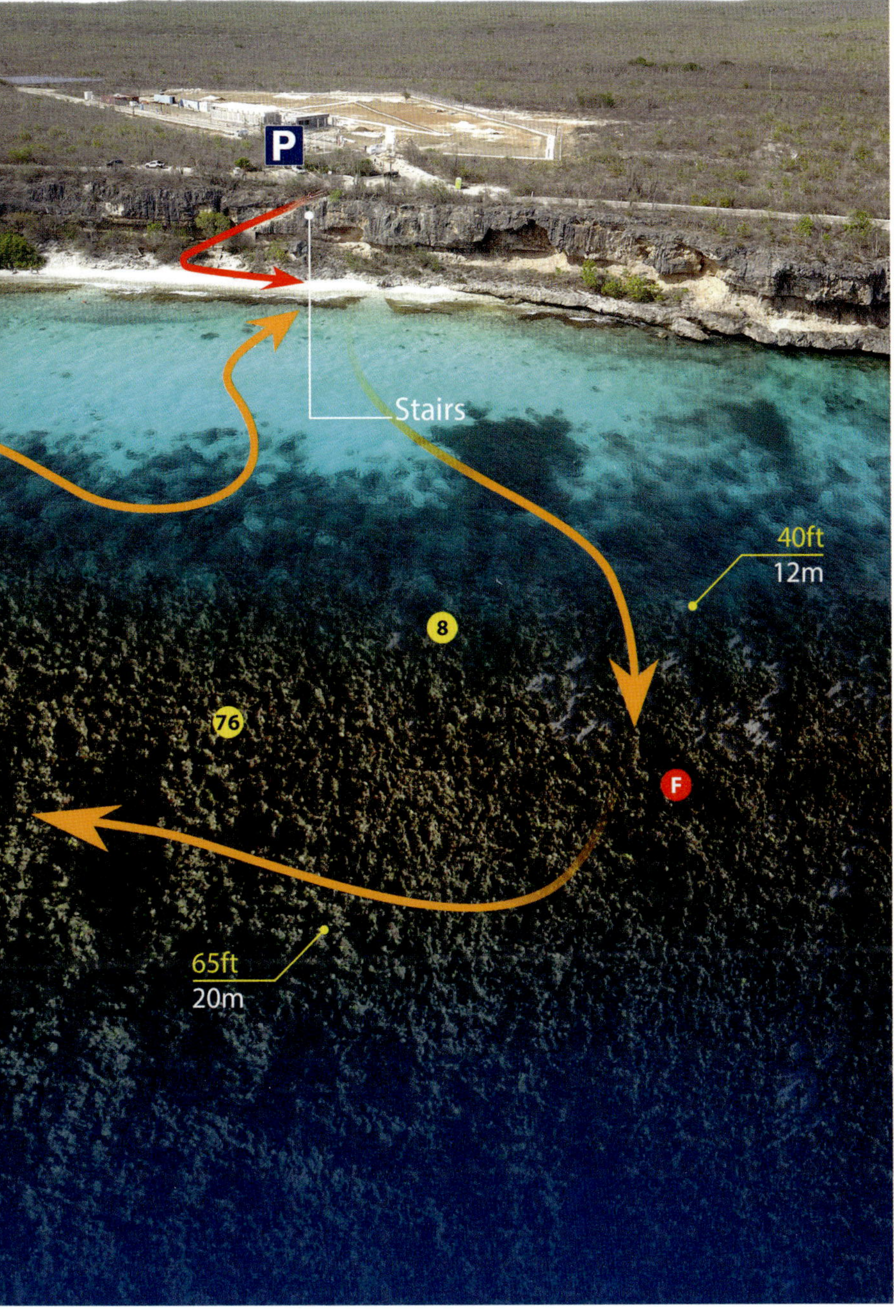

for snorkeling, has virtually no current and is one of the best places on the island to observe green sea turtles.

Weber's Joy (Witches Hut)

Difficulty ● ○ ○
Current ● ● ○
Depth ● ● ○
Reef ★★☆
Fauna ★★☆

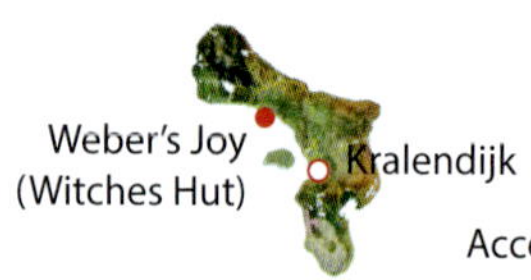

Access about 13 mins from Kralendijk
about 31 mins from Kralendijk

Level Open Water

Location
Tolo, Bonaire
GPS: 12°12'24.0"N, 68°18'59.0"W

Getting there

Weber's Joy is located about 5.3 miles (8.5 kilometers) north of Kralendijk by car—a 13-minute drive. Head north on Kaya Gob. N. Debrot past the Harbour Village Marina and Hato, where the road becomes Bulevar Gob. N. Debrot. The road moves inland at Sabadeco, also known as Santa Barbara Crowns. The highway returns to the coast at the Oil Slick Leap dive site, where it becomes known as Queen's Highway. Continue along the coastal road for just under 0.75 miles (1.2 kilometers) to reach the dive site—it is just 0.2 miles (0.3 kilometer) past the Jeff Davis Memorial dive site.

On the right-hand side of the road there will be a blue parking sign followed by an abandoned white building with a red roof. There is enough parking for several cars on either side of this building. A paved path to the dive site is located on the opposite side of the road and is marked with two yellow rocks.

Access

Divers should follow the path down the steps to the shoreline. It can get a little slippery when wet, so they must watch their step. At the end of the path is a beach consisting of coral rock, which stretches nearly 60 feet (18 meters) in length. Divers can just step off the beach and swim directly out into the water, avoiding the shallow reef immediately to the south. A mooring buoy is located 240 feet (73 meters) to the north of the beach.

Description

Some references call this site Witches Hut after the abandoned house that once graced the beach. This dive is well known to underwater photographers. It offers plenty of opportunity to get up close to colorful reef organisms, including giant anemone and their associated Pederson cleaner shrimps, corkscrew anemones, arrow crabs, octopuses and nudibranchs. Squid, parrotfish, angelfish (particularly grey angelfish and rock beauties) and soapfish are frequently seen swimming among the colorful variety of sponges and corals.

18

BONAIRE

Jeff Davis Memorial

Access: about 12 mins from Kralendijk (by car); about 30 mins from Kralendijk (by boat)

Level Open Water

Location
Tolo, Bonaire
GPS: 12°12'18.4"N, 68°18'49."W

Getting there
Jeff Davis Memorial is located 5.2 miles (8.3 kilometers) north of Kralendijk by car—a 12-minute journey. Drive north on Kaya Gob. N. Debrot past the Harbour Village Marina and Hato, where the road becomes Bulevar Gob. N. Debrot. The road moves inland at Sabadeco, also known as Santa Barbara Crowns, and returns to the coast at Oil Slick Leap, where it turns into Queen's Highway.

Divers should continue along this coastal road for a short while. A small wall runs along the left-hand side of the road by the shore and a cliff rises to the right. The road winds for another minute or so after which there is a blue parking sign on the right, followed by a lay-by with enough parking for several cars. A gravel path leads to the dive site starting on the opposite side of the road. Two yellow rocks mark the start of the path.

Access
Divers should follow the path toward the shoreline where it turns right and heads down to a small sand and coral rubble beach. Divers and snorkelers must descend a small cliff, about 6 feet (2 meters) high, which can be challenging for some people. A mooring buoy sits 300 feet (92 meters) to the south of the beach. Divers wishing to visit Kalli's Reef will have to swim even farther south, past the Jeff Davis Memorial Reef buoy. The Kalli's Reef buoy can be reached after a surface swim of about 45 minutes to the southeast.

Description
Jeff Davis Memorial boasts a relatively shallow back reef leading to a steep reef slope. The reef bottoms out at a depth of 130 feet (40 meters), which is typical of the dives on the west coast of Bonaire. The back reef has plenty to see for snorkelers and divers alike. The area is dominated by gorgonians until the reef starts, at which point it transitions into hard coral, starting at a depth of 20 feet (6 meters). Juvenile reef fishes shelter in the complex habitat created by the gorgonians and corals, and divers may even be lucky enough to find seahorses and sea turtles here. If not, divers are almost guaranteed to see all manner of parrotfish, including Queen, princess, stoplight and the rare blue parrotfish, in and around the

Rocks mark the path at Jeff Davis Memorial.

reef transition area. Divers also frequently spot pairs of butterflyfish and angelfish here.

The reef slope is steep, with large coral mounds interspersed with tube sponges. Vertical sand-bottomed chutes framed by hard corals break up the reef slope. Schools of creole wrasses stream across the face of the reef wall, while glasseye snapper shelter under the coral heads and ledges along the wall. Cleaning stations are abundant, including both shrimp stations and those managed by juvenile Spanish hogfish, providing a great opportunity for macro-photographers. As with most sites in Bonaire, the most interesting sights are higher up on the wall and into the reef transition area. There are still corals and reef fishes to see lower down the wall, but these areas lack the diversity of the shallower depths.

This site contains a Reef Renewal outplant location for staghorn coral toward the southern end of the site, in approximately 15 feet (4.5 meters) of water.

Reef Smart ©

Route

After entering the water, most divers choose to surface swim around 300 feet (90 meters) to the south to reach the buoy. They can check out the coral transplant area at the southern end of the site or simply descend the reef slope to their target depth before making their way in a north, northwest direction back toward the entry point. A large sand channel cuts into the reef toward the deeper edge of the slope, which can be interesting to explore.

Most divers continue along the reef slope as they gradually ascend. They will pass a couple of large coral mounds between the depths of 30 and 50 feet (9 and 15 meters) that provide habitat for a number of coral reef organisms

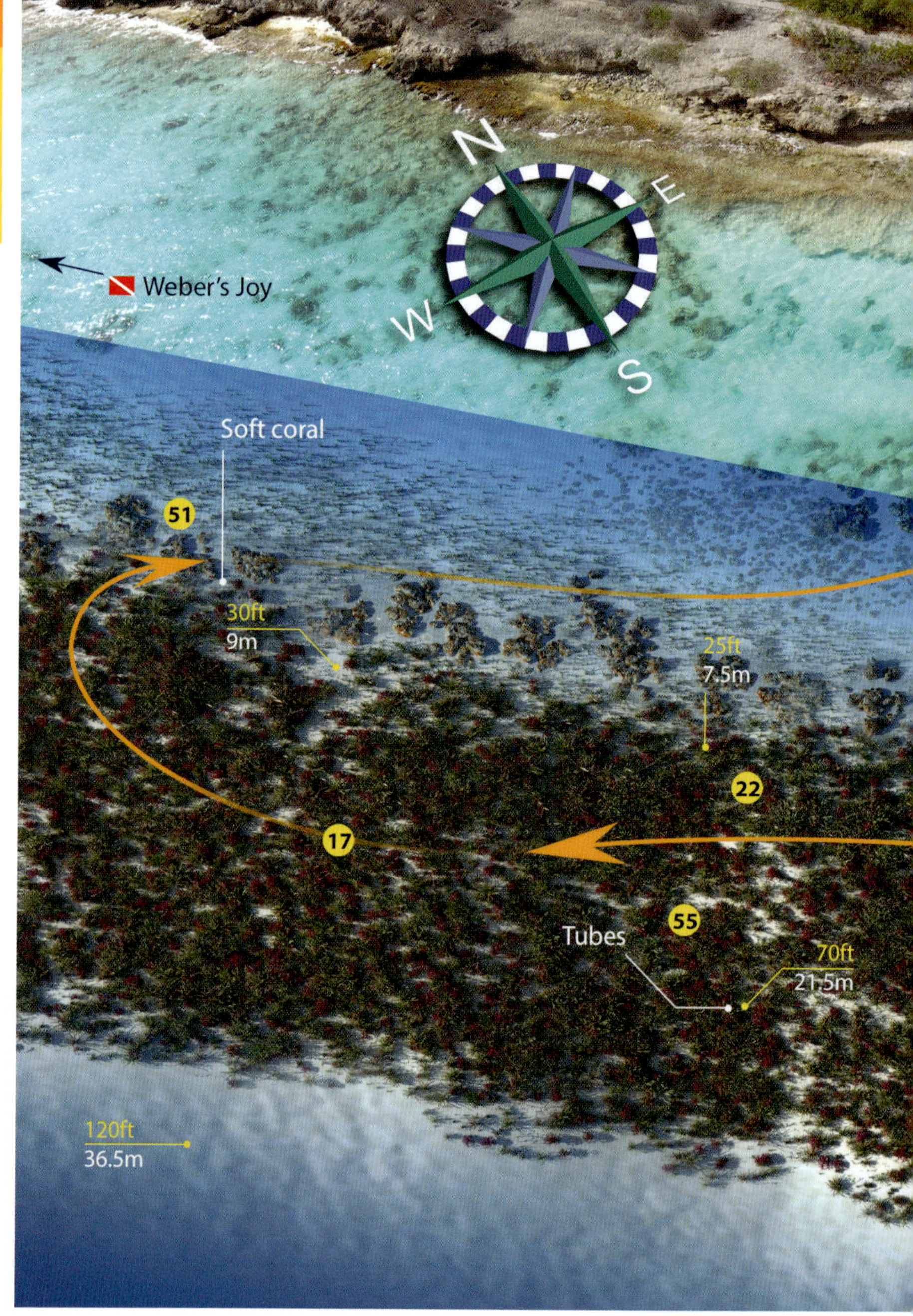

including fairy basslets, snapper and grunts.

Most divers take their safety stops in the shallow back reef area while they explore the multitude of soft corals at a depth of 20 feet (6 meters). This habitat supports trumpetfish and sharpnose pufferfish, among many other species. The greatest diversity in terms of corals and reef fishes is found on the north side of the buoy, so we recommend divers focus their snorkel or dive time there. They can then exit relatively easily at the beach.

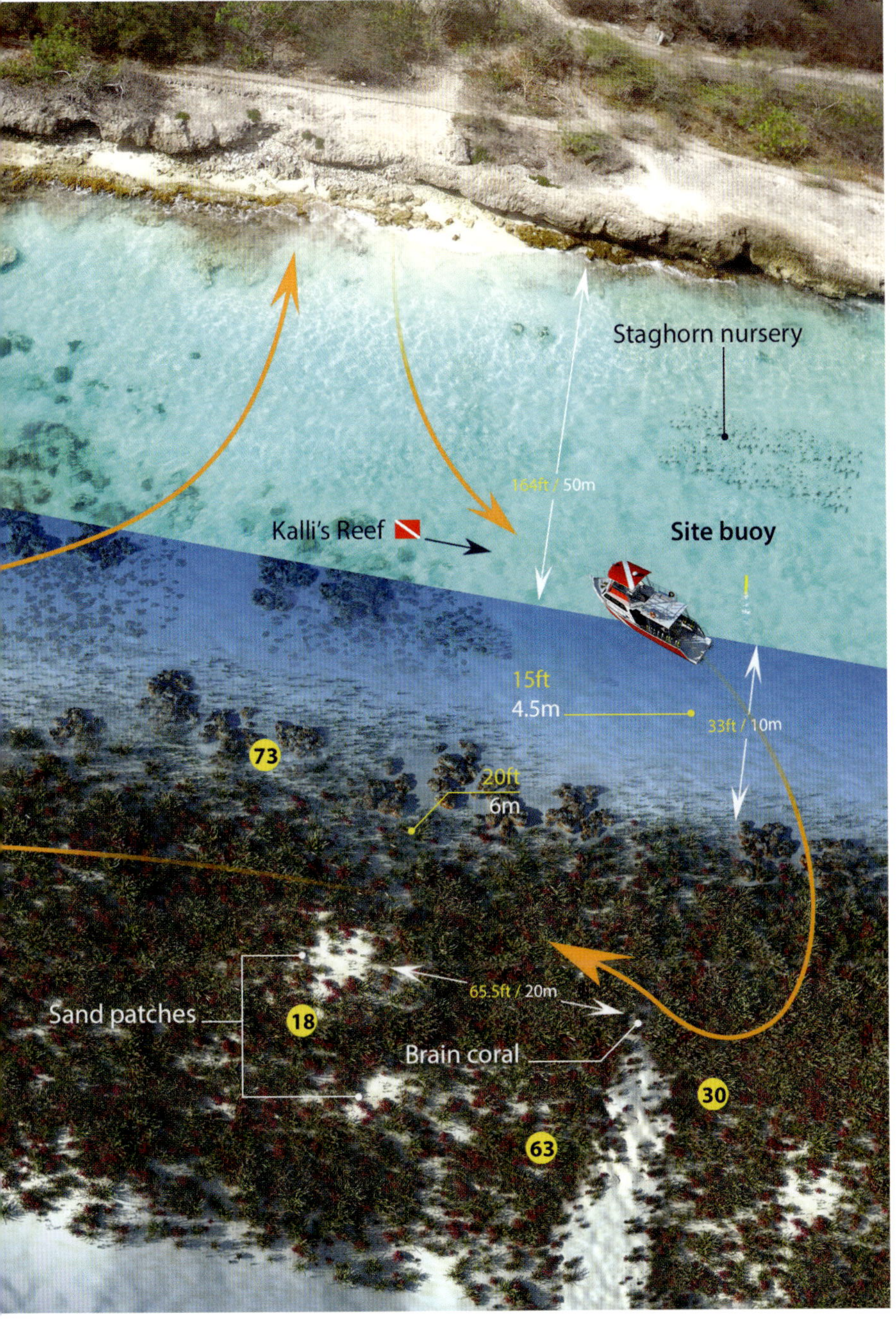
Staghorn nursery
164ft / 50m
Kalli's Reef
Site buoy
15ft
4.5m
33ft / 10m
73
20ft
6m
65.5ft / 20m
Sand patches
18
Brain coral
30
63

19 BONAIRE

Kalli's Reef

Difficulty ●●○
Current ●●○
Depth ●●○
Reef ★★☆
Fauna ★★☆

Access about 12 mins from Kralendijk
about 28 mins from Kralendijk

Level Open Water

Location
Tolo, Bonaire
GPS: 12°12'06.7"N, 68°18'37.0"W

Getting there

Kalli's Reef is located 4.8 miles (7.7 kilometers) north of Kralendijk by car—a 12-minute journey. Drive north on Kaya Gob. N. Debrot past the Harbour Village Marina and Hato, where the road becomes Bulevar Gob. N. Debrot. Just after Sabadeco, also known as Santa Barbara Crowns, the road turns sharply left toward the coast. The road passes the STINAPA headquarters and descends toward the ocean immediately ahead. Just before it reaches the shore, the road takes another

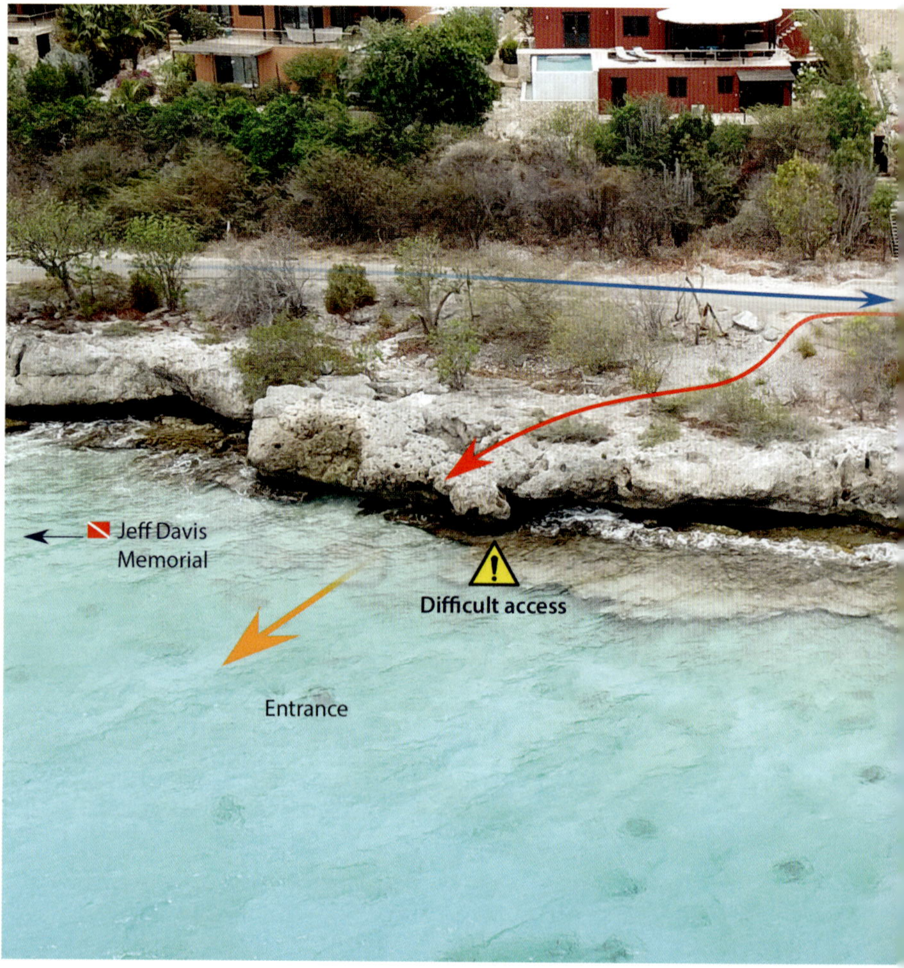

Jeff Davis Memorial

Difficult access

Entrance

sharp turn, this time to the right, and runs north along the coast. Kalli's Reef is located about 600 feet (183 meters) past the turn.

On the right-hand side of the road there is a parking sign, immediately followed by a lay-by on the side of the road next to a staircase that leads up to a house on the cliff above. There is no yellow rock here, but it is easy to spot the mooring buoy that sits just 150 feet (45 meters) off shore.

Access

On the opposite side of the road to the lay-by, a small gravel path leads down to the shore. To access the sites, divers must climb down the small cliff to the water, which can be challenging for individuals carrying heavy dive gear. For this reason, Kalli's Reef is most often accessed as a boat dive. Divers wanting to access the site from shore can also opt to swim the 0.3 miles (0.5 kilometers) south from the adjacent Jeff Davis Memorial dive site. In that case, divers should plan for the surface swim to take about 45 minutes, depending on conditions.

Description

Kalli's Reef was named after the founding manager of the Bonaire National Marine Park, Kalli De Meyer. It is a popular dive site with both snorkelers and divers thanks to its moderate currents and diverse range of fish species. Divers will likely encounter barracuda, which are very common here. Triggerfish, pufferfish, black durgons, porcupinefish, and all types of angelfish can be seen in and around large sponges and hard corals. Sea turtles are also occasionally spotted here, as are Queen and blue parrotfish.

20

BONAIRE

Oil Slick Leap

Difficulty ●●○
Current ●○○
Depth ●●○
Reef ★★☆
Fauna ★★☆

Access about 12 mins from Kralendijk
about 27 mins from Kralendijk

Level Open Water

Location
Tolo, Bonaire
GPS: 12°12'00.9"N, 68°18'30.8"W

Getting there

Oil Slick Leap is located 4.7 miles (7.5 kilometers) north of Kralendijk by car—a 12-minute ride. Drive north on Kaya Gob. N. Debrot past the Harbour Village Marina and Hato, where the road becomes Bulevar Gob. N. Debrot. Just after Sabadeco, also known as Santa Barbara Crowns, the road turns sharply left toward the coast. The road passes the STINAPA headquarters and descends toward the ocean immediately ahead. Just before the road reaches the water it takes a sharp turn to the right, heading north. At this turn, there is a gravel side road that heads left and leads to the parking lot next to Oil Slick Leap. There is plenty of parking available at this site.

Access

There is a relatively flat cliff area perched above the sea, located 75 feet (23 meters) away from the parking lot. A wooden platform built on the cliff's edge includes a metal ladder that provides access to the water, which is 10 feet (3 meters) below. This is the safest way to reach the dive site, although some divers choose to take a giant stride off the cliff edge directly into the water. Divers descending the ladder should know that the last few steps may be slippery, or even missing. Once in the water, divers should push away from the cliff edge, being careful not to accidentally kick the stands of elkhorn coral that grow close to the ladder. The buoy is located approximately 75 feet (23 meters) south of the platform.

Description

Oil Slick Leap allegedly got its name from when it was under consideration as a site for the Bonaire Petroleum Corporation (BOPEC) terminal. Fortunately for both divers and snorkelers, BOPEC was ultimately situated farther along the coast toward the northwest, allowing divers unfettered access to this fantastic site.

The view from above Oil Slick Leap.

Right from the start, this site delivers great habitat. As divers enter the water, they must be careful of the stands of elkhorn coral located just to the southeast of the ladder. The depth at the base of the ladder is 17 feet (5 meters) but an uncontrolled entry or a brief lack of attention during an exit could damage the stand of living coral. There are several recesses near the ladder that contain schools of glassy sweepers. Decorator crabs have also been found along this stretch of wall.

Aside from the handful of living elkhorn coral stands, coral rubble dominates the area between the base of the cliff and where the reef starts, interspersed with sand patches and groups of soft corals. This area provides ideal habitat for multiple cryptic species, including trumpetfish, slender filefish, and even seahorses. Stingrays and barracuda are also often observed hunting in this area.

The reef slope at Oil Slick Leap descends in a series of steps before dropping more steeply from 35 feet (10.5 meters) to over 100 feet (31 meters). The mooring buoy is anchored at a depth of 33 feet (10 meters) in a sand patch close to the edge of the drop-off. Pencil coral surrounds the sand patch, providing shelter to plenty of juvenile reef fishes. Plate-form hard corals dominate the deeper areas of the reef, mixed in with the normal complement of tube and vase sponges.

Reef Smart ©

The Reef Renewal Foundation Bonaire has placed a coral nursery and outplant site near the southern end of Oil Slick Leap, around 480 feet (146 meters) along the shore from the entry point. The array is positioned about 75 feet (23 meters) from shore, in the middle of a mix of sand, patch reef, and gorgonians, at a depth of 30 feet (9 meters).

Route

After entering the water, divers swim clear of the ladder to avoid getting pushed back against the cliff by waves and to allow other divers and snorkelers to enter and exit. When the chance presents, divers may opt to check out the stands of elkhorn coral and look for the glassy sweepers and decorator crabs along the cliff edge, if they can do so safely.

The plateau and cliff edge are great areas for snorkelers to explore as long as the wave action is not too strong. Divers should head toward the yellow mooring buoy and descend to the reef. The best route is to head southeast toward the coral nursery before looping back to the northwest toward the exit point. Much like other dive sites on the island, the best diving is in relatively shallow waters, down to a depth of approximately 60 feet (18 meters). Although the reef slope continues below that depth, it does

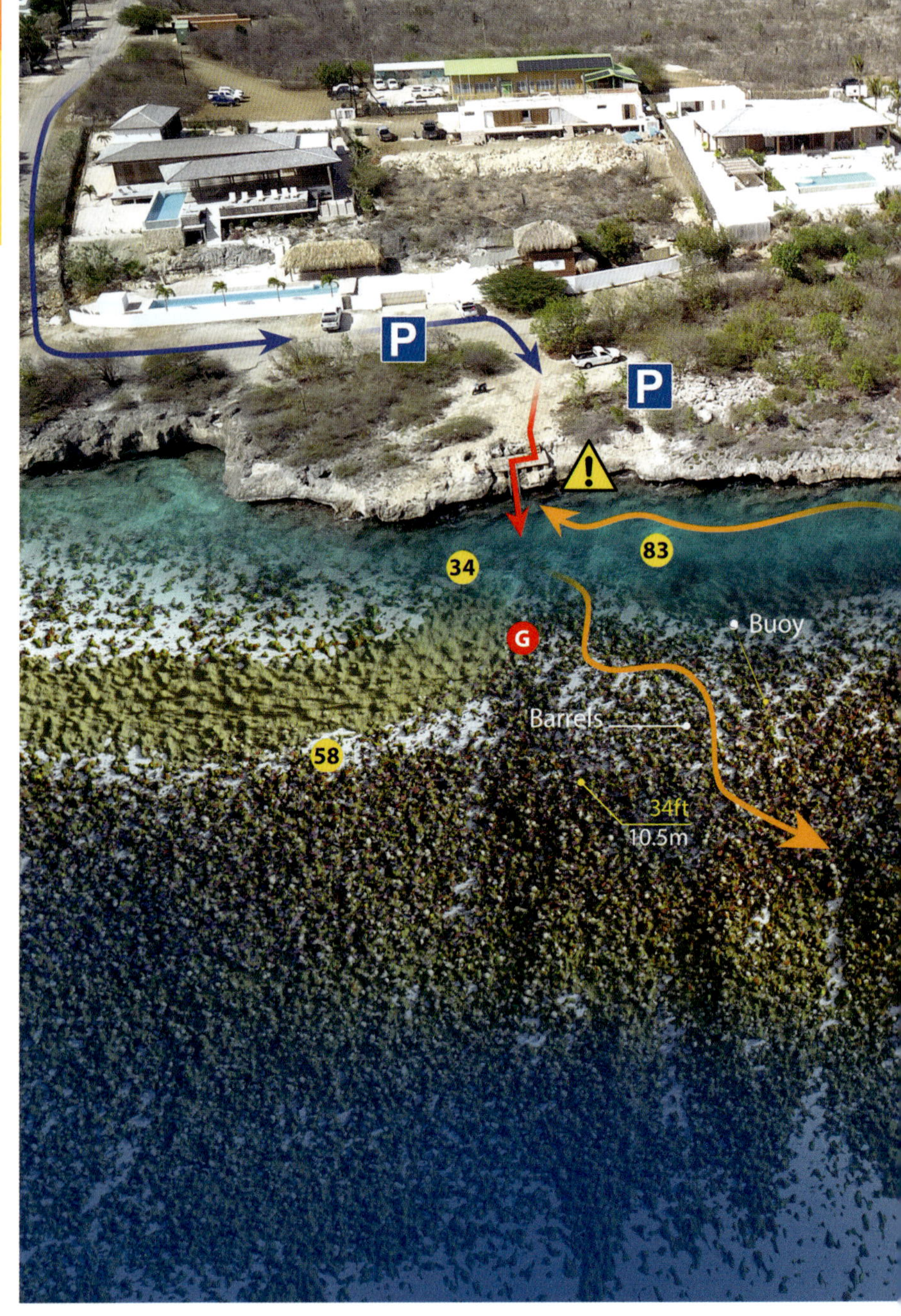

not feature the same level of biodiversity and concentration of corals as the shallower area. As divers head back past the buoy, they will encounter a large area of sand and coral rubble, which is a good landmark for returning to shore. As they wend their way through the coral rubble habitat while headed back toward the ladder, they often look for cryptic species such as scorpionfish, yellowhead jawfish and small eels such as goldentail morays.

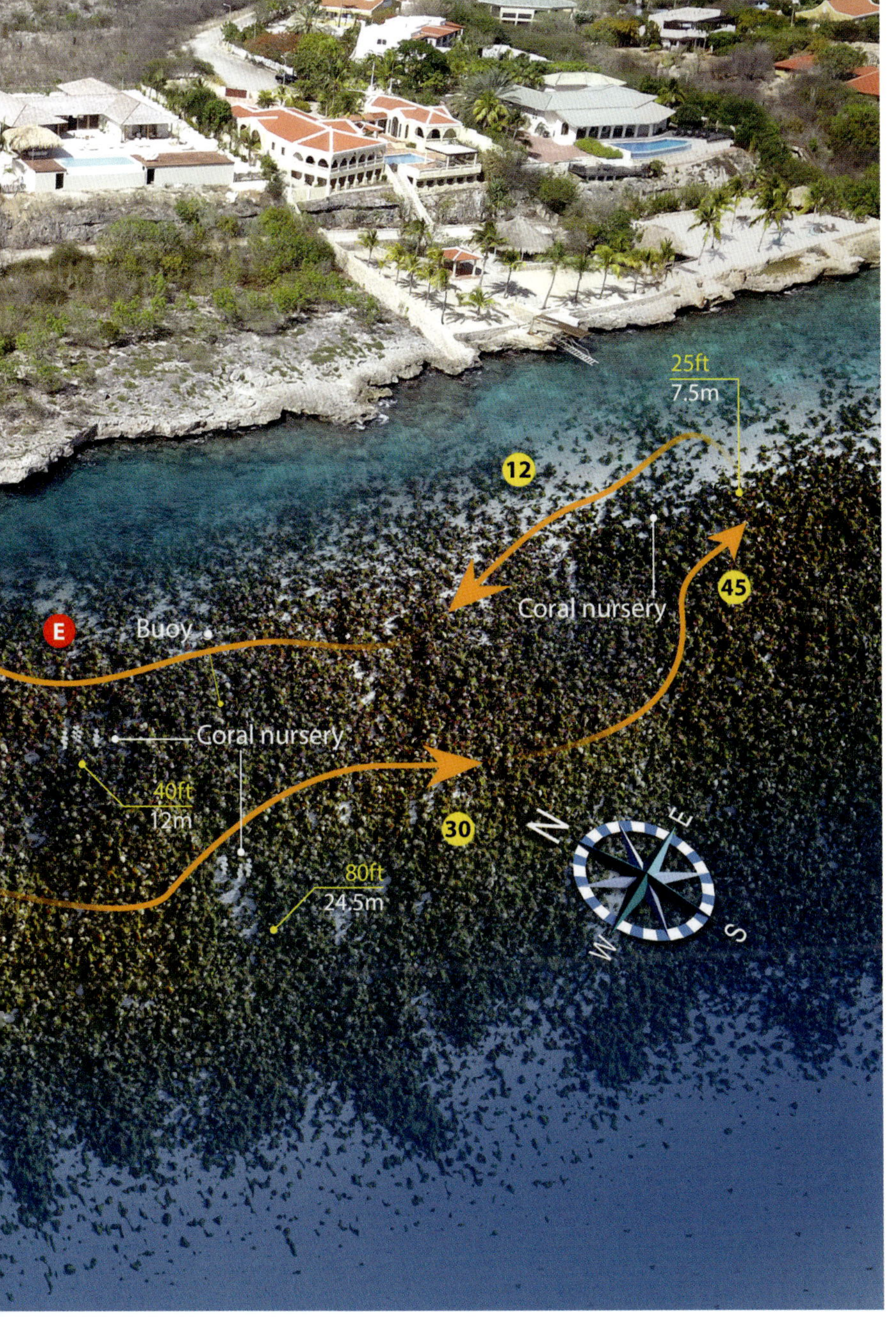
25ft
7.5m
12
Coral nursery
45
E
Buoy
Coral nursery
40ft
12m
30
80ft
24.5m
N
E
S
W

21

Barcadera

BONAIRE

Difficulty ●●○
Current ●●●
Depth ●●○
Reef ★★★
Fauna ★☆☆

Access about 26 mins from Kralendijk

Level Open Water

Location

Sabadeco, Bonaire
GPS: 12°11′54.6″N, 68°18′24.3″W

Getting there

Barcadera (also Barkadera) is a boat-only dive site located just off shore from Sabadeco, also known as Santa Barbara Crowns. It is a 4-mile (6.5-kilometer) boat ride north of Kralendijk. Coastal development in this area means the site can now only be visited by boat.

Access

The currents at Barcadera can be moderate to strong depending on the conditions. This dive site is accessible to divers of all experience levels

Oil Slick Leap

Access by boat only

unless conditions are rough.

Description

Barcadera is known for stands of elkhorn coral and yellow pencil coral. Divers will typically see schools of tangs along with plenty of parrotfish, butterflyfish, trumpetfish and Spanish hogfish. The reef is densely covered in hard corals, with a transition to plate-form corals farther down the reef slope. There are plenty of cleaning stations located throughout the site, while other species known to frequent Barcadera include squirrelfish, filefish and creole wrasses. Barracuda are also common.

SCIENTIFIC INSIGHT

Fish school for many reasons, including protection against predators and better swimming efficiency. The schools of acanthurids (the genus Acanthuridae, which includes surgeonfish, doctorfish and blue tangs) common in Bonaire and elsewhere in the Caribbean are formed largely to improve foraging success. These species feed on turf algae, which is often aggressively defended by damselfish. By forming large schools that move over the reef as one, acanthurids can overwhelm the damselfish, letting more fish in the school feed than if they were foraging alone. Divers and snorkelers are more likely to see acanthurids schooling at dawn and dusk, which also suggests that these schools might help protect the fish from predators, as dawn and dusk are periods of high predation.

N E S W

Andrea II

22

BONAIRE

Andrea II

Difficulty ●●○
Current ●●○
Depth ●○○
Reef ★★☆
Fauna ★★☆

Access about 12 mins from Kralendijk
about 21 mins from Kralendijk

Level Open Water

Location
Sabadeco, Bonaire
GPS: 12°11′29.4″N, 68°17′51.6″W

Getting there
The Andrea I and Andrea II dive sites are along the coast of Sabadeco, also known as Santa Barbara Crowns, 3.4 miles (5.5 kilometers) north of Kralendijk by car—a 12-minute drive. Head north on Kaya Gob. N. Debrot, past the Harbour Village Marina and through Hato. The coastal road turns sharply inland as it exits the town, followed by a left turn as it returns to a northerly heading. Less than 0.5 miles (0.7 kilometers) after this turn there is a yellow wall on the left-hand side of the road; this wall marks the

N E S W
Barcadera

entrance to a residential development. Yellow rocks marked with Andrea I and Andrea II sit on either side of the road at the entrance.

To reach Andrea II, divers should turn right immediately after entering the estate and follow the road north. Take the first left turn, about 600 feet (180 meters) down the road, where a yellow rock marks the route to Andrea II. The road descends a slope toward the water and into a parking lot adjacent to the beach; there is enough room for several cars. A large drop at the bottom of the slope can cause damage to vehicles, even those with four-wheel drive. So care must be taken when entering the parking lot.

Access

Divers can walk directly into the water from the shoreline parking area, taking care to step over the large rocks on the beach. The mooring buoy is located to the north of the parking lot.

Description

Andrea II experiences weak to moderate currents, which makes it the easier of the two Andrea dives. The site is well known for its plate-form coral formations at a depth of 65 feet (20 meters) as well as for the abundance of soft corals in shallower waters. Divers and snorkelers can see stands of staghorn coral as well. Divers often take time to investigate the soft coral habitat, which shelters seahorses, sea turtles and slender filefish. Parrotfish are common at Andrea II, particularly Queen parrotfish, and divers will likely see plenty of jacks hunting along the reef drop-off, along with patrolling barracuda.

Andrea I

Difficulty ●●○
Current ●●●
Depth ●●○
Reef ★★☆
Fauna ★★☆

Access: (car) about 12 mins from Kralendijk
(boat) about 21 mins from Kralendijk

Level Advanced Open Water

Location
Sabadeco, Bonaire
GPS: 12°11′17.2″N, 68°17′47.3″W

Getting there

The Andrea I and Andrea II dive sites are along the coast of Sabadeco, also known as Santa Barbara Crowns, 3.4 miles (5.5 kilometers) north of Kralendijk by car—a 12-minute drive. Head north on Kaya Gob. N. Debrot past the Harbour Village Marina and through Hato. The coastal road turns sharply inland as it leaves town, followed by a left turn as it returns to a northerly heading. Less than 0.5 miles (0.7 kilometers) after this turn there is a yellow wall on the left-hand side of the road; this wall marks the entrance to a residential development. Yellow rocks marked with Andrea I and Andrea II sit on either side of the road at the entrance.

To reach Andrea I, divers must turn left immediately after entering the estate and follow the road south. After about 0.2 miles (0.3 kilometers), the road turns right and heads toward the water. There is a stone wall in front of the intersection and a narrow track that leads down and to the right in the direction of a beach that has plenty of parking.

Access

From the parking lot, divers can walk 130 feet (40 meters) north between the small trees and bushes to a painted rock that indicates the safest place from shore to enter and exit the dive site. Kick straight out from the shore to avoid the fire coral stands to the left and right. Before descending, divers should take another look at the shore so they can return to the same location. The mooring buoy is anchored slightly to the north of the parking area, but divers can descend directly onto the reef and start exploring. This dive and snorkel site is accessible to those with more experience due to the strong currents and the challenge of navigating back to the point of entry.

Description

Andrea I is known for its schools of tangs and surgeonfish, along with plenty of brown and blue chromis. The site boasts its share of hard and soft corals, including fire corals that flank the entry point, and a broad complement of sponges that draw regular visits from sea turtles. Divers should look for banded butterflyfish and bar jacks, as well as various species of parrotfish, including midnight and rainbow parrotfish.

Petrie's Pillar

Difficulty ●●○
Current ●●○
Depth ●●○
Reef ★★★
Fauna ★★☆

Access about 12 mins from Kralendijk
about 20 mins from Kralendijk

Level Open Water

Location
Sabadeco, Bonaire
GPS: 12°11′10.6″N, 68°17′48.9″W

Getting there

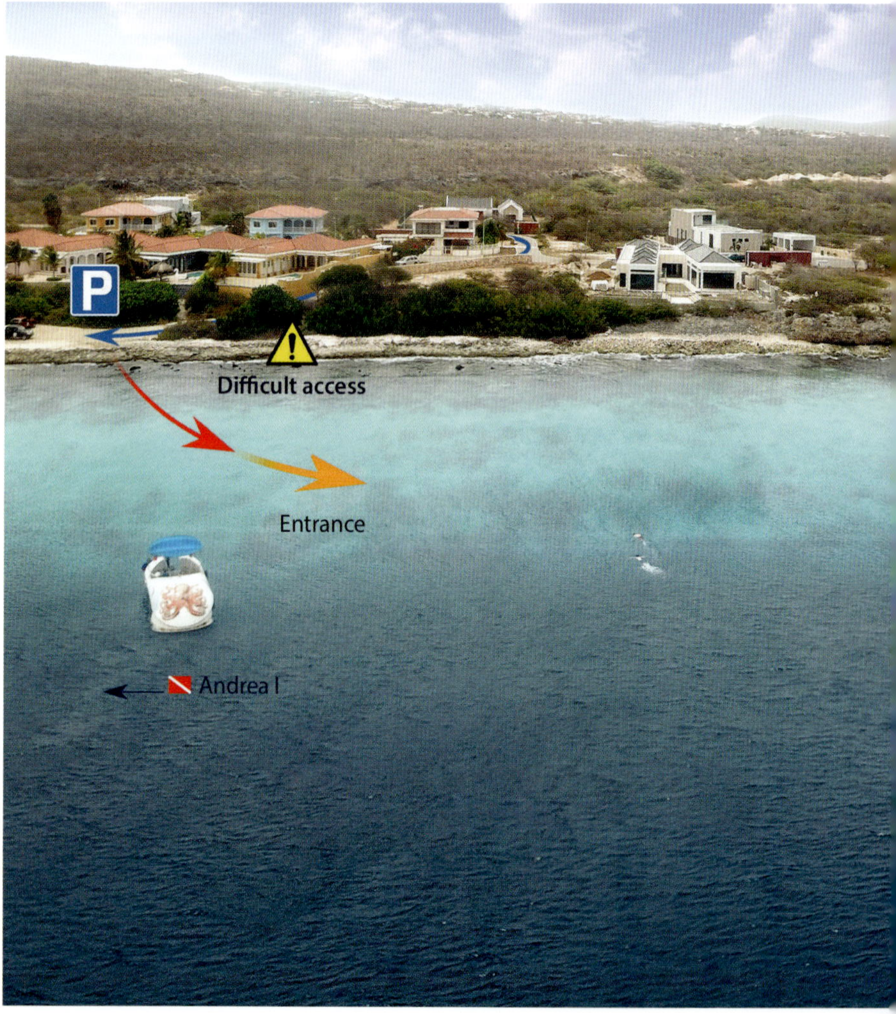

Petrie's Pillar is located between Hato and Sabadeco, just 2.8 miles (4.5 kilometers) north of Kralendijk by boat. This site is best accessed by boat because it is adjacent to a small cliff that makes it dangerous to reach from the shore. However, the site can be reached by surface swimming from nearby Andrea I. (To access this site from the shore, follow the driving directions to Andrea I on the preceding page, then read the access information below.)

Access

The Petrie's Pillar mooring buoy is visible from the Andrea I dive site parking lot. From the parking lot, divers can walk 130 feet (40 meters) north between the small trees and bushes to a painted rock that indicates the safest place from shore to enter and exit the dive site. They can then kick straight out from the shore to avoid the fire coral to the left and right.

The buoy at Petrie's Pillar is just over 750 feet (230 meters) to the south of the entry/exit point for Andrea I, which is a significant distance for some divers. It is important that divers check the current before they commit to the swim and consider diving another site if there is a strong current that makes returning to Andrea I a challenge.

Description

This site often experiences more moderate currents than nearby Andrea I. The site gets its name from the pillar corals that are found here (local lore holds that Captain Don, who named many of Bonaire's sites, named this site after a friend as a wedding gift). Stands of elkhorn coral are also common, and the site is popular with snorkelers since the coral grows very close to shore. Snorkelers and divers are likely to encounter parrotfish, as well as schools of tangs and surgeonfish, squid and the occasional sea turtle. Frogfish, soapfish and scrawled filefish are also regular visitors to this reef.

Small Wall

Difficulty ● ○ ○
Current ● ○ ○
Depth ● ● ○
Reef ★★☆
Fauna ★★★

Access about 16 mins from Kralendijk

Level Open Water

Location

Hato, Bonaire
GPS: 12°10′47.1″N, 68°17′37.0″W

Getting there

Small Wall is located about 2.3 miles (3.7 kilometers) north of Kralendijk by boat, just off shore from the Black Durgon Inn. Unfortunately, coastal development in this area has eliminated the shoreline access at this site, meaning divers can only get there by boat. Check with a local dive center to see when they are next visiting the site.

Access

The main section of Small Wall is located just south of the yellow mooring buoy, which is anchored on a sandy seabed at a depth of 15 feet (4.5 meters), and 27 feet (8 meters) from the reef line. There is a second, smaller section of wall located just north of the buoy. This site is easily accessible by boat and is a great dive for novice to advanced divers. It also makes for an interesting night dive.

Description

Small Wall gets its name from the most interesting feature at this site: a small wall positioned in the middle of the reef slope. The inshore part of the site is dominated by coral rubble and sand. This habitat gives way to reef consisting of a mix of hard and soft corals interspersed with sand patches at around 150 feet (46 meters) from shore, and at a depth of 18 feet (6 meters). Here the reef descends at a gentle slope, increasing dramatically in steepness at a depth of around 37 feet (11 meters), which marks the top of the wall.

The wall bottoms out at a depth of around 55 feet to 60 feet (17 to 18 meters), where a narrow sand channel runs parallel to shore. About halfway along the base of the wall, at a depth of 60 feet (18 meters), divers will see a cave that may hold a resting nurse shark. The cave measures 13 feet (4 meters) in from the opening and it has a sandy floor.

Just beyond the main sand channel, the reef continues deeper at a slightly gentler slope, eventually bottoming out at a depth of 115 feet (35 meters). This deeper reef slope is dominated by plate-form corals and large elephant ear sponges. Divers will likely encounter tarpon on the deeper reef slope, while the wall itself offers a colorful mix of coral heads and wire coral, along with plenty of reef fish, including parrotfish, basslets, grunts, snapper, small grouper and even seahorses. Large mixed schools of surgeonfish and tangs are often found in the upper sections of the reef.

Route

The mooring buoy sits between the two sections of wall. It can be interesting to explore both sections during this dive. However, the large southern section has the cave at its mid-point and is by far the more interesting of the two sections.

RELAX & RECHARGE

Between 2 Buns is located on Kaya Gob. N. Debrot, just south of the Harbour Village Marina. It is a small café that has a range of breakfast and lunch options for busy divers and snorkelers who want to refuel while they explore the island. Between 2 Buns serves great coffee, pastries, smoothies and the kind of deluxe sandwiches that people like to photograph and post to social media before they consume. They also have free internet.
Visit: **Between2BunsBonaire.com**

If the current allows, divers generally start out by heading north and exploring the smaller section of wall before cutting back to visit the larger southern section. The two walls are separated by approximately 180 feet (55 meters) of patchy coral reef where schooling surgeons and tangs are often found.

As they reach the second wall, divers often descend to the base of the wall and swim along the sand channel until they reach the cave, or drop below the sand channel and explore the lower reef slope with its elephant ear sponges and plate-form corals. Divers should be sure to check out the cave, but should always leave sleeping sharks alone.

At its southern end of the wall, the sand channel ascends to a depth of 43 feet (13 meters) and heads toward shore, effectively cutting off the wall from the rest of the reef—this marks a decent turning point.

The wall at Small Wall offers a spectacular experience for divers, but so too does the reef slope above the wall. As divers return to the mooring buoy, they should keep an eye open for the cryptic seahorses that are regularly seen among the soft corals and sea whips along the upper edge of this dive site.

A diver approaches the anchor on Small Wall.

blue-sea.cz/Shutterstock ©

Site buoy
15ft
4.5m
6
26 / 8m
25ft
7.5m
Petrie's Pillar
39ft / 12m
36ft
11m
Anchor
36ft
11m
Block
Barrels
30
60ft
18m

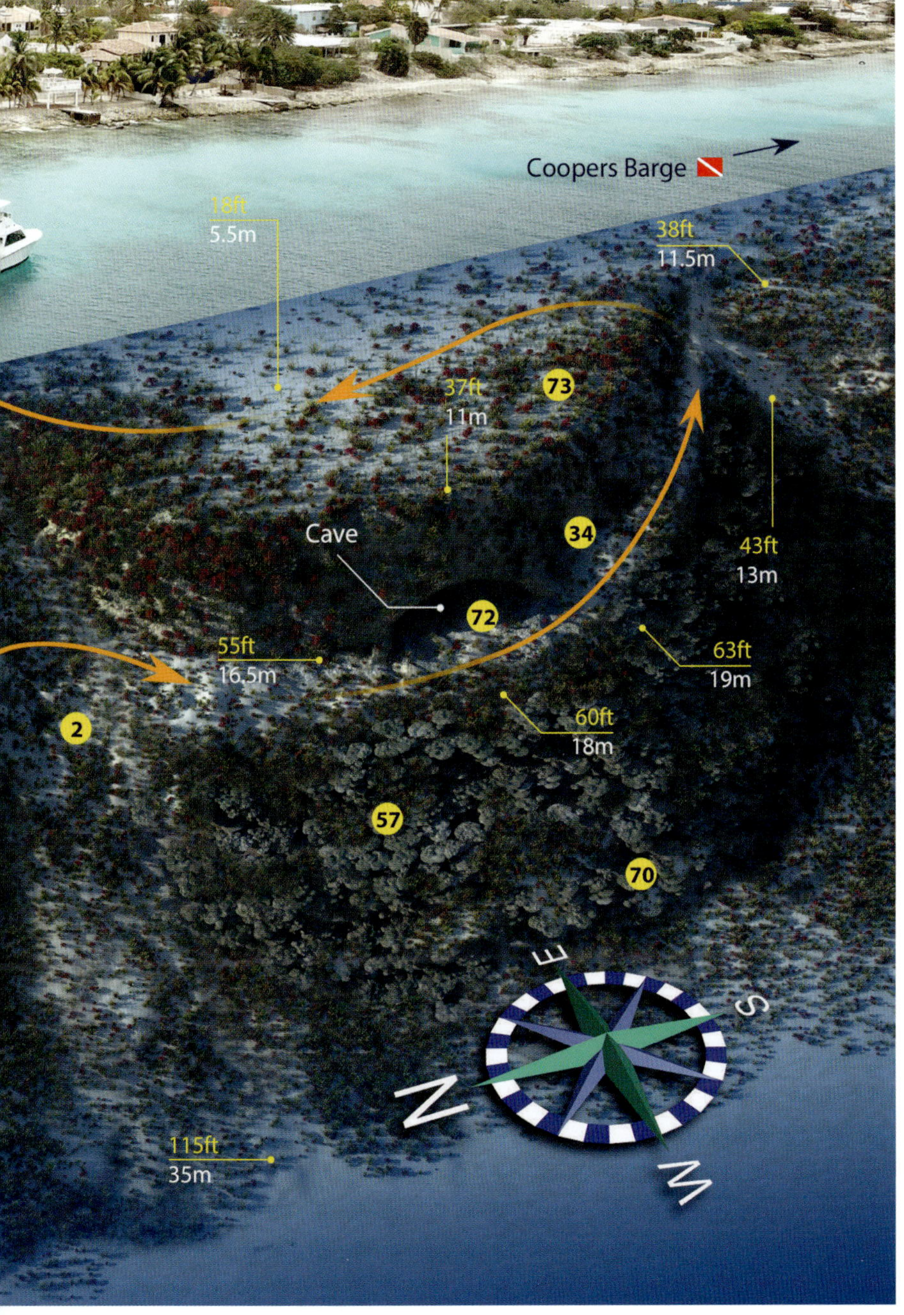
Coopers Barge
18ft
5.5m
38ft
11.5m
37ft
11m
Cave
43ft
13m
55ft
16.5m
63ft
19m
60ft
18m
115ft
35m
E
S
N
W

25A

Coopers Barge

BONAIRE

Difficulty ●●●
Current ●●○
Depth ●●●
Reef ★☆☆
Fauna ★☆☆

Access about 7 mins from Kralendijk
about 14 mins from Kralendijk

Level **Technical / Advanced Open Water**

Location

Hato, Bonaire
GPS: 12°10'31.4"N, 68°17'31.1"W

Getting there

Coopers Barge is located directly in front of Bonaire's desalination plant in Hato, which is about 2 miles (3.2 kilometers) north of Kralendijk. Members of the public are not permitted on the grounds of the desalination plant, so the only way to access the site is either by boat or by swimming from Cliff (see the "Getting there" information for Cliff on page 120).

Access

A short path with several steps that are lined with yellow painted rocks leads from the parking lot to the sea next to Dive Friends Bonaire. A yellow rock with an arrow, located on the sand and rubble beach, indicates the best spot to enter the water. There is a pipe underwater that cuts a path through the abundant blade fire coral close to shore. Divers can follow this pipe to reach the reef safely and head north to reach *Coopers Barge*, which lies directly between the two large commercial ship mooring buoys that mark the northern and southern ends of this site.

SAFETY TIP

Coopers Barge is a deep dive that sits beyond recreational SCUBA diving depth limits. Bottom time on air is extremely limited at this depth and divers can easily slip into a decompression dive if they are not careful. As such, we recommend that this site only be visited by technical divers with training in deep diving. Additionally, divers should note that access to this site is not permitted if a ship is located on the moorings.

Description

Coopers Barge, also known as Barge 101, is an unmarked site and one of the few technical dive sites on Bonaire. Originally a flat-bottomed tugboat used to transport drinking water from Curaçao, *Coopers Barge* sank in 1972 just off shore from the Bonaire desalination plant.

The wreck initially settled in shallower waters, but an early salvage attempt ended up leaving it at the bottom of the reef slope in deeper water and resting perpendicular to the reef. The angled stern

Tarpon are a common site on *Coopers Barge*.

DID YOU KNOW? 

For centuries, drinking water in Bonaire was available only through rainwater collection and by a limited number of wells in the interior of the island—most of which produced brackish water. Bonaire supplemented its water supply by importing drinking water from Curaçao until water shortages in the 1960s made it clear that Bonaire's growing population could no longer be supported by these limited means. Construction of a desalination plant in 1963 allowed Bonaire to produce drinking water from seawater through a process known as thermal desalination, which involves boiling seawater to produce a pure water vapor. The downside of this process is that it also produces a warm water residue with a high concentration of salt, which can be harmful to marine life when discharged directly into the ocean. The original desalination plant was replaced with the one currently in use today, which produces fresh drinking water through reverse osmosis—a process that involves passing seawater through a semi-permeable membrane at high temperature without generating residue that ends up back in the ocean.

points toward shore at a depth of around 125 feet (38 meters), while the rounded bow sits in deeper waters at 150 feet (46 meters). Deck level ranges from 115 to 140 feet (35 to 42.5 meters).

Sponges and soft corals, including sea whips, have colonized the hull of the barge. Many reef fish now inhabit the wreck, including snapper, black margates, porcupinefish, and large numbers of tarpon, as well as territorial

sergeant majors that can be seen guarding their colored egg patches during the breeding season.

The wreck's hull is intact although there is no superstructure present. Open hatches in the deck theoretically allow for access to the interior of the wreck, but penetration is strongly discouraged.

Route

Divers should enter the water at the Cliff dive site and surface swim in a northwest direction along the coast toward the southern-most

mooring buoy of the desalination plant. Before reaching the buoy, divers should start descending to the reef and continue swimming northwest along the reef slope at a depth of about 20 meters (65.5 feet). The barge should come into view, lying on the sand just off the deep edge of the reef. Divers typically tour the wreck and observe the marine life, before ascending to a shallower depth and heading back in the direction of the Cliff dive site.

42
115ft
35m
70
Stern
123ft
37.5m

Name:	*Coopers Barge*	**Last owner:**	Unknown
Type:	Tugboat	**Sunk:**	1972
Previous names:	Barge 101		
Length:	100ft (30m)		
Tonnage:	Unknown		
Construction:	Unknown		

The Cliff

Difficulty ● ○ ○
Current ● ○ ○
Depth ● ○ ○
Reef ★★☆
Fauna ★★☆

Access about 6 mins from Kralendijk
about 13 mins from Kralendijk

Level Open Water

Location

Hato, Bonaire
GPS: 12°10'28.0"N, 068°17'24.4"W

Getting there

The Cliff is located 1.9 miles (3.1 kilometers) north of Kralendijk by car. Head north on Kaya Gob. N. Debrot from Kralendijk past the Harbour Village Marina and straight on over the roundabout by the Trans World Radio studios. Immediately after the Hamlet Oasis Resort there is a gate on the left marked The Hamlet and signage for Dive Friends Bonaire. The side road runs to the sea and ends in a parking lot with plenty of space next to Dive Friends Bonaire. The gate is often locked outside of dive center hours (8:00am to 5:00pm daily), but the parking area and dive site are still accessible through the Hamlet Oasis Resort.

Access

A short path leads from the parking lot to the sea next to Dive Friends Bonaire, which has several steps lined with yellow rocks. Once on the sand and rubble beach, divers will see a yellow rock with an arrow indicating the best spot to enter the water. An underwater pipe cuts a path through the abundant blade fire coral close to shore. Divers should follow this pipe to reach the reef safely. The buoy is located at the southern end of the site adjacent to a monument of a dive flag at half-mast. Visibility is generally good and currents are usually mild. This site is suitable for all divers.

Description

The Cliff is a steep fringing reef that becomes a wall dive in several places. The Wall, which is covered in sea whips, starts at a depth of about 25 feet (7.5 meters) and drops sharply down to a depth of 55 feet (17 meters). The wall is undercut in several places, and a narrow sand path runs along its base. Below the sand path the reef continues to slope less steeply down to a sandy seafloor at about 120 feet (36.5 meters). Large elephant ear sponges, plate-form star corals, and scroll corals can be found between small sand patches in the deeper parts of the reef. Garden eels and sand tilefish can be found in the sand at the base of the reef although divers do not need to venture this deep. Large fish, such as tarpon and horse-eye jacks, cruise the deeper parts of the reef. Graysbies

Colorful creole wrasses school above a coral reef.

are particularly common around the steep walls where brown and blue chromis (a favorite food of graysbies) school above the reef.

Snorkelers also find this a very enjoyable site, with plenty of colorful fish, such as butterflyfish, angelfish, and even some large rainbow parrotfish. Small moray eels, gobies, and blennies can also be found hiding among the blade fire coral in the shallow parts of this site. And in the shallows above the wall, snorkelers can check out the dive memorial (complete with a dive flag at half-mast) that commemorates "all divers who have gone before us."

Route

Once divers pass through the fire coral close to shore, they will notice the reef starts to slope gradually into deeper water. Divers should head south as they descend and will notice that the reef becomes a wall about 150 feet (46 meters) in length until it reaches a wide sand channel running perpendicular to shore. From there, divers should take the time to drop slightly deeper down the reef slope in order to observe the plate-form coral and elephant ear sponges and look for large predatory fish, such as tarpon. The second wall begins after the sand channel and is longer than the first section.

Andrew Jalbert/Shutterstock ©

Swimming along the sand ledge at the base of the second wall at a depth of around 55 feet (17 meters) provides a decent vantage point to observe many reef organisms, including trumpetfish, angelfish, snapper, grunts, and parrotfish. Divers should also

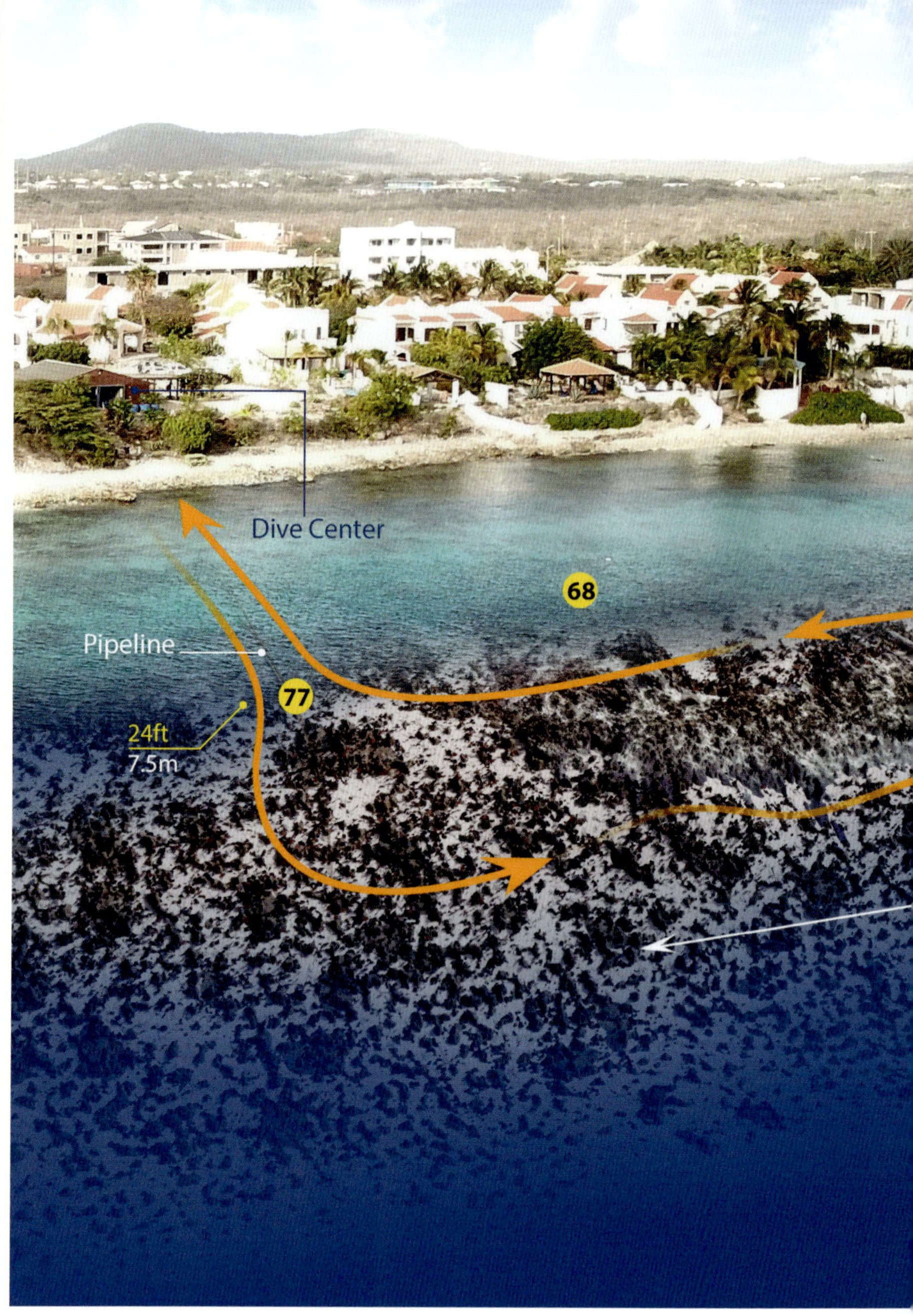

look for corkscrew anemones with their associated Pederson cleaning shrimp.

There is another sand channel at the end of the second section of reef. Take this channel to return to the top of the reef slope and the dive memorial at a depth of 25 feet (7.5 meters). Divers can return to the entry/exit point along the sand, where they may notice palometas and even the occasional stingray or eagle ray.

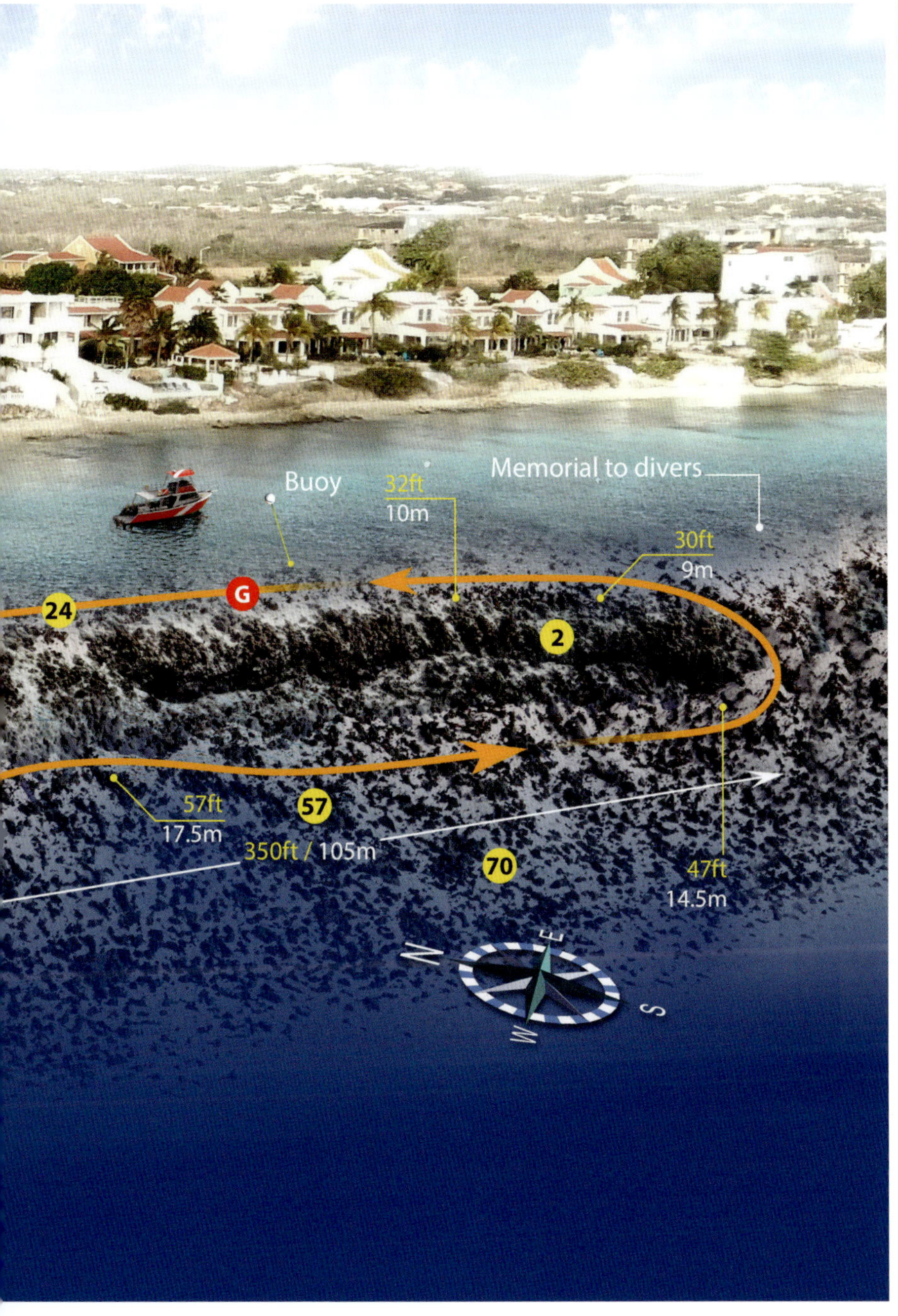
Buoy
32ft
10m
Memorial to divers
30ft
9m
24
G
2
57ft
17.5m
57
350ft / 105m
70
47ft
14.5m
N
E
S
W

La Machaca

Difficulty ●○○
Current ●○○
Depth ●○○
Reef ★★☆
Fauna ★★☆

Access about 4 mins from Kralendijk
about 12 mins from Kralendijk

Level Open Water

Location
Hato, Bonaire
GPS: 12°10′20.0″N, 68°17′18.6″W

Getting there

La Machaca is a small wreck located immediately off the jetty at Captain Don's Habitat—a dive resort located approximately 1.6 miles (2.6 kilometers) north of Kralendijk by car. Head north on Kaya Gob. N. Debrot from Kralendijk, past the Harbour Village Marina and straight on over the roundabout by the Trans World Radio studios. Turn left off the main road into Captain Don's Habitat where visitors will find plenty of parking. Divers who are not staying at that resort are charged a small access fee to use the rinse tanks and showers, but the fee is sometimes waived during low season. Visitors should check in at reception or the dive center when they arrive.

La Machaca can also be reached by swimming from Buddy Dive Resort, immediately to the south, which does not charge an access fee (use the "Getting there" information for Reef Scientifico and Buddy's Reef on page 128).

Access

Divers can enter the water by walking down the steps of the smaller of the two jetties. The larger jetty is more commonly used for dive-boat access. It is possible to take a giant stride from the end of the smaller jetty, but the water here is slightly shallower than at the nearby Buddy's Reef jetty, so it is important to ensure that any jump entry is shallow. Captain Don's Habitat has placed a line on the seabed in front of the smaller jetty to help divers navigate from the jetty to the reef and back again.

Description

The wreck of *La Machaca* is a popular site with both snorkelers and divers given the ease of access, mild currents and the opportunity to see plenty of reef fishes, not to mention the availability of refreshments and other facilities at the resort. The highlight is the small 45-foot (14-meter) wreck of *La Machaca* that sits upside down on the sandy seafloor at a depth of 40 feet (12 meters). Gorgonians have colonized the wreck and divers may be lucky enough to spot the resident green moray eel that is said to live in the wreck.

The back reef, between the jetty and the wreck, consists mainly of sand and coral rubble, but divers and snorkelers can encounter plenty of marine life, including stingrays, yellowhead jawfish, and even the occasional octopus. The reef starts taking shape at around 200 feet (60 meters) from shore and drops gradually to a depth of more than 100 feet (30 meters). The reef supports a variety of boulder

La Machaca is shallow enough to be viewed by snorkelers.

corals and tube sponges. Divers will see schools of creole wrasses as well as plenty of parrotfish weaving through the coral heads. As the reef slope gets deeper, the boulder corals give way to plate-form corals mixed in with sea whips and giant, orange, elephant ear sponges. Snapper and tarpon are common in the deeper areas of the reef.

With its well-lit entry and exit points, this site is popular as a night dive, when divers and snorkelers may see moray eels and sleeping parrotfish, as well as large tarpon that hunt the smaller fish attracted to dive lights.

Route

Most divers and snorkelers can easily explore *La Machaca* and much of the neighboring reef in a single outing by following a roughly circular route. Enter the water at the jetty and follow the line in the water to reach the reef. *La Machaca* is located slightly to the south of the line and should be clearly visible as divers reach the upper reef area.

Divers generally head south from the wreck to explore Reef Scientifico / Buddy's Reef; or alternatively, head north toward Cliff. Most divers

SAFETY TIP

Shore diving is a big part of what makes Bonaire so accessible to divers. With mooring buoys located out at the reef line, it is relatively safe for divers to swim out and drop in on most sites without a surface marker buoy (SMB). The rules of the marine reserve limit boat navigation to the darker water beyond the sand back reef. However, dive sites located closer to downtown Kralendijk, and particularly sites with active piers such as Captain Don's Habitat, have a higher risk of boat traffic in shallower areas. Pay close attention while entering and exiting the water. Also, check in with staff when diving at a resort or in a location where there is an on-site dive operator before entering the water in case they have any advice or tips that could improve safety.

Stubblefield Photography/Shutterstock ©

should be able to reach the dive memorial located at the southern end of the Cliff dive site before having to turn around.

At the end of their dive, divers typically follow the line to return to the jetty. However, they often save some air to explore the back reef area as they return to shore. This habitat has plenty of cryptic marine life, including stingrays, jawfish, and octopuses.

Name:	*La Machaca*	**Last owner:**	Unknown
Type:	Locally-built boat	**Sunk:**	Unknown
Previous names:			
Length:	45ft (14m)		
Tonnage:	Unknown		
Construction:	Unknown		

Reef Scientifico / Buddy's Reef

Difficulty ● ○ ○
Current ● ○ ○
Depth ● ○ ○
Reef ★☆☆
Fauna ★★☆

Access about 4 mins from Kralendijk
about 11 mins from Kralendijk

Level Open Water

Location

Hato, Bonaire

Reef Scientifico

GPS *(The reef)*: 12°10'17.4"N, 68°17'21.4"W

Buddy's Reef

GPS *(Unloading area)*: 12°10'14.9"N, 68°17'17.3"W

Getting there

Reef Scientifico and Buddy's Reef combine to form the house reef of Buddy Dive Resort, located approximately 1.5 miles (2.4 kilometers) north of Kralendijk by car. Head north on Kaya Gob. N. Debrot from Kralendijk past the Harbour Village Marina. Buddy Dive Resort is located just north of the roundabout by the Trans World Radio studios. Once at Buddy Dive Resort, divers can make their way to the water where they can unload their gear at a small turning circle between the dive center and the Blennies Restaurant. Due to the limited parking here, all vehicles must park nearer the main road. Buddy Dive Resort does not charge a fee for access or use of their facilities, but divers should check with the dive center or resort reception before accessing the site.

Access

Once the car is safely parked by the entrance, away from the unloading area, divers can gear up and access the water by walking down the steps on either side of the smaller jetty, or taking a giant stride off the end. The larger, L-shaped, jetty is more commonly used for dive-boat access. Buddy Dive Resort has placed a line on the seabed in front of the smaller jetty to help divers navigate from the jetty to the reef and back again.

Description

Buddy's Reef is a popular dive and snorkel site that provides a relaxed and pleasant experience with mild currents and convenient access both day and night. Just north of Buddy's Reef is another

Reef Smart ©

A view of the jetties at Buddy Dive Resort from Blennies Bar & Restaurant.

FEATURED OPERATOR

Buddy Dive Watersports, located at Buddy Dive Resort, is one of the most well-known and respected operators on Bonaire. This exceptional PADI 5-star resort and Career Development Center provides every service a diver or snorkeler could possibly need, including equipment and tank rentals, dive courses up to, and including, instructor level, and of course, guided shore and boat dives, led by their professional, multilingual, staff. Buddy Dive Watersports has guests and visitors well and truly covered, and there's even a bar and two restaurants to relax in and enjoy Bonaire's spectacular sunsets.

Tel: +599-717-5080
Email: info@buddydive.com
Visit: **Buddydive.com**

dive site called Reef Scientifico, which is a section of reef marked by a small grid used by researchers to monitor coral cover over time. Between Buddy's Reef and Reef Scientifico, there are multiple features anchored to the sandy seafloor such as frames used for diver buoyancy control training. There are also numerous coral nurseries and outplant sites located here, managed by the Reef Renewal Foundation Bonaire (see pages 18 and 19 for more information).

Despite being labeled as two separate sites, Buddy's Reef and Reef Scientifico are essentially contiguous sections of the same reef slope that stretches from the Buddy Dive Resort property to the wreck of *La Machaca* and onward to the north.

The transition from sand and coral rubble to patch reef begins at around 150 feet (45 meters) from shore, at a depth of about 35 feet (10.5 meters). From the transition zone, the slope descends to more than 100 feet (30 meters) to the sandy seafloor. The top section of the reef slope is dominated by sponges and boulder corals. A mix of gorgonians adds to the complexity of the reef, creating habitat that supports a variety of reef fishes, including filefish, trumpetfish, grunts, parrotfish and small grouper.

As the reef slope gets deeper, the boulder corals give way to plate-form corals, interspersed with sea whips and elephant ear sponges. Although the slope offers an opportunity to go deep, the best diving is above a depth of 65 feet (20 meters). Divers should be sure to check out the back reef as they return to the jetty. Jawfish, octopuses, and squid can be found in the sandy areas and grey snapper are always present beneath the jetties.

This site is also very popular as a night dive thanks to the well-lit entry and exit points, and accessible staircases that are just as easy to navigate at night as they are during the day. The reef offers divers a different view at night, including moray eels and large tarpon that tend to congregate around night divers to hunt the small fish that are attracted to their dive lights.

Route

Divers generally follow the submerged line out from the smaller of the two jetties and descend the reef slope to their target depth. They then choose to head north or south, depending on the direction of the current and what they want to see. Heading north allows them to check out Reef Scientifico and the wreck of *La Machaca*, while heading to the south, the reef slope continues

RELAX & RECHARGE

Exploring the reef in front of Buddy Dive Resort is often a relaxing way to spend the day, with simple access as well as showers and rinse tanks readily on hand. But if you want to take the experience to the next level (literally) then head upstairs from the dive center and stay for dinner at **Ingridients Restaurant**. This peaceful establishment has developed a reputation for fine dining, great service and spectacular views, especially if you can arrive in time to watch the sun set into the clear blue ocean. The cuisine is essentially Mediterranean, with elements of French, Spanish and Italian dishes, but using local ingredients where possible, such as lionfish, red snapper, barracuda and tuna.
Visit: **Ingridientsrestaurant.com**

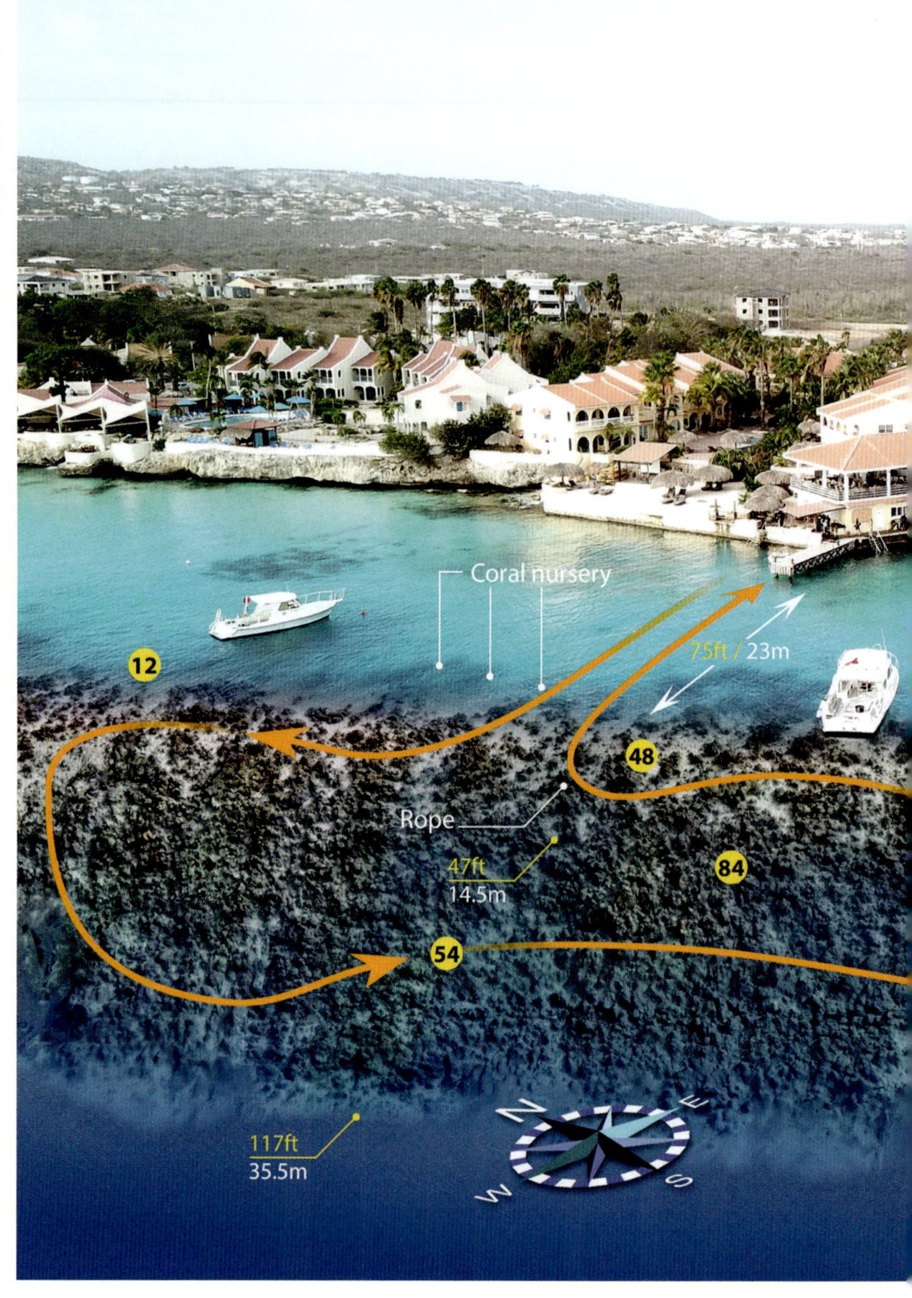

uninterrupted all the way to Bari Reef.

Coral nursery
78
Coral nursery
20ft
6m
52
117ft
35.5m

Bari

Difficulty ● ○ ○
Current ● ● ○
Depth ● ● ○
Reef ★★☆
Fauna ★★☆

Access about 4 mins from Kralendijk
about 9 mins from Kralendijk

Level Open Water

Location

Kralendijk, Bonaire
GPS (*Public access*): 12°10′02.0″N, 68°17′13.1″W

Getting there

Bari (sometimes referred to as Bari Reef) is located 1.25 miles (2 kilometers) north of Kralendijk—a drive of about four minutes. Divers should head north on Kaya Gob. N. Debrot, past Harbour Village Marina and turn left at the roundabout next to Trans World Radio studios. Enter the Isidel Beach Park, which has public access to the water and where there is plenty of parking. Alternatively, divers and snorkelers can access this site through Scuba Do Bonaire, located within Chogogo Dive & Beach Resort Bonaire, immediately to the south of Isidel Beach Park.

Access

Entering the water at either Isidel Beach Park or Chogogo Dive & Beach Resort Bonaire is relatively easy. Both access points feature a small sandy beach that transitions into a sand and rubble plateau that gets deeper very gradually. The site typically experiences constant current that ranges from mild to moderate. The direction of the current is almost always from north to south, so divers usually begin their dive heading north, into the prevailing current. Alternatively, divers can head south and explore features that are often considered part of Front Porch. However, they may need to walk back along the beach to the entry point if the current is strong. Visibility is usually great at this site.

SCIENTIFIC INSIGHT

Biodiversity is a term used to describe the variety of life in a particular habitat or ecosystem. It is the hallmark of a healthy environment, since more biodiverse systems tend to be more productive, more stable and altogether more robust than systems that support fewer species, regardless of how abundant those species are. Biodiversity is an important factor in an ecosystem's ability to withstand or rebound from negative events, such as storms, disease outbreaks and the introduction of an invasive species—such as the introduction of lionfish into the Western Atlantic.

Description

The adjacent sites of Bari Reef and Front Porch are great for divers and snorkelers of all experience levels and are known for their incredible diversity of coral reef species. The

A snorkeler enjoys the company of a green sea turtle.

FEATURED OPERATOR

Scuba Do Bonaire is a 5-star Padi Dive Resort located on the beach at Chogogo Dive & Beach Resort. The Scuba Do family also includes a dive shop on the neighboring island of Curaçao. Scuba Do offers certification courses, guided dives, and equipment rentals for divers of all levels. Some of Bonaire's best shore accessible dive and snorkel sites are on the Scuba Do schedule, which can also include boat accessible sites if desired. Their house reef, Bari, is one of the best sites on the island to start your adventure, with a vibrant underwater reef teeming with life, including sea turtles.

Tel: +599-777-3200
Email: info@scubadobonaire.com
Visit: **Scubadobonaire.com**

reef slope starts nearly 150 feet (45 meters) from shore and consists predominantly of hard corals and a range of sponge species. The top of the reef is approximately 30 feet (9 meters) deep and descends to the sandy seafloor at a depth of between 80 and 100 feet (24 and 30 meters).

Vertical sand channels descend all the way to the seafloor, breaking up the reef slope and providing interesting structure to explore. The reef is generally considered to be better quality on Bari Reef, which supports a higher density of reef fish, including schooling schoolmaster snapper

Jag_cz/Shutterstock ©

and French grunts. Divers will also spot stoplight parrotfish, Spanish hogfish, French angelfish, rock beauties and the occasional spotted moray eel and tarpon in the deeper parts of the reef. Divers may find it interesting to explore the back reef area during their safety stop, given the varied habitat that supports razorfish, peacock flounders and octopuses and frogfish.

Snorkelers generally focus their attention on the remnants of a collapsed concrete pier near the water's edge in front of Scuba Do Bonaire, which is often referred to as the "Aquarium." This area supports large schools of fish, including grunts,

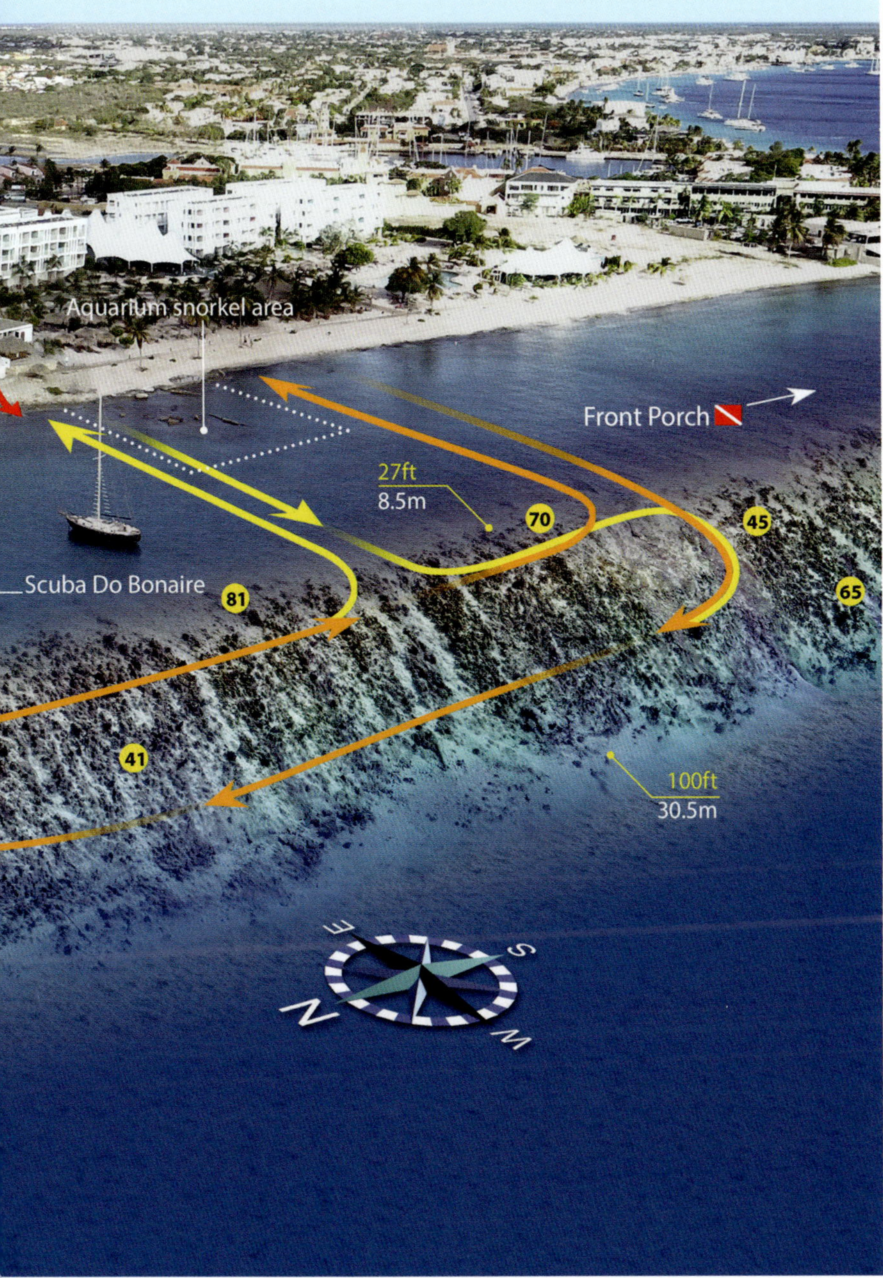

goatfish, chromis, sergeant majors, wrasses, surgeonfish and redlip blennies.

Route

The best route will depend on the current, with the most common direction being along the shoreline toward the north before returning to the entry point. Divers usually drop down the reef and start shallowing as they head north, using the back reef area for their safety stop. Snorkelers usually spend their time exploring the area known as the Aquarium, located in front of Scuba Do Bonaire.

Front Porch

Difficulty ● ○ ○
Current ● ● ○
Depth ● ● ○
Reef ★ ☆ ☆
Fauna ★ ★ ★

Access: about 4 mins from Kralendijk (by car); about 7 mins from Kralendijk (by boat)

Level Open Water

Location

Kralendijk, Bonaire
GPS: 12° 9′51.89″N, 68°17′14.47″W

Getting there

Front Porch (which is sometimes referred to as Eden's Rubble) is located just under one mile (1.4 kilometers) north of Kralendijk—a drive of about four minutes. Divers should head north on Kaya Gob. N. Debrot, past Harbour Village Marina and then take the first left toward Eden Beach Resort. The turn is well marked, and there is plenty of parking. The Wannadive dive center is located within the resort and welcomes visitors.

Access

There is a small beach in front of Eden Beach Resort that provides easy access to Front Porch. The site typically has a constant current that ranges from mild to moderate. The direction of the current is almost always from north to south, so divers usually begin their dive heading north, into the prevailing current. Visibility is usually great at this site.

The wreck of the *New York* lies at the bottom of the reef slope at Front Porch.

FEATURED OPERATOR

Wannadive is a Five Star PADI IDC Dive Center with locations at both Eden Beach Resort and the Grand Windsock Resort. They offer every dive service imaginable, from dive training to expert equipment repair. They also have a competitive retail shop and an enormous stock of rental dive equipment. Wannadive offers both boat and guided shore dives and their dedicated, multilingual, crew can handle every dive and snorkel request, from the casual 'once a day' diver to the hard core 'never dry up, nitrogen addict'.

Tel: +599-717-8884
Email: info@wannadive.com
Visit: **Wannadive.com**

Description

The adjacent sites of Bari Reef and Front Porch are great for divers and snorkelers of all experience levels and are known for their incredible diversity of coral reef species. The reef at Front Porch starts just 70 feet (22 meters) from shore, sloping gradually from a depth of 30 feet (9 meters) down to approximately 100 feet (30 meters) on the deeper edge of the reef.

The reef at Front Porch is significantly patchier than at the adjacent site of Bari, with large sand and rubble channels descending from the shallow back reef plateau. The patchy habitat hosts an incredible range of reef creatures, however, including frogfish, seahorses, and octopuses, as well as the occasional eagle ray.

Front Porch hosts multiple artificial structures, including scaffolding, concrete blocks, barrels, and metal beams. Divers and snorkelers will notice the large cylindrical mooring structure that sits on the seabed at a depth of 40 feet (12 meters) near the northern end of the site, as well as a Reef Renewal nursery and coral outplant site at a depth of approximately 20 feet (6 meters).

There are also two small shipwrecks at Front Porch. The deeper of the two wrecks is the tugboat called *New York*, which rests upside down at the base of the reef slope near the northern edge of the site, at a depth of 90 feet (27.5 meters). Garden eels have colonized the sand at the base of the reef and divers may also spot stingrays here, as well as tarpon, yellowtail snapper, French angelfish, bar jacks, and barracuda.

To the south, the wreck of the *Baka di Laman II* lies at the base of the reef slope but in slightly shallower water than the nearby *New York*. The *Baka di Laman II* (which is often referred to as the *Willy Bakanal* or the *Sea Cow* by local divers) sank during Hurricane Lenny in 1999 and currently rests on its port side with its bow pointing up the reef slope. It sits at a depth of approximately 75 feet (23 meters). A third wreck, called Our Confidence, is located just to the south of Front Porch, just around the corner from where the reef slope sticks out into the channel. This third

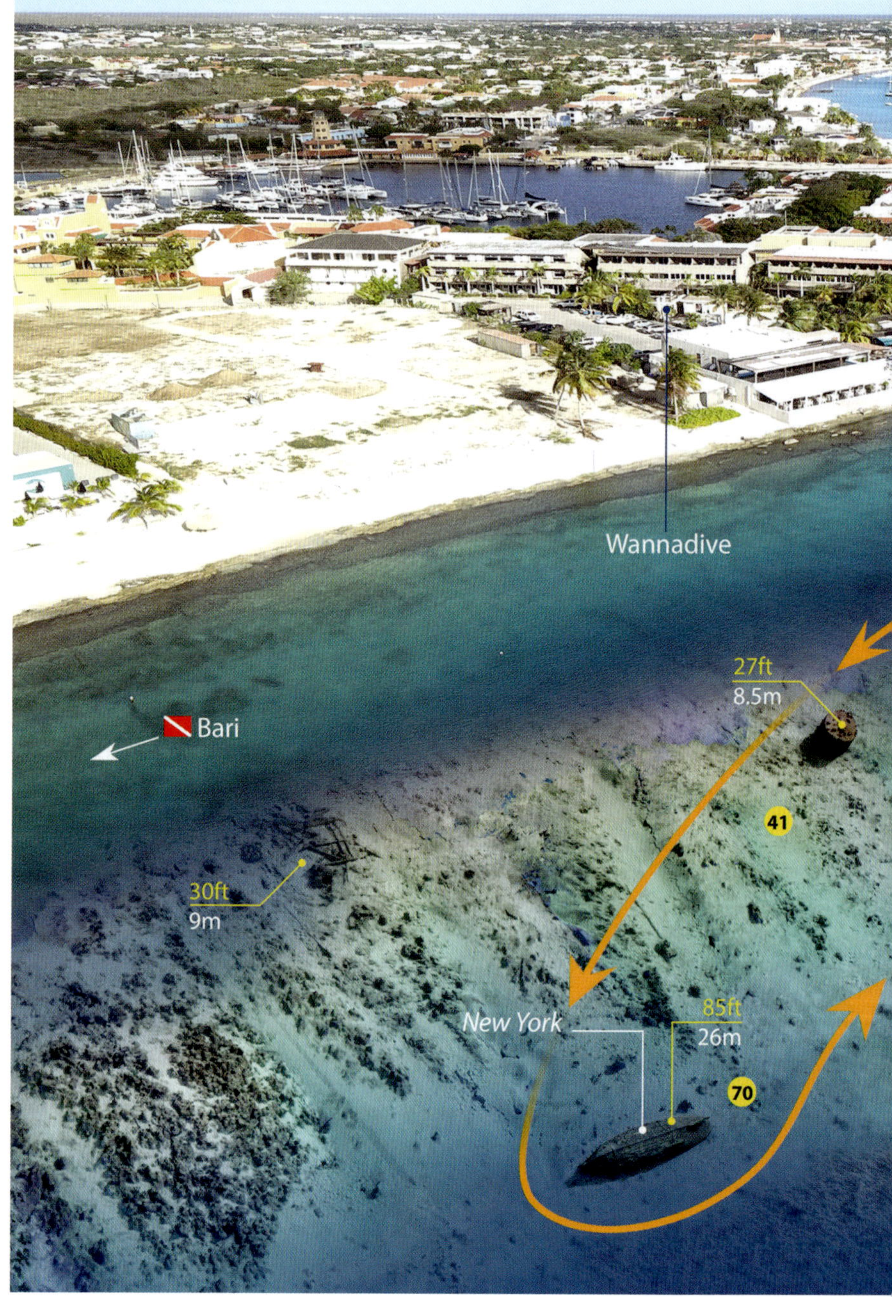

wreck is mostly just a degraded wooden sailboat hull that rests at a depth of around 45 feet (14 meters). As it lies far from the main route used to explore Front Porch, this third wreck is rarely visited.

Route

Most divers enter the water adjacent to the jetty in front of Eden Beach Resort and head north into what is usually the prevailing current. Increasing in depth gradually, divers will usually pass the giant cylindrical mooring structure en route to

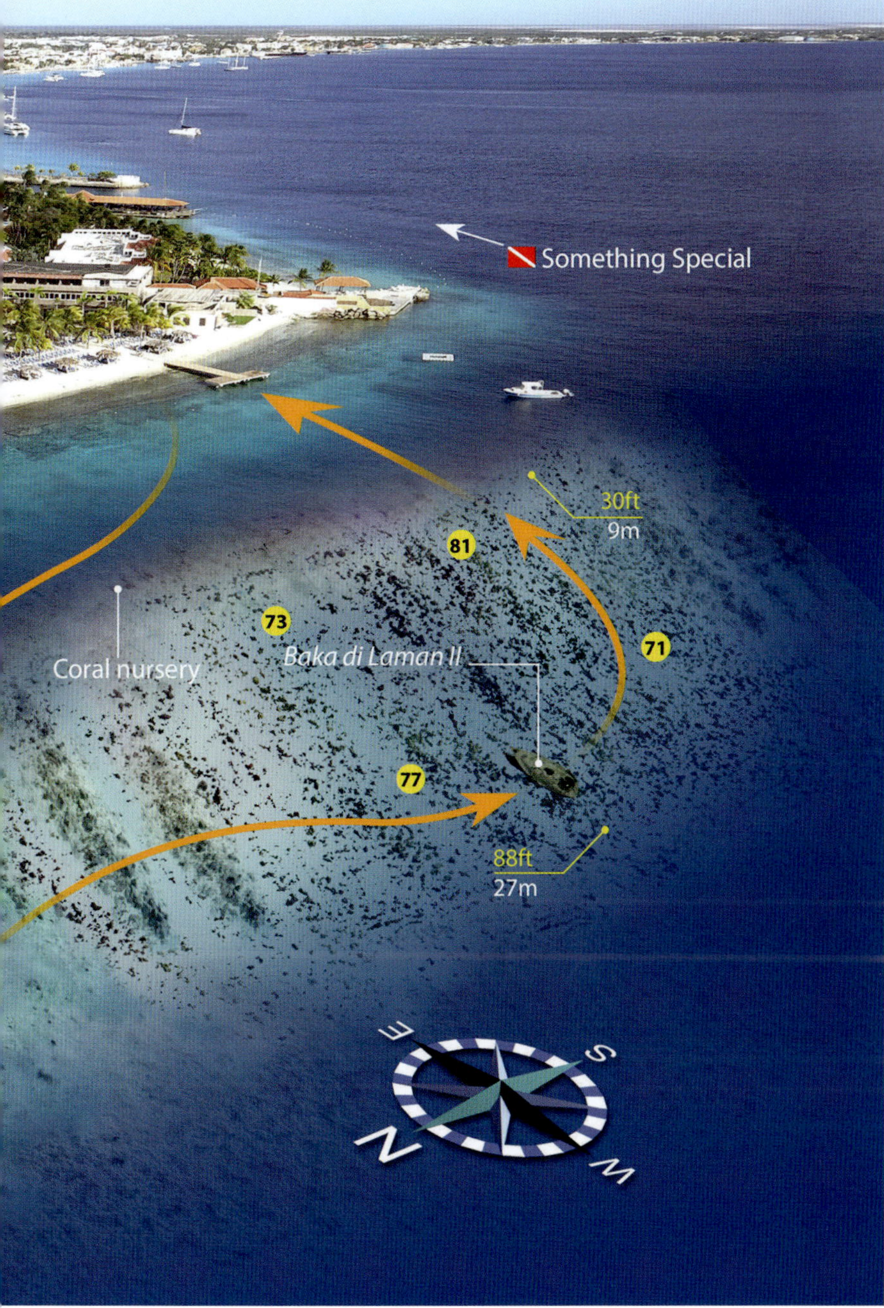

the wreck of the New York at the bottom of the reef. Divers usually explore this wreck and then head south, shallowing slightly, as they drift to intercept the wreck of the Baka di Laman II—an eight to ten-minute swim. Directly inshore of this wreck is an area of slightly denser reef structure, where divers can find a range of different reef creatures and conduct their safety stop. Snorkelers usually explore the back reef plateau and may find sailfin blennies, rosy razorfish, and giant anemones, which often include Pederson cleaning shrimp in their tentacles.

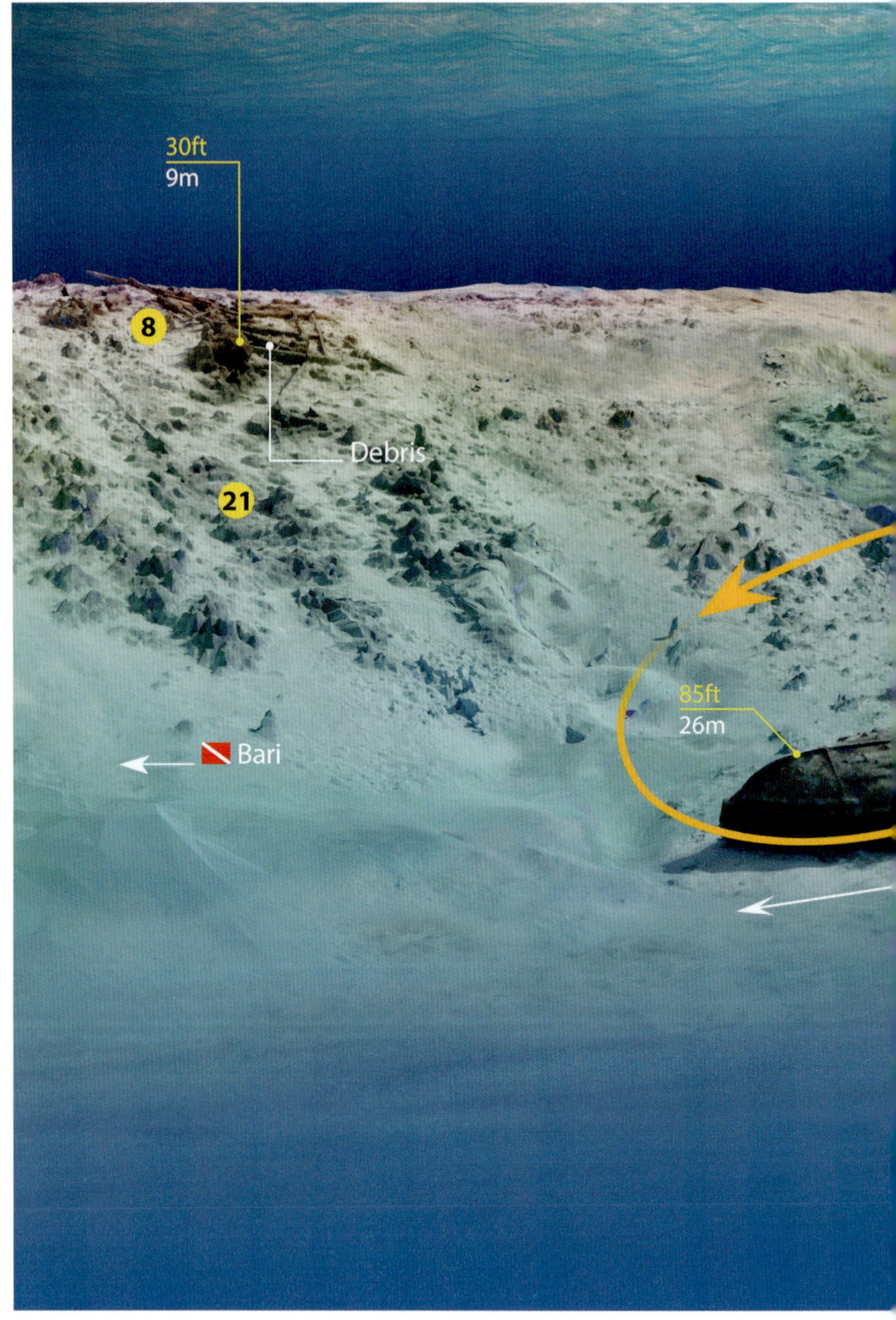
30ft
9m
8
Debris
21
Bari
85ft
26m

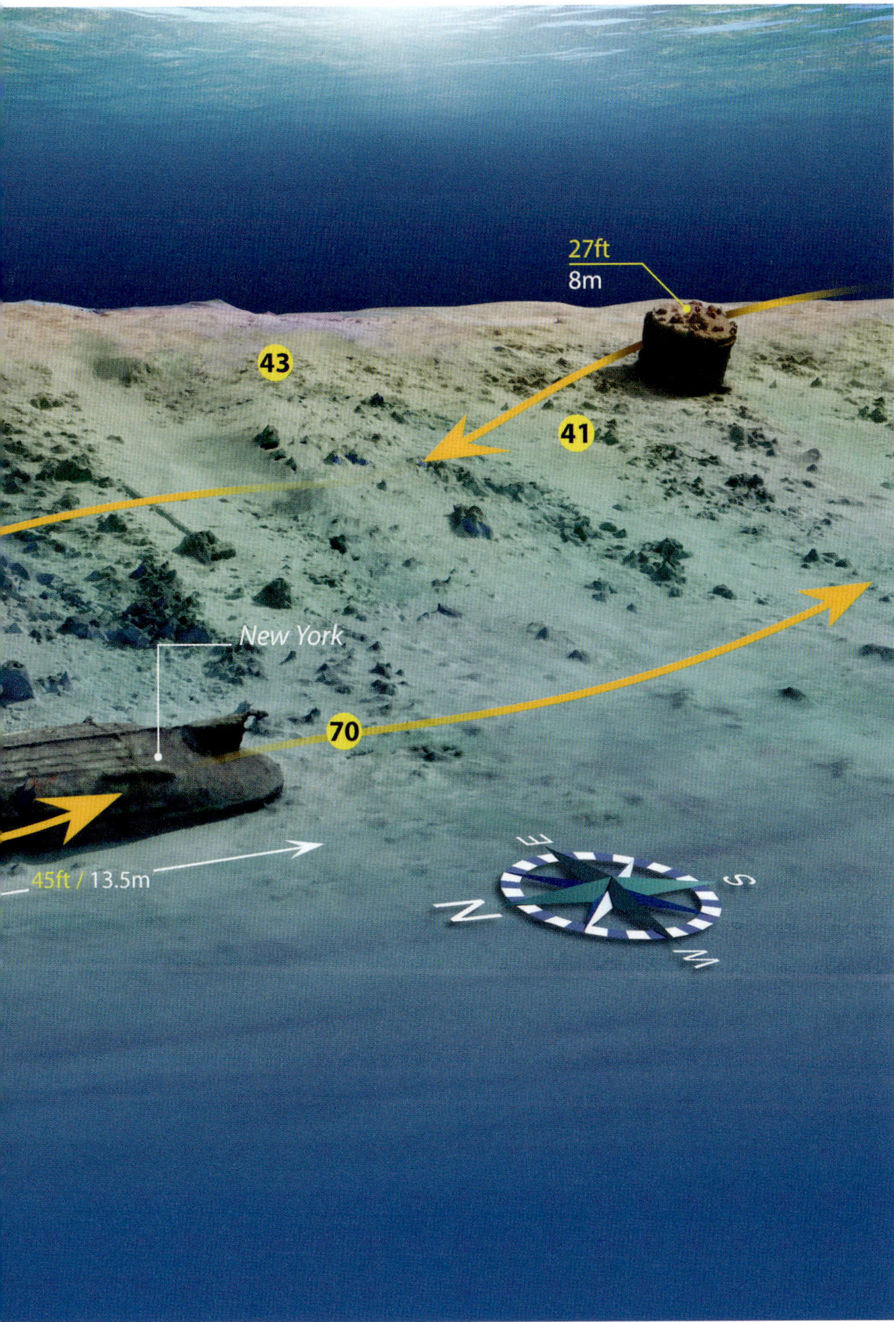

Name:	*New York*	**Last owner:**	Unknown
Type:	Tugboat	**Sunk:**	Unknown
Previous names:	Unknown		
Length:	43ft (13m)		
Tonnage:	Unknown		
Construction:	Unknown		

32

BONAIRE

Something Special (Pali Grande)

Level Open Water

Location
Kralendijk, Bonaire
GPS (*parking*): 12°09′43.1″N, 68°16′59.9″W

Getting there

From downtown Kralendijk head north toward the Harbour Village Marina, about 0.8 miles (1.3 kilometers) on Kaya Gob. N. Debrot—a journey of about two minutes by car. There is a parking lot on the left side of the road followed by a small side road located just before the restaurant Between 2 Buns. This side road leads to the shore access for the dive and snorkel site Something Special.

Access

Divers should make their way down the small sand and gravel slope to the beach and enter the water next to the white wall. They can surface kick out to the yacht moorings before descending and heading north. The yellow mooring buoy is located about 330 feet (100 meters) to the north, close to the edge of a large sand channel. This site is an area of high boat traffic, so divers should stay close to the bottom. Snorkelers should not venture too far out from the mooring buoys.

Description

Something Special is also known as Pali Grande. The English name is believed to originate from the near guarantee that divers and snorkelers will see "something special" when they enter the water. The site's close proximity to the harbor has probably impacted the level of coral cover on the reef. The site has a limited number of hard corals and sponges, along with anemones sprinkled throughout the area. However, the site is better known for its wide variety of reef fish, particularly elusive and cryptic bottom-dwelling species such as frogfish, scorpionfish, sailfin blennies, and yellowhead jawfish. But divers should not think that this site is only for small creatures; it is not uncommon to see eagle rays and sea turtles cruise through.

Frogfish are often hard to spot when hiding in the reef.

The area between the shoreline and the drop-off stretches 200 feet (60 meters) and consists primarily of gravel and coral rubble. At a depth of nearly 30 feet (10 meters), the reef starts to drop away at a fairly steep angle, getting a little steeper and almost wall-like, at the northwestern end of the site. Some corals are even undercut in places. To the north, a large sand channel containing garden eels interrupts the reef. This channel provides a good reference point to turn and head back south. Divers and snorkelers should avoid crossing the sand channel; it marks the entrance to the Harbour

ECO TIP 

When conducted responsibly and sustainably, aquariums can help the public develop a greater appreciation and understanding of coral reefs. But all too often, the aquarium trade involves the illegal and unsustainable poaching of organisms from living reefs. Frogfish and seahorses are particularly lucrative targets in the aquarium trade because of their unique appearance. While frogfish are not themselves threatened, seahorse populations have declined across much of their distribution, in part due to harvesting for the aquarium trade. Bonaire has strict rules prohibiting the collection and removal of anything living or dead from the reef—which includes dead pieces of coral found on Bonaire's beaches.

Sarawut Kundej/Shutterstock ©

Village Marina where boat traffic increases significantly.

A coral nursery managed by Reef Renewal Foundation Bonaire is located at a depth of about 20 feet (6 meters), approximately 400 feet (122 meters) from the shore access point. (See pages 18 and 19 for more information.)

Route

Divers generally swim out from the beach and slightly to the west, toward the mooring buoys, passing the coral nursery. From there they descend to the reef and head northwest along the slope. They typically make their way along the reef toward the sand channel and return following a slightly shallower route.

The best area of this reef to explore is along the sand-to-reef transition where frogfish and anemones can be found among the coral heads and sailfin blennies and jawfish can be found in the sand. This is not a large site—a circular route can take less than 30 minutes to complete. The ideal way to explore this site is therefore to do so slowly and carefully. Bottom time is not an

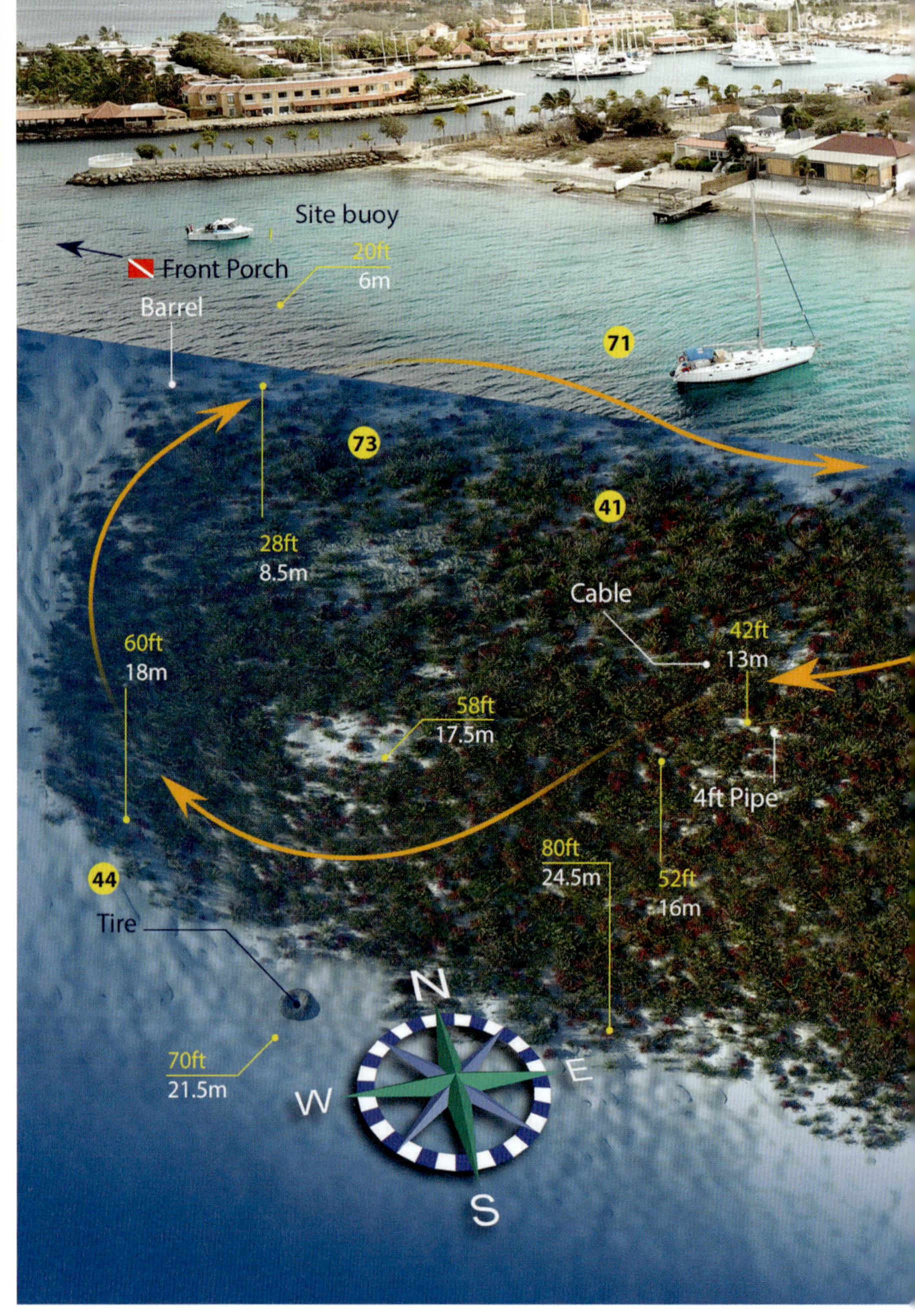

issue in the upper reef area, so divers can take their time to explore this amazing site.

Coral trees nursery
98.5ft / 30m
12
Calabas Reef
19ft
6m
38
74 81
100ft
30.5m

34

Calabas Reef

Difficulty ●○○
Current ●●○
Depth ●●○
Reef ★☆☆
Fauna ★★☆

Access about 5 mins from Kralendijk

Level Open Water

Location
Kralendijk, Bonaire
GPS: 12°08'30.5"N, 68°16'33.1"W

Getting there

Calabas Reef can be accessed from shore through the Divi Flamingo Beach Resort and Casino, as well as through two public access points. To access the site through Divi Flamingo Beach Resort and Casino, head south on Kaya International from downtown Kralendijk. Turn right at the roundabout and head west toward the coast on Kaya Industria. After about 0.15 miles (0.25 kilometers), the road ends at a junction adjacent to the Divi Flamingo Beach Resort and Casino. The resort charges a small access fee for those planning to stay and use the facilities, such as the pool and beach chairs.

There are also two public access points for Calabas Reef. Divers can turn left at the junction in front of Divi Flamingo Beach Resort and Casino and continue south along Julio A. Abraham Boulevard for about 0.19 miles (0.3 kilometers). On the right-hand side, just after the Carib Inn, there is a small track called Kaya Alemania that leads to the waterfront. There is no parking on this side street, so divers should unload their gear and park back on Julio A. Abraham Boulevard. A second public access is located just 230 feet (70 meters) farther south on Julio A. Abraham Boulevard. This southern part of the site is often referred to as Sebastian's Reef, after the restaurant located there. The total distance from downtown is only about half a mile (0.8 kilometers), but the drive can take at least five minutes, depending on traffic.

Access

Calabas Reef is easily accessible from the jetty at the Divi Flamingo Beach Resort, where steps lead directly into the water. This simple and well-lit entry and exit point also makes this dive site great for night diving. The relatively shallow

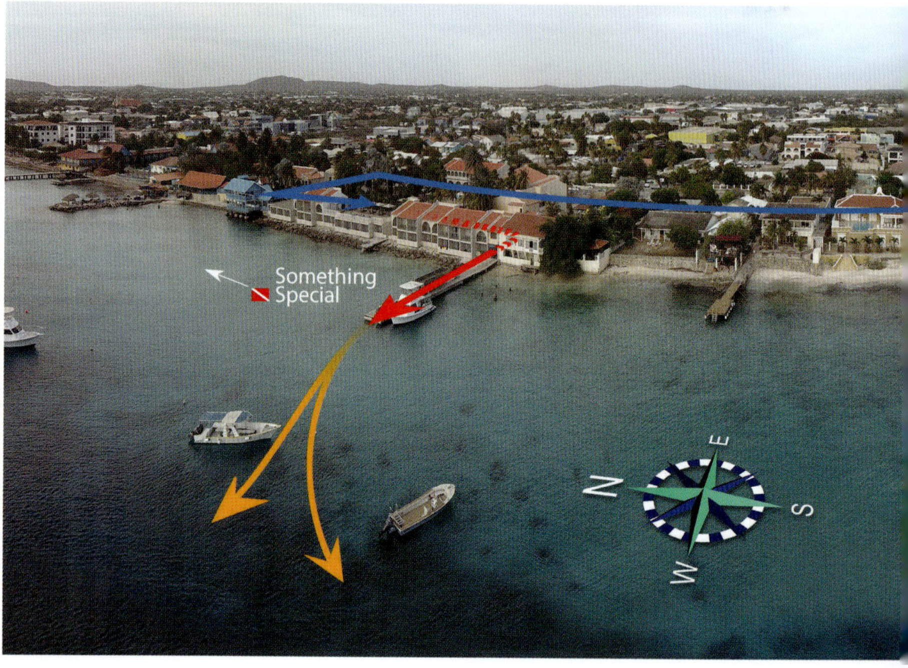

Something Special
N
E
S
W

FEATURED OPERATOR

With their dive center and retail store located just steps from Calabas Reef, **VIP Diving** is proud to call the popular dive site their home reef. The dive professionals at VIP lead daily dive excursions at Calabas Reef, including night dives with UV lights, which provide a completely unique underwater experience. With small groups, usually consisting of just four people, personalized attention is assured, and divers can expect an unforgettable experience from start to finish.

Tel: +599-701-7701
Email: info@vipdiving.com
Visit: **Vipdiving.com**

reef in front of the resort provides a decent experience for snorkelers as well.

The reef is arguably of better quality to the south, nearer to the two public access points. Here, divers and snorkelers must descend a shallow slope to reach the gravel and sand beach. They must then carefully negotiate the rutted and flat reef area at the waterline. Once in the water, sand stretches out to the reef line.

Divers and snorkelers should be aware that boat traffic is often higher in this stretch of coastal water than elsewhere in Bonaire. There is no buoy or yellow rock at this site.

Description

Calabas Reef (sometimes spelled Kalabas Reef) is located just south of downtown Kralendijk. The reef has probably suffered from its proximity to the heavy boat traffic, including cruise ships, to and from the Town Pier to the north, but it still offers divers and snorkelers an easily accessible reef to dive, particularly for those staying at the nearby Divi Flamingo Beach Resort and Casino. The site is known for its schools of goatfish, grunts and snapper, but also for parrotfish, sea turtles, rays, squid and seahorses. Both Calabas and Sebastian's Reef have coral nurseries and outplanting sites managed by the Reef Renewal Foundation Bonaire.

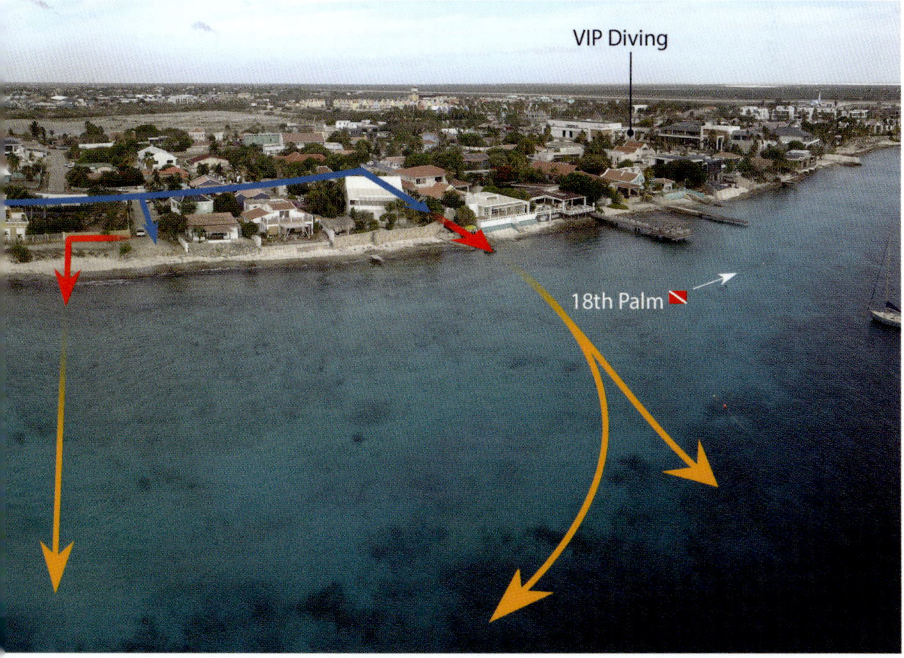

35

BONAIRE

18th Palm

Difficulty ●○○
Current ●○○
Depth ●●○
Reef ★☆☆
Fauna ★★★

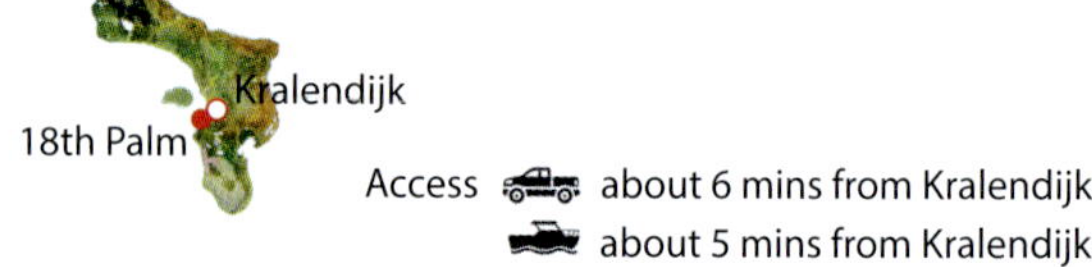

Access about 6 mins from Kralendijk
about 5 mins from Kralendijk

Level Open Water

Location

Kralendijk, Bonaire
GPS: 12°08′16.6″N, 68°16′35.0″W

Getting there

The 18th Palm dive and snorkel site lies just off shore of the Van der Valk Plaza Beach & Dive Resort Bonaire, which sits between the airport and downtown Kralendijk. To reach the resort, drive south from Kralendijk along Julio A. Abraham Boulevard. Take the sharp left turn after approximately 0.6 miles (1 kilometer) followed by the first right into the resort. Access to the reef is free unless divers wish to use the facilities. Visitors can purchase an all-inclusive day pass at the front desk that provides access to the pool and beach, and includes lunch, bar snacks, drinks (including house wine and beer), and snorkeling equipment.

Access

Toucan Diving is located within the resort and can provide support for those wishing to explore 18th Palm reef, including equipment

The sun sets beyond the beach at Van der Valk Plaza Beach & Dive Resort.

FEATURED OPERATOR

Toucan Diving is a PADI 5-Star Resort conveniently located in the Van der Valk Plaza Beach Resort Bonaire. Whether you are an experienced diver, or it is your first time in the water, the dedicated team at Toucan Diving will provide a safe, fun and, above all, unforgettable diving experience. There is no better place to explore the underwater world than the 18th Palm house reef, with its clear waters, bountiful corals and countless colorful reef fish.

Tel: +599-717-2500
Email: diveshop@bonaire.valk.com
Visit: **Toucandiving.com**

Van der Valk Plaza Bonaire
TOUCAN DIVING

rental and guided tours. They also have small buggies that divers can use to carry their gear to the beach. Divers and snorkelers often gear up on the promenade next to the beach. Accessing the reef from here involves simply walking across approximately 130 feet (40 meters) of beach to the shoreline. The bottom changes from sand to coral rock at the waterline, which can be slippery in places. Divers and snorkelers will need to walk around a small breakwater that runs from north to south approximately 30 feet (9 meters) from the edge of the water. The water shallows gradually, and can be rutted on the bottom in places, but transitions to sand at about waist deep. The swim out to the reef slope is about 200 feet (61 meters). On their way out, divers will pass a large stand of blade fire coral on their right-hand side in relatively shallow water.

ReefSmart ©

Description

18th Palm is also sometimes known as 18 Palms. The name originates with the 18 palm trees that stand tall along the beach. This site is known for its gentle current and its fantastic marine life, both large and small. Divers and snorkelers can see everything from large tarpon and barracuda to cryptic frogfish and octopuses. Snapper, grouper and angelfish are also regularly found here, making this a great spot for divers and snorkelers of all experience levels.

The reef line starts as a gentle slope that gradually steepens before reaching a sand plateau at a depth of around 100 feet (30 meters). To the north, the site transitions into an area often known as Sebastian's Reef, after the restaurant located there. To the south, the deep edge of the reef extends significantly out to sea and has a noticeable hook toward the north. Stingrays and eagle rays can be spotted here and even manta rays have been recorded cruising along the reef.

A buoy line runs from north to south enclosing the back reef area located along the southern stretch of the reef. There are numerous structures located along the sand interface here, from a diver buoyancy test to a coral restoration nursery and an outplant site.

Route

The current is usually minimal at 18th Palm, which means divers can head in either direction, often choosing to explore both sides of the site via two separate dives. The reef is similar in both directions. The northern area is more commonly explored from shore and the southern area is a popular area for divers to be dropped by boat. Snorkelers usually remain within the buoyed back reef area. The area of blade fire coral near the beach is particularly interesting to explore as this area hosts large numbers of small

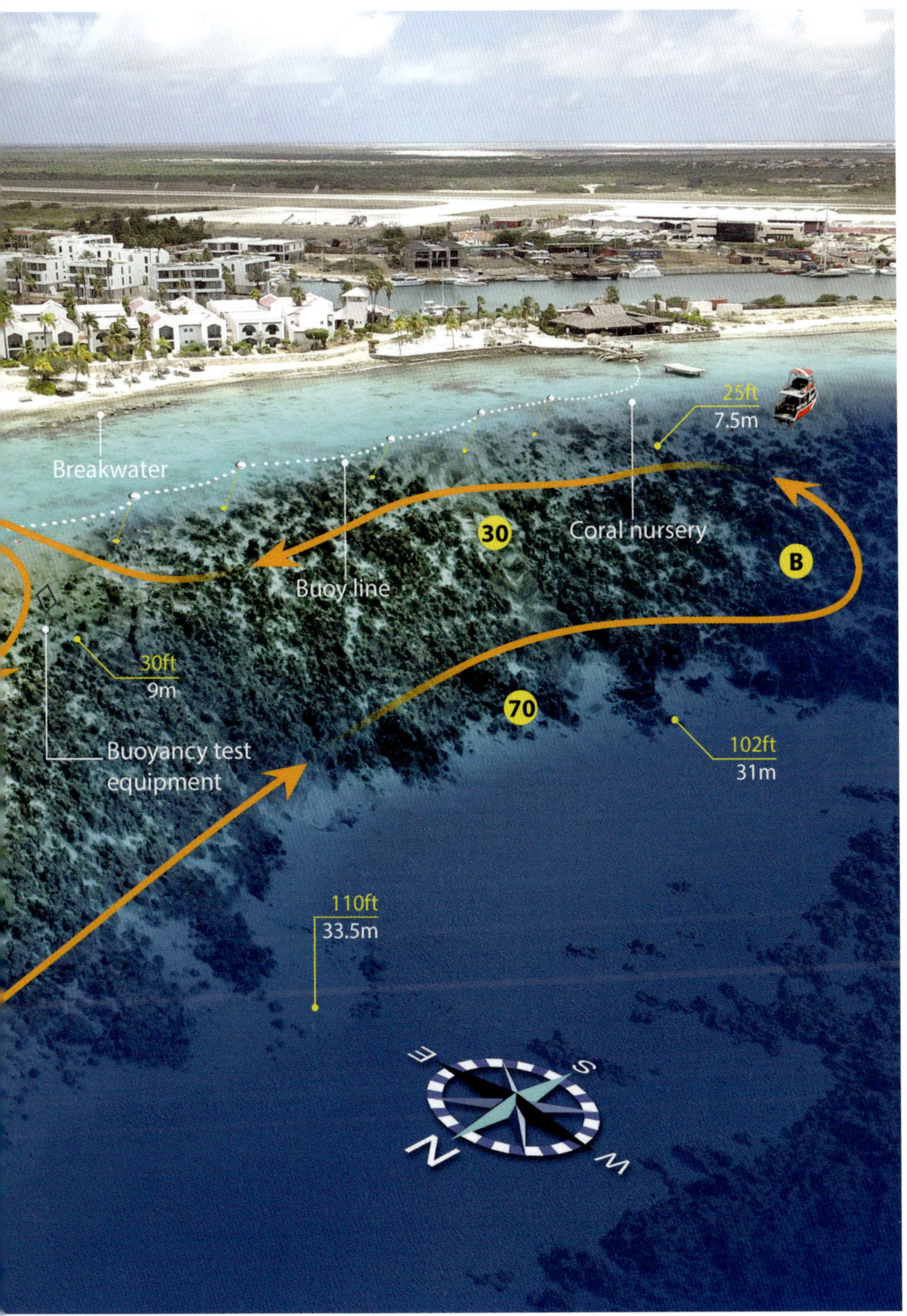

species, including wrasses, grunts, goatfish, and damselfish, among others.

Windsock

Difficulty ●○○
Current ●●○
Depth ●●○
Reef ★☆☆
Fauna ★★☆

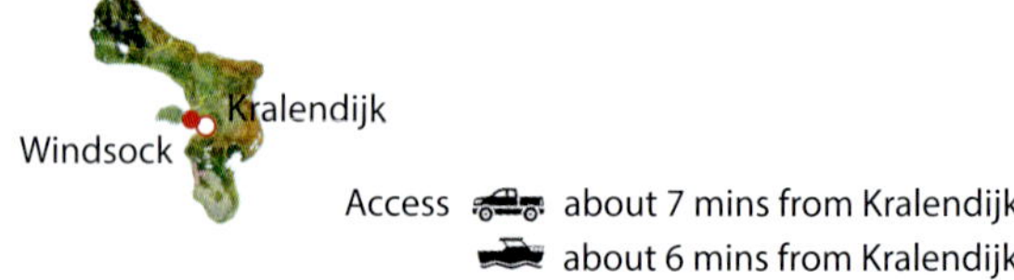

Access about 7 mins from Kralendijk
about 6 mins from Kralendijk

Level Open Water

Location

Belnem, Bonaire
GPS: 12°07′58.3″N, 68°16′54.7″W

Getting there

Windsock is located at the end of the airport runway, which is the origin of this site's name. Drive south from Kralendijk on Kaya International, which becomes EEG Boulevard at the airport. There is a large jetty located at the point where the road bends slightly left and runs adjacent to Playa Palu di Mangel, also known as Donkey Beach. Yellow painted rocks are located on the side of the road and there is plenty of parking.

Access

Access to the water is relatively simple along this stretch of the coast. Pass through the shrubs to the beach—a distance of about 70 feet (20 meters) from the road. Be careful not to trip on any small rocks or accidentally step on the spiky branches of the acacia trees that are abundant in this area. The water's edge may be rutted in places, so divers and snorkelers should watch their step when entering and exiting the water. Fortunately, the seas are generally calm here, particularly in the sheltered area just south of the pier.

Description

The reef at this site starts out as turf-covered sand and rubble, which gradually slopes down to a depth of 25 feet (7.5 meters). The shallowness of the back reef means that snorkelers will have no problem observing the habitat and its creatures from the surface. From the back reef, the slope transitions into patchy reef before becoming a

Yellowhead jawfish are often seen close to their burrow in the rubble-filled back reef.

Peter Leahy/Shutterstock ©

RELAX & RECHARGE

Bonaire has multiple great restaurants, but it also boasts some delicious food trucks that hungry divers can enjoy during their surface intervals. For those who love fresh fish, **Kite City** is a must. This food truck is conveniently located on Te Amo beach just north of the Windsock dive and snorkel site.

Nuno and Co. serve up a wide selection of fish, including perennial favorites such as wahoo, mahi mahi and snapper, They also serve burgers and salads. The food is simple, fresh and incredibly tasty. You can take out if you like, but the best option is usually to "eat in" on the beach and enjoy the view. Your food will come on a proper plate, rather than ecologically insensitive plastic or polystyrene. We also recommend the chilled homemade watermelon juice, which really quenches the thirst.
Visit: **2cook4.com**

Reef Smart ©

The popular Kite City food truck offers beach-side dining.

predominantly hard coral reef, interspersed with gorgonians and sponges.

The reef gradually descends to a sandy bottom at 95 feet (29 meters) at the north end of the beach, adjacent to the jetty, which extends around 150 feet (46 meters) into the water. The density of corals is lower at this site than at some of the sites farther south and the coral heads are also smaller, although there are still plenty of reef fish to see, including black margates, Bermuda chub and plenty of chromis schooling above the reef. This site also offers the opportunity to see larger pelagic species out in deeper waters as they patrol just off the reef slope.

The base of the slope gets deeper to the south, bottoming out at around 115 feet (35 meters). As a result, divers should watch their depth when taking a southern route. Currents tend to be mild at this site and generally move in a northerly direction.

Route

Given that access points exist all along the beach, divers and snorkelers can choose multiple different routes at this site. We recommend entering the water just south of the pier and swimming toward the south. If a ship is docked at the jetty, divers and snorkelers will need to adjust their route or choose another site, as it is unsafe to venture near a commercial boat moored next to the pier.

If the jetty is free of activity, it can be interesting to check out the pylons of the pier, which hosts numerous grey snapper and Bermuda chub. Divers should then descend the reef slope, keeping an eye on depth and on the sandy bottom for the eagle rays and stingrays. Barracuda are known to frequent the lower sections of the slope as well. Once target depth is reached, divers should turn southward, scanning the reef for angelfish, grunts and filefish. The middle of the reef slope is the best area to explore.

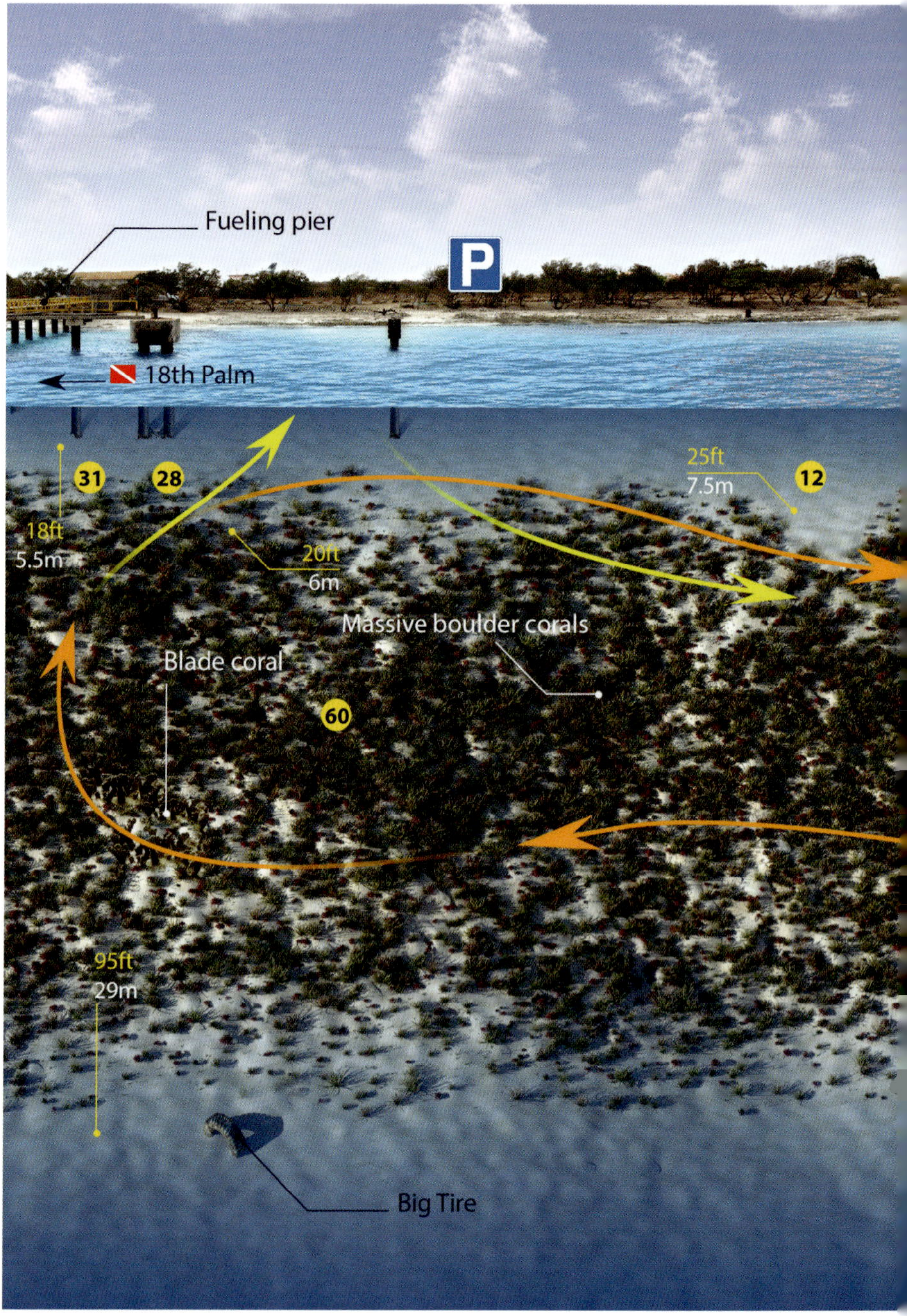

Divers should rise slowly to extend their bottom time—although this section of reef is small enough and shallow enough that divers should have plenty of bottom time to spare. The back reef is a great place to conduct a safety stop, and divers and snorkelers can often find yellowhead jawfish and sailfin blennies in the sand and rubble here.

P
Site buoy
Corporal Meiss
64
51
30ft
9m
74
81
S
E
W
N
115ft
35m

37

BONAIRE

Corporal Meiss (North Belnem)

Difficulty ● ○ ○
Current ● ○ ○
Depth ● ● ○
Reef ★ ☆ ☆
Fauna ★ ★ ☆

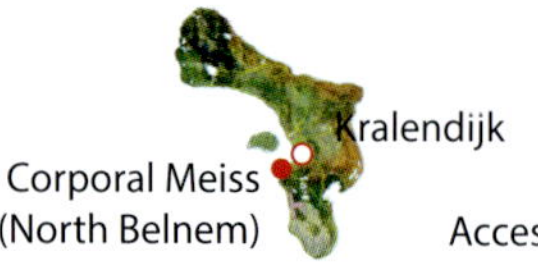

Access about 7 mins from Kralendijk
about 7 mins from Kralendijk

Level Open Water

Location
Belnem, Bonaire
GPS: 12°07′52.3″N, 68°17′01.2″W

Getting there

Corporal Meiss is an oft-overlooked shore dive and snorkel site located adjacent to Windsock at the southern end of Palu di Mangel Beach, also known as Donkey Beach. Drive south from Kralendijk on Kaya International, which becomes EEG Boulevard as it passes the airport. Divers should continue past the jetty that marks the north end of Windsock and pull over where the fence marking the end of the runway cuts back away from the road. They will notice a yellow rock that says Corporal Meiss on it. There is plenty of parking on either side of the road.

Access

There are several paths from the road through the shrubs to the shoreline, both immediately at the end of the runway and also farther south nearer the white wall of the Bonairian Restaurant. The

P
Entrance
Windsock
E S N W

last few yards to the water's edge are the trickiest, with a shallow gravel slope that can give way underfoot when wearing heavy dive gear. The beach is rocky and rutted in places, but access to the site is not too challenging relative to others. The back reef is largely sand and patch reef, and the yellow mooring buoy is located 200 feet (61 meters) off the beach.

Description

While Corporal Meiss, also sometimes known as North Belnem, offers an interesting level of biodiversity, most divers seem to skip this site in favor of Windsock to the north or Bachelor's Beach to the south. As such, the site is rarely crowded with other divers. It is easy to access, and simple and rewarding to explore. Barracuda are often found patrolling the deeper parts of this reef, while sea turtles and octopuses are also common here, as well as soapfish and small snake eel species such as the golden spotted eel and the sharptail eel.

RELAX & RECHARGE

Cactus Blue is another of Bonaire's premier food trucks. It is located on the main road adjacent to the Corporal Meiss dive and snorkel site, and it serves delicious wraps and burgers. But it is the fresh lionfish burger that most people crave. The food truck operates from 11:00am to 3:00pm, but getting there before noon is essential for anyone looking to eat lionfish, as the supply is limited and they sell out fast. There is plenty of shade under the divi trees that line the beach at this spot, so "eat in," relax and soak up the atmosphere. For those still hungry, try the homemade chocolate and peanut dessert they call Flamingo Droppings.
Visit: **Cactusblue.us**

Bachelor's Beach

Bachelor's Beach (Fondu Di Kalki)

Difficulty ● ○ ○
Current ● ○ ○
Depth ● ● ○
Reef ★★☆
Fauna ★★☆

Access: about 8 mins from Kralendijk (by car); about 11 mins from Kralendijk (by boat)

Level Open Water

Location

Belnem, Bonaire
GPS: 12°07'31.9"N, 68°17'14.0"W

Getting there

Drive south from Kralendijk on Kaya International, which becomes EEG Boulevard as it passes the airport. Bachelor's Beach is located in a gap between the houses that line this stretch of coast, about half a mile (just under one kilometer) past the end of the airport runway. Pass through the intersection with Kaya IR. Randolph Statius van Eps on the left, as it heads to the east coast. Just 50 feet (15 meters) after this intersection, there is a large open area on the right-hand side of the road, which is the parking lot adjacent to Bachelor's Beach. Two yellow painted rocks are present in the parking lot.

Access

Bachelor's Beach is reached by descending the set of stairs located in the middle of the cliff overlooking the water. Divers may need to use the rocks to descend the last few steps to the beach. It is possible to simply walk down the beach and into the water. The mooring buoy is located about 300 feet (91 meters) directly out from the beach.

RELAX & RECHARGE

King Kong Burger is a food truck located at Bachelor's Beach. They only serve burgers, hot dogs and fries, but boy do they do those well. There is a reason King Kong Burger is consistently voted the number one restaurant in Bonaire. They offer a range of ways to vary, or "pimp out," your standard burger by adding elements such as brie, bacon, honey and nuts. The fries are also outstanding and can be "juiced" with a little truffle paste and Parmesan, or, in the case of their famous Mosquito Repellent Fries, tossed with garlic and fresh parsley. They even have outstanding veggie burgers and hot dogs. Do not miss this Bonaire highlight.

Description

The name Bachelor's Beach applies to both the popular white sand beach at this location and

The white sand and inviting water at Bachelor's Beach.

the reef that sits just off shore. This site is popular for both diving and snorkeling, with a relatively shallow back reef protected from wave action and currents.

The beach itself, known as Fondu di Kalki in Papiamento, is narrow—only 20 feet (6 meters) wide. But the white sands continue out to the reef line that sits 300 feet (91 meters) away, lending the waters of the small bay a vivid turquoise color. The sandy back reef is far from devoid of life, however, with peacock flounders, grunts, and goatfish common throughout.

There are large stands of staghorn, elkhorn, and blade fire coral in the back reef, as well as patches of gorgonians. The back reef slopes gently out to the mooring buoy, which is located at a depth of 30 feet (9 meters). At this point the reef transitions to denser coral on the reef slope, with numerous brain and star coral mounds interspersed with soft corals. The complexity of the reef here helps support many more species of reef fishes, including trumpetfish, schools of chromis and creole wrasses, pufferfish, and parrotfish, to name just a few. Divers often describe Bachelor's Beach as having something for everyone.

The lack of current, relative shallowness of the reef and the easy, convenient access to the site also makes this a preferred site for night divers. In fact, visiting Bachelor's Beach during both day and night offers the opportunity to see very different versions of the same reef. At night, divers can see spotted moray eels on the prowl and yellowline arrow crabs out looking for bristleworms and tube worms. Night divers can also expect company from large tarpon, which often approach night divers to hunt the small fish that congregate in and around their dive lights.

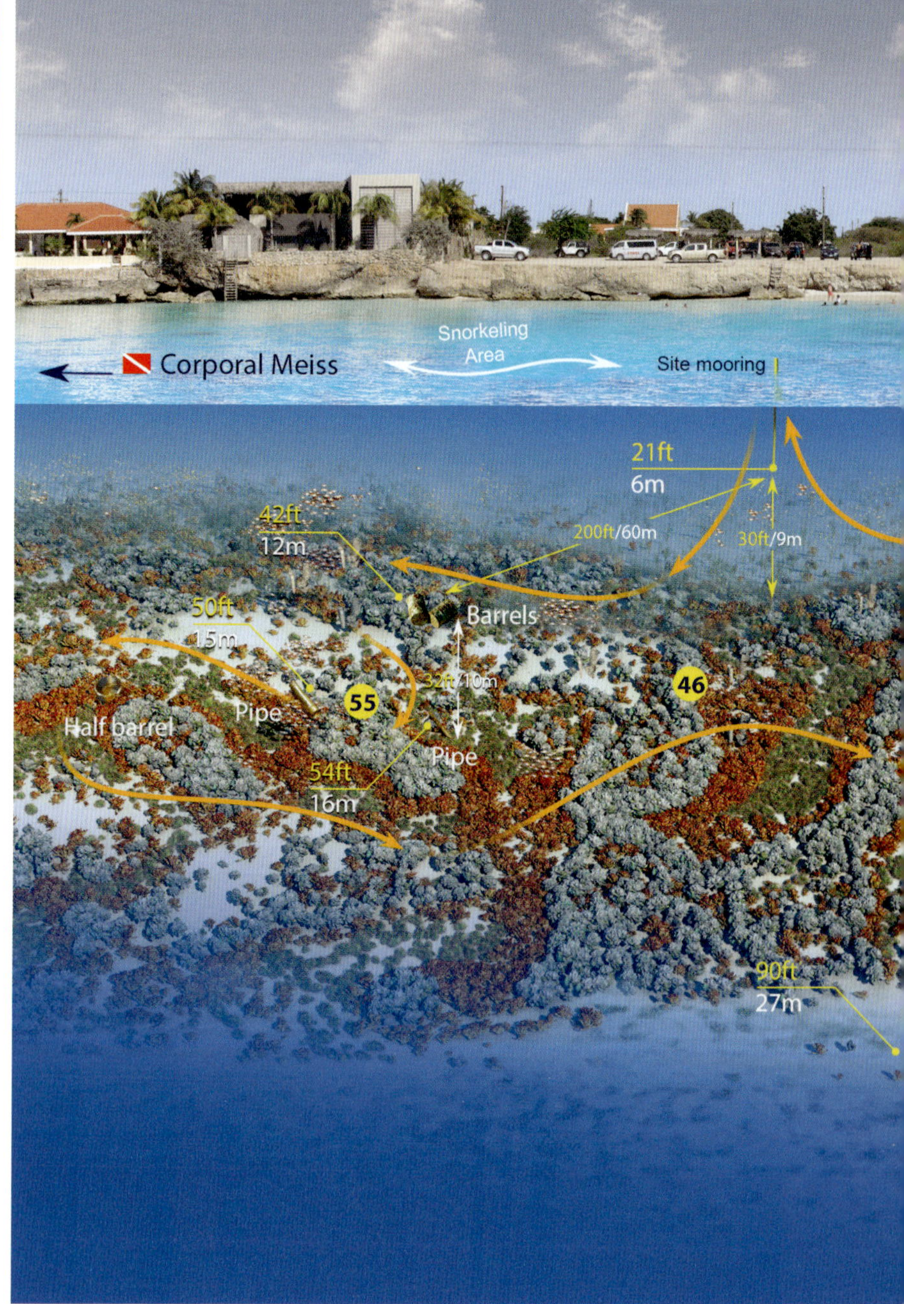

Route

The route is the same for both night and day dives. Divers can make their way out toward the buoy, enjoying the back reef and its creatures as they go. Once at the buoy, they can descend to the reef slope and head either left or right. To the north divers will notice several objects, such as discarded barrels and pipes. To the south a large pillar coral rises above the rest of the reef like a tower, and provides a useful reference point for where to turn around.

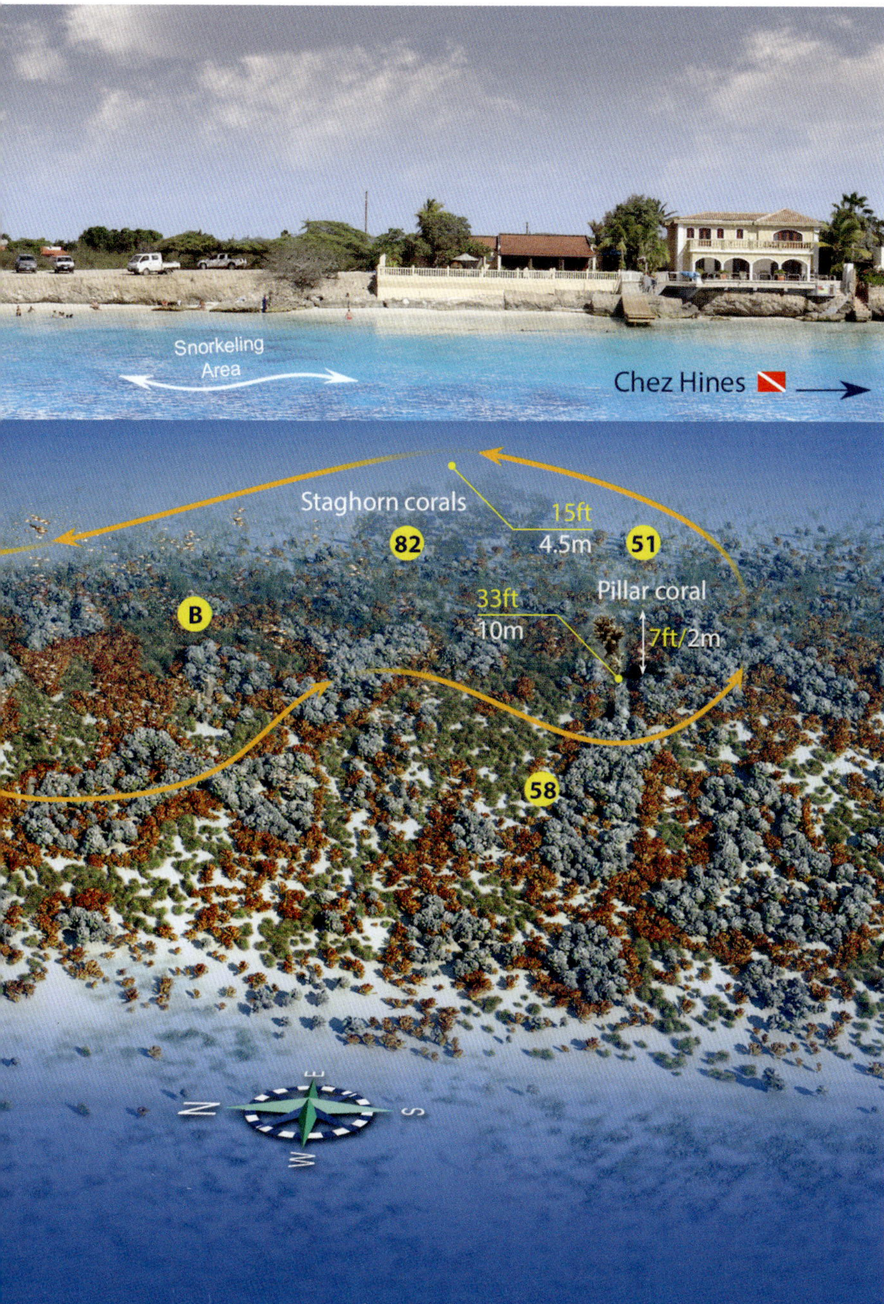

There is plenty to see in the shallows at Bachelor's Beach and it is worth spending some time checking out the back reef, particularly the large stands of staghorn coral. A coral outplant site managed by Reef Renewal Bonaire is located in the back reef, south of the beach. The deeper parts of this reef are also interesting to explore, particularly the deep edge where the reef transitions to sand. The reef is patchier than at other sites and occurs at a depth of around 90 feet (27 meters). Hamlets, tiger grouper, and even cubera snapper have been spotted in the deeper areas of this reef.

39 BONAIRE

Chez Hines

Difficulty
Current
Depth
Reef
Fauna

Access about 15 mins from Kralendijk

Level Open Water

Location
Belnem, Bonaire
GPS: 12°07'08.8"N, 68°17'37.0"W

Getting there

Chez Hines is a boat-access dive and snorkel site located between Bachelor's Beach and Delfin's Beach. Consult with a local dive center to see when they are next visiting this site in their schedule.

Access

This site is great for both snorkelers and divers, but the currents can be strong at times. Advanced and tech divers may want to check out the deeper second reef. Although it is not as clearly defined as the second reefs that are present along the sites to the south, it can still be interesting to explore.

Description

Chez Hines is another dive site that used to be readily accessible as a shore dive, but coastal development has since limited access. Sometimes referred to as South Belnem, this site offers divers the opportunity to choose a range of depths. For those individuals who wish to remain in shallower waters, whether snorkeling or diving, the shallow plateau at this site has plenty of hard soft coral to explore. The site is best known for regular sightings of sea turtles, parrotfish, cowfish, filefish and trumpetfish.

Divers with the experience to visit deeper waters can descend all the way to the bottom of the reef at a depth of 120 feet (37 meters). There they can explore the deep second reef, where green morays, nurse sharks, tiger grouper and black grouper have been spotted.

Lighthouse Point

Difficulty ●●●
Current ●●○
Depth ●●○
Reef ★★☆
Fauna ★★☆

Access about 11 mins from Kralendijk (by car)
about 18 mins from Kralendijk (by boat)

Level Open Water

Location
Belnem, Bonaire
GPS: 12° 6′51.23″N , 68°17′45.20″W

Getting there

Drive south from Kralendijk on Kaya International, which becomes EEG Boulevard at the airport. The adjacent resorts of Delfins Beach and Lighthouse Beach are located just under 2 miles (3 kilometers) from the airport—a drive of about 4 minutes. The Lighthouse Point dive and snorkel site can be accessed from either of these properties, or from a public access point just south of Lighthouse Beach Resort.

Access

The back reef at Lighthouse Point is particularly wide—about 500 feet (150 meters)—which requires a very long surface swim for those planning to explore this site from shore. Entering the water from the jetty at Delfins Beach Resort is perhaps the easiest way to explore the site as it cuts approximately 150 feet (46 meters) from the swim in either direction. Divers and snorkelers are free to access the site by asking permission from the resort. Dive Friends Bonaire is located at

The jetty at Delfins Beach is a great entry point to the Lighthouse Point dive and snorkel site.

the site and can provide equipment rentals and guided tours if desired. Lighthouse Point can also be visited by boat. Check with local operators for their schedules. Visibility is usually great at Lighthouse Point, but currents can be strong, so divers should plan accordingly.

Description

Lighthouse Point is located at the westernmost point of this section of Bonaire's coastline. The site gets its name from the Punt Vierkant Lighthouse, which was originally a wooden structure built in 1931 and then replaced with a concrete lighthouse a decade later. The current lighthouse is now incorporated into Lighthouse Beach Resort.

Diving from the jetty at Delfins Beach Resort is the best way to explore this site from shore. Divers and snorkelers can gear up on shore and head down the jetty, where there is a staircase that provides easy access to the water. The depth is about 15 feet (4.5 meters) at the end of the jetty.

Currents tend to run north at this site, so heading into the current involves swimming south toward the point where the permanent mooring buoy is located. The current can be strong here, sometimes too strong to swim against. In this situation, shore divers and snorkelers usually walk south along the beach from the jetty, enter the water farther south and conduct a drift dive that finishes up back at Delfins jetty to the north. The sand can get quite hot on this walk down the beach, however, so booties are essential.

The seabed in the back reef consists largely of sand. This habitat transitions to soft corals at a depth of about 20 feet (6 meters). The soft corals host plenty of trumpetfish, slender filefish, and schooling goatfish and grunts. There are also numerous giant anemones in this area, and hawksbill sea turtles are a common sight.

The seabed slopes gently down to about 30 feet (9 meters) before transitioning to a steeper sloping reef dominated more by hard corals and sponges, particularly orange elephant ear sponges, which are scattered along the slope. The deep edge of the reef hits sand at a depth of about 115 feet (35 meters). A subsurface buoy is located on the bottom edge of the reef, directly opposite the Delfins jetty, and this landmark can help divers navigate back to the jetty. Adjacent to this buoy is a large barrel where a green moray often hides.

The moderate to strong current helps support high biodiversity at this site. Divers may also spot stingrays and snake eels, graysbies and coneys, schoolmaster snapper, and multiple butterflyfish and parrotfish species.

Route

If the current is not too strong, the best way to explore Lighthouse Point from Delfins Beach is to head into the current, which usually means swimming south. Divers should drop down the reef slope initially, before gradually shallowing throughout their dive and turning back to head north once at the halfway mark with their air supply. The shallow back reef on the way from the reef back to the jetty is a great place to conduct the safety stop while having plenty of interesting habitat to explore. If the current is strong, it is possible to drift dive this site either from the southern part of Delfins Beach, or from the public access point south of Lighthouse Point Resort. Snorkelers usually explore the shallower back reef and the soft coral zone that lies inshore of the reef slope.

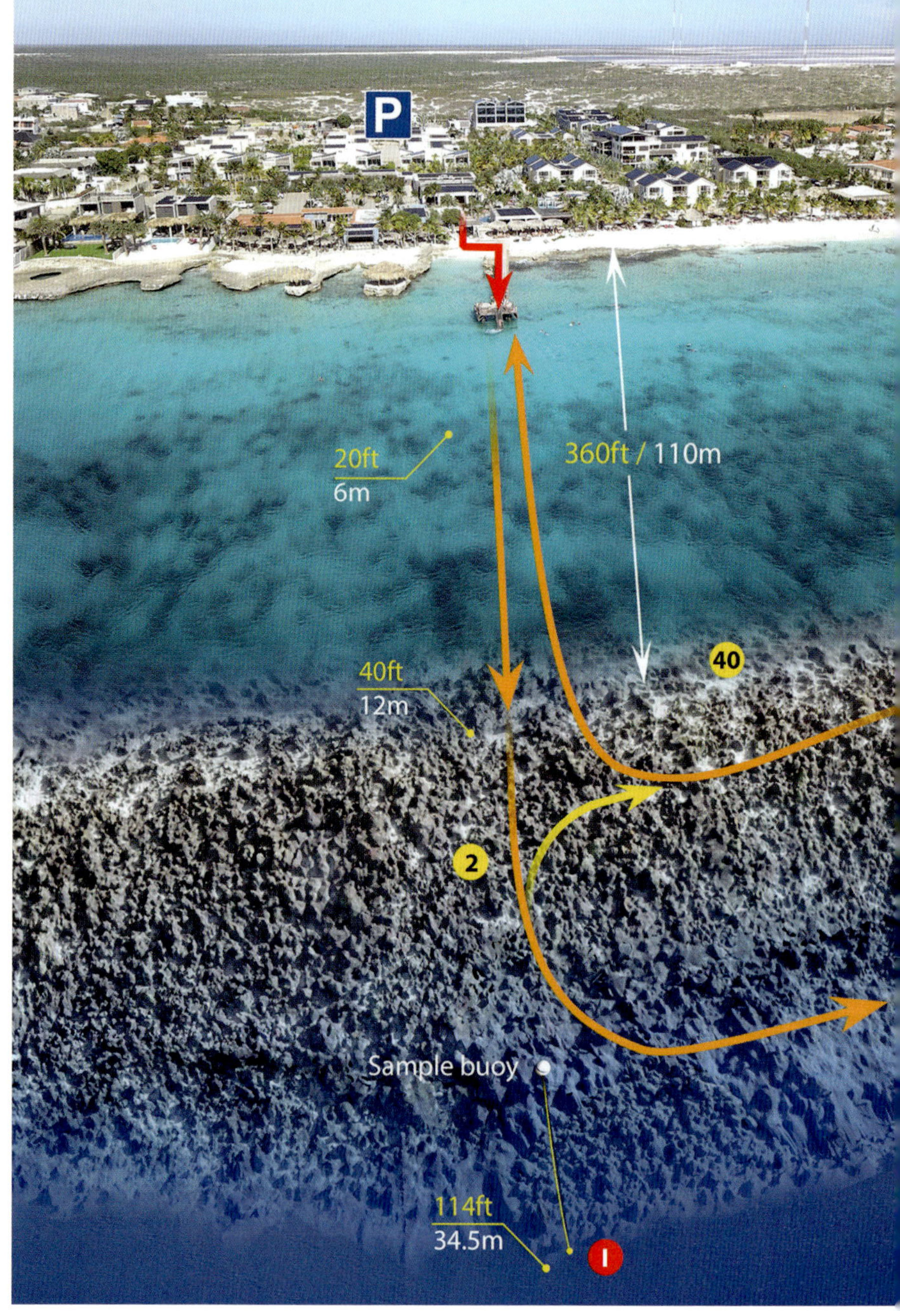
P
20ft
6m
360ft / 110m
40ft
12m
40
2
Sample buoy
114ft
34.5m

LIGHTHOUSE POINT

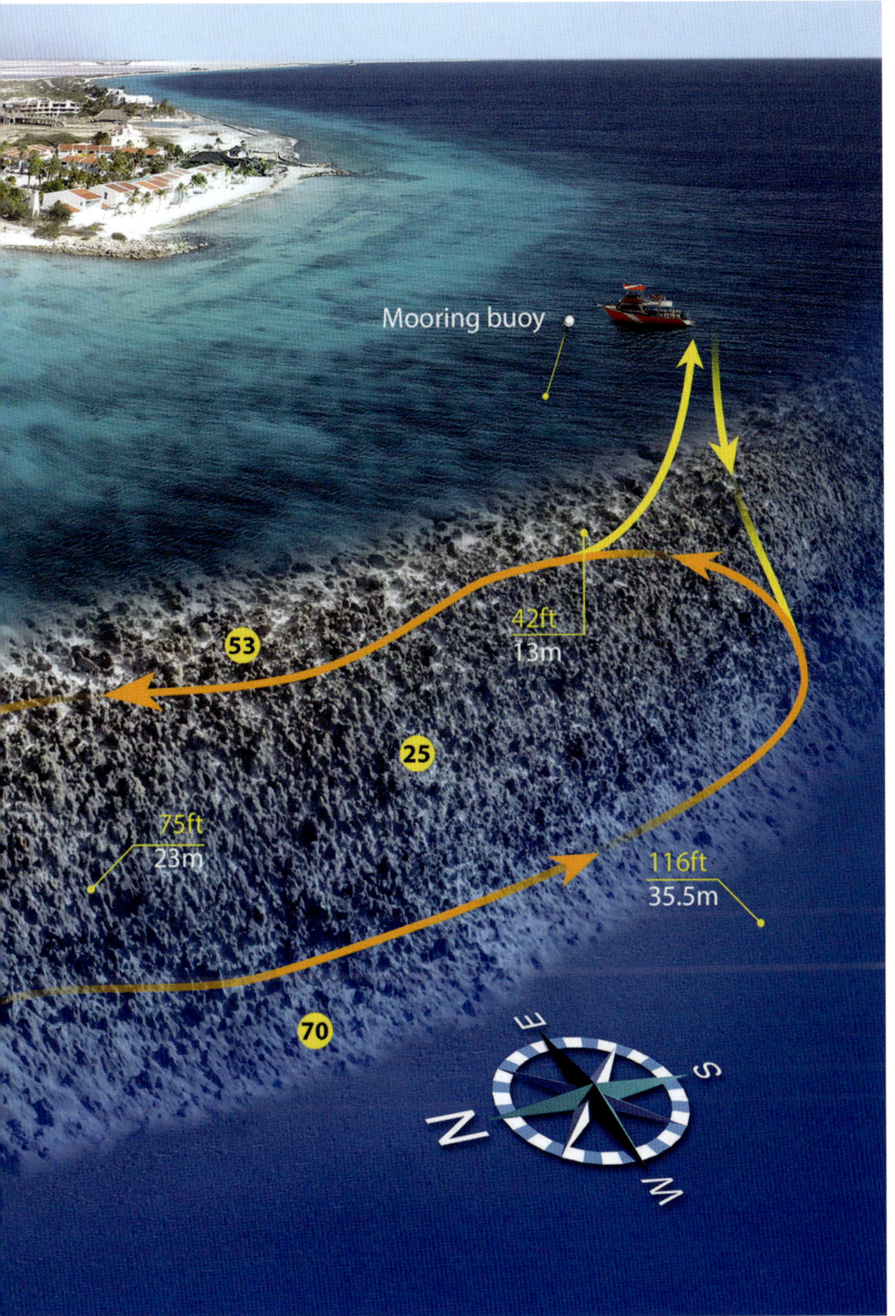

41 Punt Vierkant

BONAIRE

Difficulty ●●○
Current ●●●
Depth ●●○
Reef ★★☆
Fauna ★★☆

Access about 11 mins from Kralendijk

Level Open Water

Location
Belnem, Bonaire
GPS: 12°06'35.0"N, 68°17'31.1"W

Getting there
Drive south from Kralendijk on Kaya International, which becomes EEG Boulevard as it passes the airport. Just over 2 miles (3.4 kilometers) after the airport—a drive of about 4 minutes—is a partially constructed hotel. Now abandoned, this building is known as the Esmeralda Ruins. Just south of these ruins sits the Ocean Oasis Beach Club. The best access point for the Punt Vierkant dive site is immediately south of the beach club. Pull

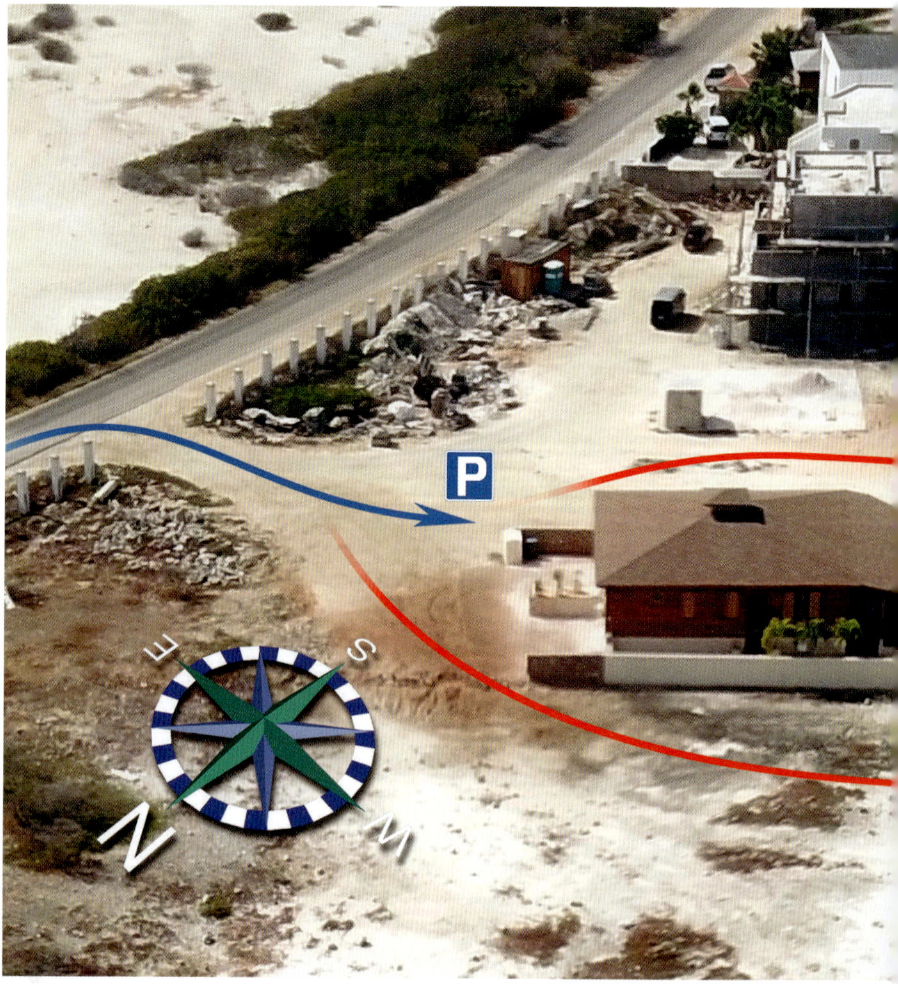

off the main road and park next to the newly constructed house adjacent to the shore.

Access

The walk from the parking lot to the shore is only about 100 feet (30 meters), but there are numerous rocks and a rutted reef ledge with holes that can lead to a twisted ankle and fall, so divers should take care as they enter the water. There is no mooring buoy at this site.

Description

Punt Vierkant means "Square Point" in Dutch, possibly a reference to the 90 degree angle formed by the point along this section of the coastline. Punt Vierkant is sometimes subjected to strong currents because it is located near where the coastline sticks out. It is the first of the southern sites to boast a clearly defined double reef system, which is characteristic of many southern dive sites. Punt Vierkant is actually the point where the double reef starts, and if divers head north from this site they may see where the two reefs join. The first reef slope descends to a sand channel at 85 feet (26 meters), the second reef rises slightly before continuing down to depths of over 120 feet (35 meters).

This site is known for its profusion of hard and soft corals in shallow waters, including fire corals, and a dense reef slope featuring brain and star corals. Large schools of creole wrasses are found here, along with some pelagic species, such as horse-eye jacks, bar jacks, and rainbow runners. Sand tilefish and stingrays are sometimes found between the two reefs.

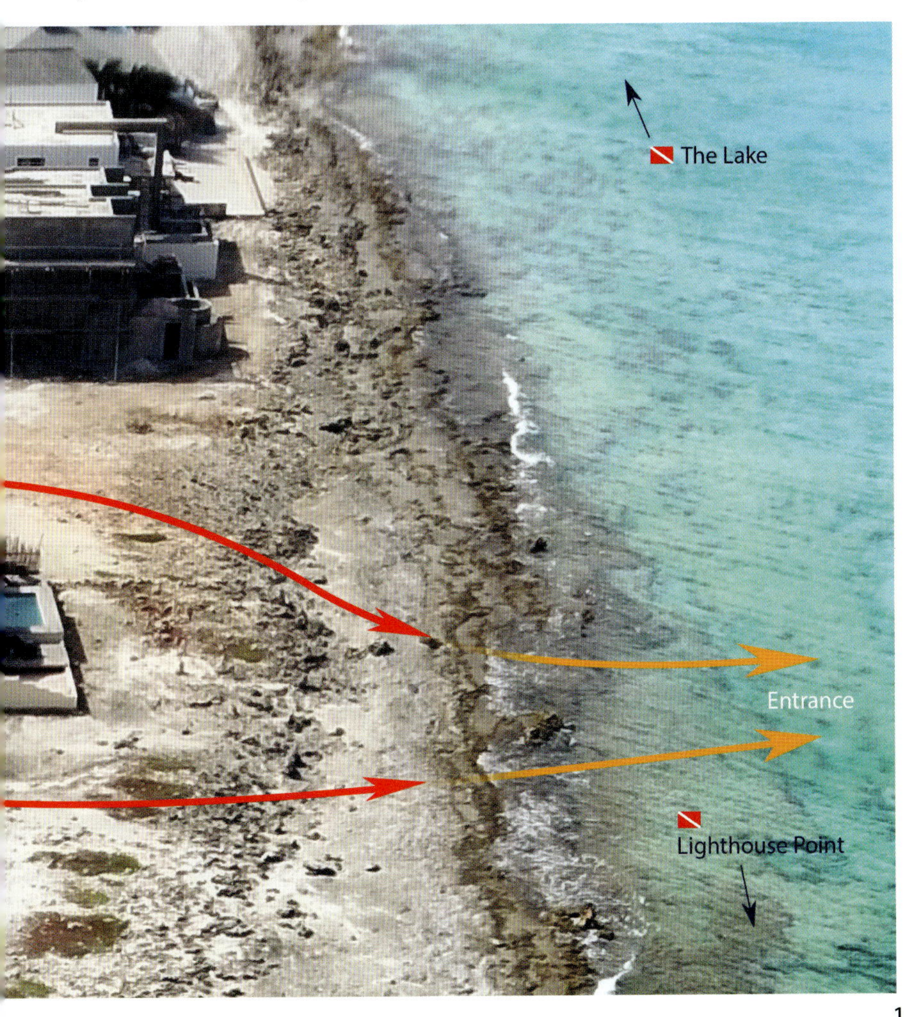

42 The Lake

BONAIRE

Difficulty ●●○
Current ●●○
Depth ●●●
Reef ★★☆
Fauna ★★☆

Access about 11 mins from Kralendijk
about 22 mins from Kralendijk

Level Open Water

Location
Belnem, Bonaire
GPS: 12°06′26.4″N, 68°17′23.5″W

Getting there

Drive south from Kralendijk on Kaya International, which becomes EEG Boulevard as it passes the airport. After Bachelor's Beach, the road bends slightly away from the coastline for about 0.75 miles (1.2 kilometers) before returning to the shore just before The Lake dive site. There is a sand and rubble parking area next to the water, immediately after the row of houses on the right-hand side of the road. The site is marked with two yellow rocks at the entrance to the parking lot. The site is just under 2.5 miles from the airport (3.8 kilometers)—a drive of about 5 minutes.

Access

Divers can gear up and walk from the parking lot to the water's edge. There are a few rocks to step over to enter the water, but access is relatively easy compared to other sites. A sand and rubble channel that is roughly 40 feet (12 meters) wide provides access through the reef. The yellow mooring buoy is located on the shoreward edge of the reef and slightly south of the parking lot.

Description

The Lake gets its name from the "lake" of sand that sits in between the first and second reef slopes at this site. Starting from the beach, the seabed is dominated by sand and coral rubble before it gives way to soft corals and patch reef, roughly 250 feet (75 meters) from shore. From there, the slope of the reef steepens, descending from a depth of 30 feet (9 meters) down to the sand channel at around 70 feet (21 meters), located in the middle of the site. The northern end of the channel is wider and deeper than the south, bottoming out at 77 feet (23.5 meters), while the southern end narrows, bottoming out at a depth closer to 68 feet (20.5 meters). Around the edge of the sand channel, numerous large coral mounds, or bommies, rise 10 to 15 feet (3 to 4.5 meters) above the reef and provide complex habitat for snapper, grunts, black margates and other reef fish.

Please do not remove any conch shells.

The second reef starts on the far side of the sand channel, cresting at a depth of 65 feet (20

DID YOU KNOW?

The "double reef" term is a misnomer in that these two reef slopes are not technically two separate reefs. Digging down through the sand that separates the two slopes would uncover dead coral, because the channel between the two is a shallow ledge in the buttress zone of this living reef where sand has collected over time. (Please do not dig down in the sand.)The different corals and sponges that inhabit the upper slope, or first reef, represent the normal differences due to depth—it is just that the separation of a sand channel makes the transition between shallow and deep corals more noticeable.

meters) before dropping down to a final depth of 100 feet (30.5 meters). Both reef slopes have very complex surfaces that provide plenty of hiding places for reef fish. Divers have the chance to see a wide range of species in the different habitats at this site. For example, sand tilefish, conch, stingrays, and garden eels can be found in the sand, while slender filefish and flamingo tongues can be found in the shallower areas dominated by soft corals.

Route

From the beach, divers generally swim out toward the mooring buoy in a southwestern direction. From there, they descend the first reef slope pausing to explore the big coral mounds

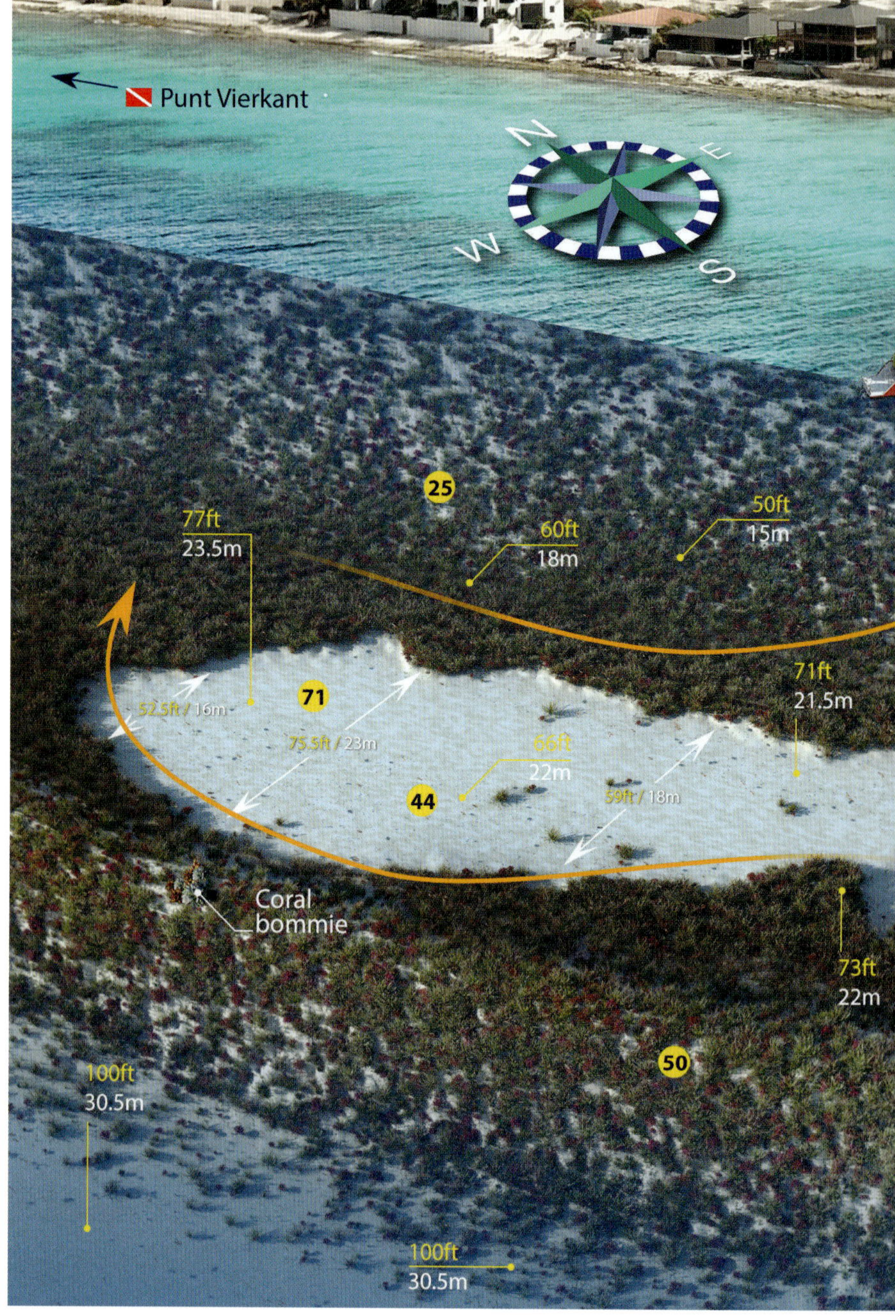

and pillars that rise above the reef. Once they reach the sand channel, divers usually head south along the nearshore side, exploring the sand-to-reef transition zone. Once they reach the southern end of the sand channel, divers typically switch over to the second reef and start heading back north.

Divers should consider dividing their bottom time between exploring the boundary between sand and reef, as well as visiting the coral heads and sponges found on the second reef slope.

Most divers turn back toward shore after they reach the northern terminus of the sand

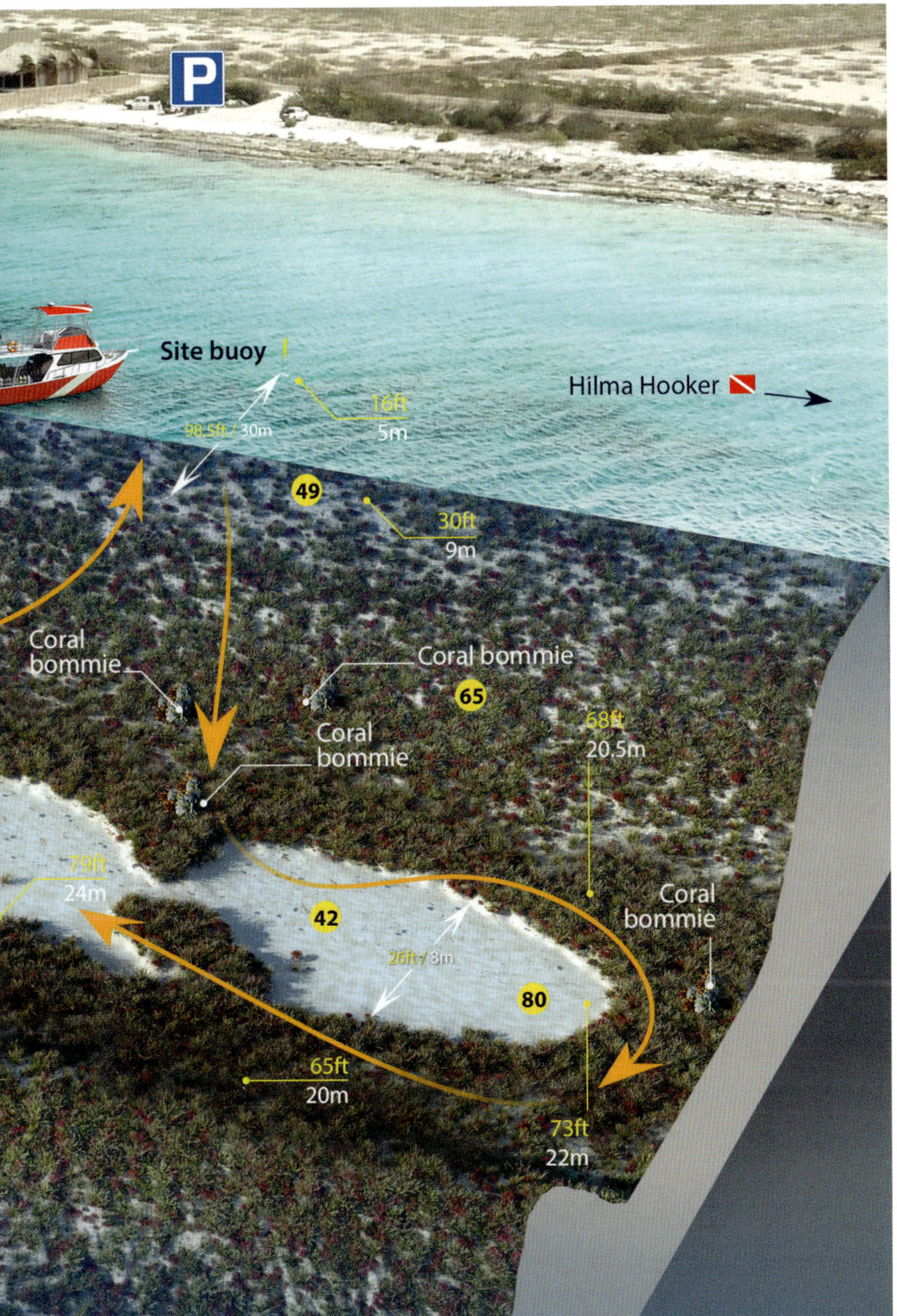

channel. They slowly ascend the first reef slope and take their three-minute safety stop as they cruise over the back reef zone with its abundance of soft corals.

43

BONAIRE

Hilma Hooker

Difficulty ●●○
Current ●○○
Depth ●●○
Reef ★☆☆
Fauna ★★☆

Access about 12 mins from Kralendijk
about 23 mins from Kralendijk

Level Open Water

Location

Belnem, Bonaire
GPS: 12°06′16.5″N, 68°17′15.0″W

Getting there

Drive south from Kralendijk on Kaya International, which becomes EEG Boulevard as it passes the airport. After Bachelor's Beach, the road bends slightly away from the coastline for about 0.75 miles (1.2 kilometers) before returning to the shore just before The Lake dive site. *Hilma Hooker* is located just under 0.2 miles (0.3 kilometers) beyond The Lake dive site, right next to the large Trans World Radio antennae. Divers should pull off the road on the right-hand side next to the yellow rock that marks the site and descend the gravel slope to the parking lot next to the water. The large shrub in the middle of the parking lot is often used as a place to turn around. Most divers back their cars up to the shoulder that runs between the parking lot and the shore to unload their dive gear and enter the water.

Access

Divers should gear up and descend the small, 30-foot (9-meter) slope to the water's edge. The slope can be a little tricky to negotiate in some spots, and the last 15 feet (4.5 meters) to the water is deeply rutted with large boulders. There is a real risk of falling down. Once in the water, divers should surface swim out to the yellow mooring buoys that mark the bow and stern of the wreck before descending.

Description

Hilma Hooker is one of Bonaire's most popular dive sites and the island's best-known wreck. Built in 1951 in the Netherlands, the freighter was originally named *MV Midsland* and began her service with a shipping company that operated out of Rotterdam. She changed her name and her ownership multiple times throughout the 1960s and 1970s before sinking off the coast of the Dominican Republic in July 1975. She was raised and resold that same year, before ultimately assuming the name *Hilma Hooker* under Colombian ownership.

Accounts of the story that led to her sinking vary from person to person, but most people agree that *Hilma Hooker* experienced problems with her rudder as she was passing the coast of Bonaire. She had to be towed to Kralendijk's harbor, at which point the authorities realized she was sailing without official papers. The authorities decided to search her after learning both the FBI and Interpol suspected she was being used to smuggle illegal drugs. During

SAFETY TIP

Divers are advised not to attempt penetration of the *Hilma Hooker*. The position of the wreck on its side can lead divers to become disoriented during penetration attempts, which can be dangerous. Additionally, the maximum depth of 100 feet (30.5 meters) leaves little margin for error, particularly if diving on air and using a single tank set-up. Finally, although the wreck was sunk deliberately, it was not prepped for penetration, and thus much of the wreck's interior, particularly the engine room, contains unstable debris that can easily snag or entangle a diver.

their search, they found 25,000 pounds (11,300 kg) of marijuana hidden behind her bulkheads. The authorities impounded the ship and tried to identify her owners, with little to no success.

After several months, and amid growing concerns about the vessel's ability to stay afloat, the port authorities towed *Hilma Hooker* away from Kralendijk's main pier. After consulting with local divers and the Bonaire Tourism authority, the ship was moored in her current position, which was considered a relatively safe place for the ship to sink, with respect to the local ecosystem and navigation, should this occur before the owners could be identified.

Soon after she was moved (a mere five days by some accounts), her aging hull began to take on water faster than her failing pumps could bail, and on September 12, 1984, *Hilma Hooker* sank beneath the waves for the last time, settling on her starboard side at the base of the first reef slope.

A diver explores the *Hilma Hooker*.

Aquapix/Shutterstock ©

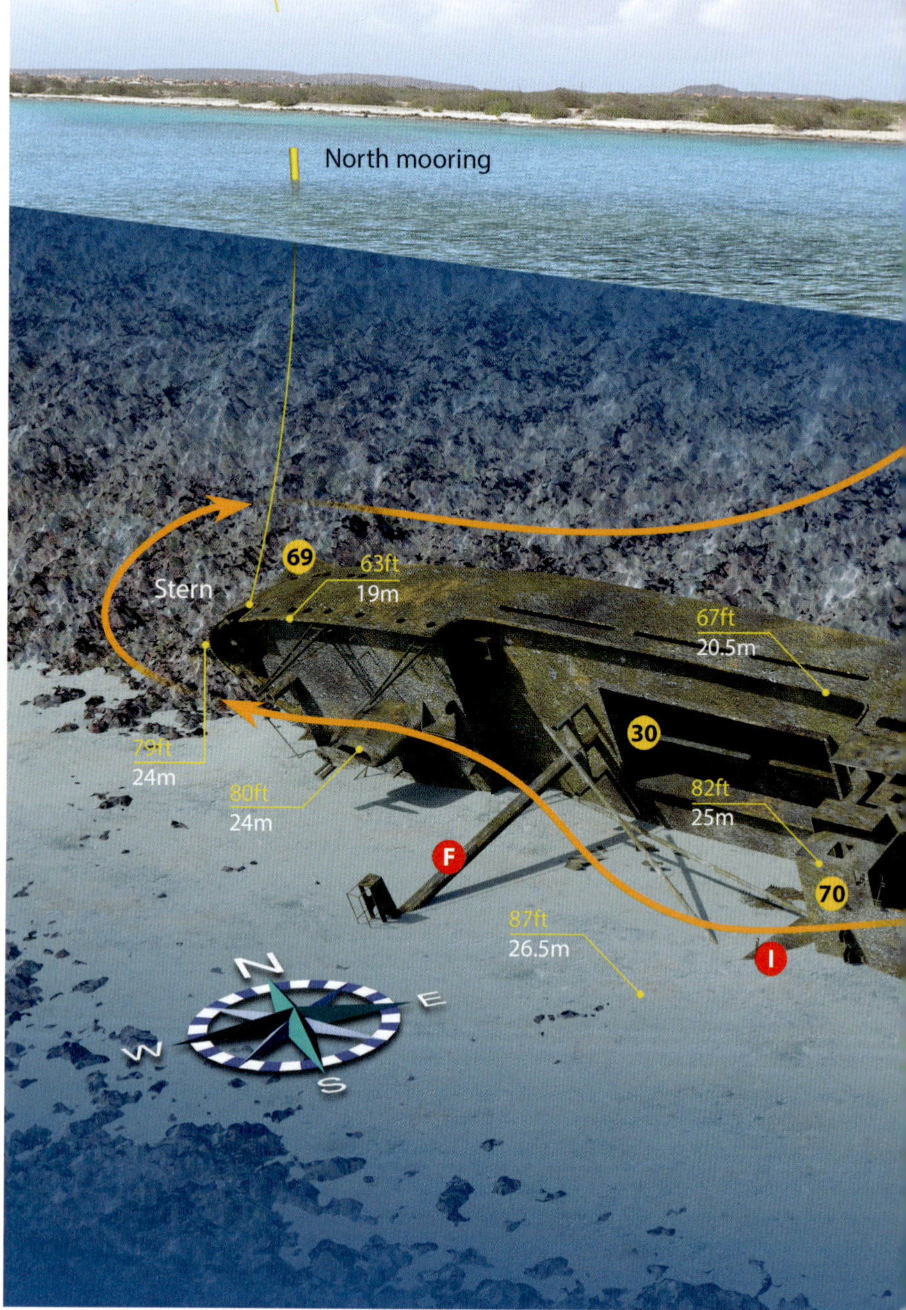

The wreck sits in the sand channel between the first and second reef slopes that is the hallmark of this stretch of the Bonaire coastline. At a depth of less than 100 feet (31 meters) and within swimming distance from shore, *Hilma Hooker* is ideally situated for boat and shore divers of all experience levels.

Divers can enjoy the first reef slope as they approach and leave the wreck on their shore dive, but the star attraction of this site is definitely the wreck itself. *Hilma Hooker* is in good condition, protected as it is from strong currents by the two nearby reefs. It is fully encrusted with soft corals and sponges,

particularly around the exposed propeller. The superstructure and masts are intact as well as the main hold, but the wreck was not properly prepared for scuttling as an artificial reef so authorities strongly advise against penetration due to entanglement risks.

Route

The wreck's bow and stern are marked by southern and northern mooring buoys, respectively. As divers approach *Hilma Hooker*'s keel, they typically head south toward the bow and then circle around to the deck side of the wreck. They often make their way from the

bow back toward the stern, checking out the superstructure and masts as they lie on their sides against the sandy seafloor. Along the way, divers should keep watch for the plentiful marine life that has colonized the wreck, including green moray eels, tarpon, snapper, angelfish, and parrotfish. Patrolling barracuda also frequent the water column above the masts. Once they reach the bow, most divers will circle back around to the keel before ascending the reef slope toward shore. The swim back along the back reef can make for an interesting safety stop.

Name:	*Hilma Hooker*	**Tonnage:**	1,027grt
Type:	Freighter	**Construction:**	Krimpen aan den IJssel, Netherlands, 1951
Previous names:	*MV Midsland, MV Mistral, MV William Express, MV Anna C, MV Doric Express*	**Last owner:**	San Andrés Shipping, Colombia
Length:	235ft (72m)	**Sunk:**	September 12, 1984

44

BONAIRE

Angel City

Difficulty ●●○
Current ●●○
Depth ●●○
Reef ★★★
Fauna ★★☆

Access about 13 mins from Kralendijk
about 25 mins from Kralendijk

Level Open Water

Location
Cargill Salt Works, Bonaire
GPS: 12°06′13.4″N, 68°17′13.3″W

Getting there

Drive south from Kralendijk on Kaya International, which becomes EEG Boulevard as it passes the airport. After Bachelor's Beach, the road bends slightly away from the coastline for about 0.75 miles (1.2 kilometers) before returning to the shore just before The Lake dive site. Angel City is located just after *Hilma Hooker* and adjacent to the large Trans World Radio antennae.

Divers should pull off to the right-hand side of the main road, next to the yellow rock that marks the site, and descend the gravel slope to the parking lot next to the water. Most divers back their cars up to the shoulder that runs between the parking lot and the shore in order to unload their dive gear and enter the water more easily. There are several large coral piles here, which help mark the site. Angel City is just over 2.5 miles from the airport (4.2 kilometers)—a drive of about 5 minutes.

Access

Divers should gear up and follow the sand and gravel path that leads down to a small sandy beach by the waterline. They may need to step around several large rocks, but access at this site is relatively easy compared to other sites. Several stands of blade fire coral can make navigating the channel out to the reef slightly challenging, so divers should make sure they have their face masks on as they enter the water. The reef is marked with a yellow mooring buoy.

Description

Angel City is another dive site that features Bonaire's famous double reefs, and one where the reef starts relatively close to shore. The site gets its name from the profusion of friendly angelfish that frequent both the back reef and the reef slopes. French and Queen angelfish are the most common, but the particularly rare flameback angelfish has also been documented here.

The back reef slopes gently out toward the mooring buoy, which sits at a depth of 15 feet (4.5 meters). Stands of staghorn coral can be found south of the buoy along the transition between back reef and reef slope. This zone holds a mix of gorgonians and hard corals, which creates a complex seafloor that helps attract a variety of reef fishes—one of the reasons this site makes for good snorkeling.

Divers can count on seeing angelfish at Angel City.

To the south end of the site, the first slope bottoms out at a depth of just 60 feet (18 meters). To the north, the sand channel lies a little deeper, closer to 80 feet (24 meters). As with most double reef sites, the primary sand channel runs parallel to shore. However, the channel is much narrower at this site than elsewhere, which has allowed bridges of coral to connect the two reefs in several places. As a result, this site is a little harder to navigate than adjacent double reef sites since it is easier to get disoriented if divers do not regularly check their compasses.

The second reef slope is dominated by hard corals and sponges and offers plenty of rugosity (a measure of the complexity of the reef) that has attracted a diverse assemblage of reef species. Multiple large brain coral mounds offer points of interest worth exploring as divers cruise along the reef crest at a depth of just 48 feet (14 meters), which is significantly shallower than other double reef sites. Divers are likely to see plenty of morays, porcupinefish, yellowtail snapper, and schooling horse-eye jacks, which are relatively common on the second reef.

Route

Snorkelers have plenty to explore in the back reef, including the stands of staghorn coral along the reef transition area. There is excellent snorkeling in the area immediately to the north and south of the buoy.

Divers should enter the water and swim out toward the mooring buoy. They typically descend the first reef slope until they reach the sand channel where conch and stingrays are common, and then turn right to head in a northerly direction. Divers should remember that the sand channel is deeper to the north, which means they will need to monitor their depth. Less experienced divers should stick to the south end of the site so that they can experience the second reef without getting too deep. For those divers who can go deeper, they can cross over to the second reef at the northern end of the site once

they pass a set of three coral bridges that span the sand channel, as well as a set of coral pillars on the reef slope above. Once on the second reef, they can turn to head in a southerly direction.

Divers can continue in this direction, alternating between exploring the reef slope with its large coral mounds and the transition between sand and reef of the main channel. Once they reach the coral bridge at the southern end of the sand channel, they should cross back over to the first reef slope and make their way back up the reef slope toward the buoy and the back reef. This site offers the opportunity to take a safety stop while

exploring the back reef area, and divers should keep an eye open for giant anemones and their associated Pederson cleaner shrimp.

45

BONAIRE

Alice in Wonderland

Difficulty ● ○ ○
Current ● ○ ○
Depth ● ● ●
Reef ★★☆
Fauna ★★☆

Access about 13 mins from Kralendijk
about 26 mins from Kralendijk

Level Open Water

Location
Cargill Salt Works, Bonaire
GPS: 12°05′59.9″N, 68°17′06.7″W

Getting there

Drive south from Kralendijk on Kaya International, which becomes EEG Boulevard as it passes the airport. After Bachelor's Beach, the road bends slightly away from the coastline for about 0.75 miles (1.2 kilometers) before returning to the shore just before The Lake dive site. Alice In Wonderland is located about halfway between The Lake and Salt Pier, and just under 3 miles from the airport (4.7 kilometers)—a drive of about 6 minutes.

As divers approach the end of the first salt pond, they will notice a small yellow hut on the left-hand side of the road, just before the large Cargill sign. They should take the track on the opposite side of the road, where a yellow rock marks the site, and drive down into the gravel parking lot. Most divers back their cars up to the shoulder that runs between the parking lot and the shore to unload their dive gear and enter the water more easily.

Access

There is a white sand and rubble beach that makes entering the water at this site relatively easy. The wave action is also low, but several large boulders and reef holes exist in the shallows, which can pose tripping hazards on the way out. The site is marked with a yellow mooring buoy about 300 feet (91.5 meters) off the beach.

Description

Alice in Wonderland is another of Bonaire's spectacular double reef dive sites. The back reef includes a mix of gorgonians and a few isolated hard corals at an average depth of around 15 feet (4.5 meters). From there the reef gradually slopes toward the drop-off, which starts at a depth of 25 feet (7.5 meters). Soft corals and sea fans dominate this section of the reef, all the way down to where the slope meets the sand channel at a depth of around 90 feet (27.5 meters). The white sand channel runs parallel to shore and varies in width from nearly 165 feet

(50 meters) at its southern end, to just 26 feet (8 meters) in the north where two coral patches extend from either side. Patches of hard corals are sprinkled throughout the sand channel creating interesting islands in the otherwise open space. Garden eels pepper the sand channel with a higher density at the southern end of the channel.

The second reef crests at a depth of 60 feet (18 meters) before descending to over 130 feet (40 meters). Plate-form corals dominate this section of reef, along with scattered sponges. Large brain corals are worth exploring on this section of the reef, along with a few giant anemones. Horse-eye jacks, triggerfish, and barracuda can frequently be spotted patrolling the waters above the second reef slope, while green moray eels hide in the reef below.

Lucky divers may see spotted eagle rays near the reefs in Bonaire.

Priya Talwar/Shutterstock ©

Route

Snorkelers will have plenty to see in the back reef, particularly in the vicinity of the mooring buoy. Divers will want to swim out to the drop-off zone before descending the first reef slope to the second reef. They can choose a clockwise or counter-clockwise route to explore this site. Divers should take care and consider using a

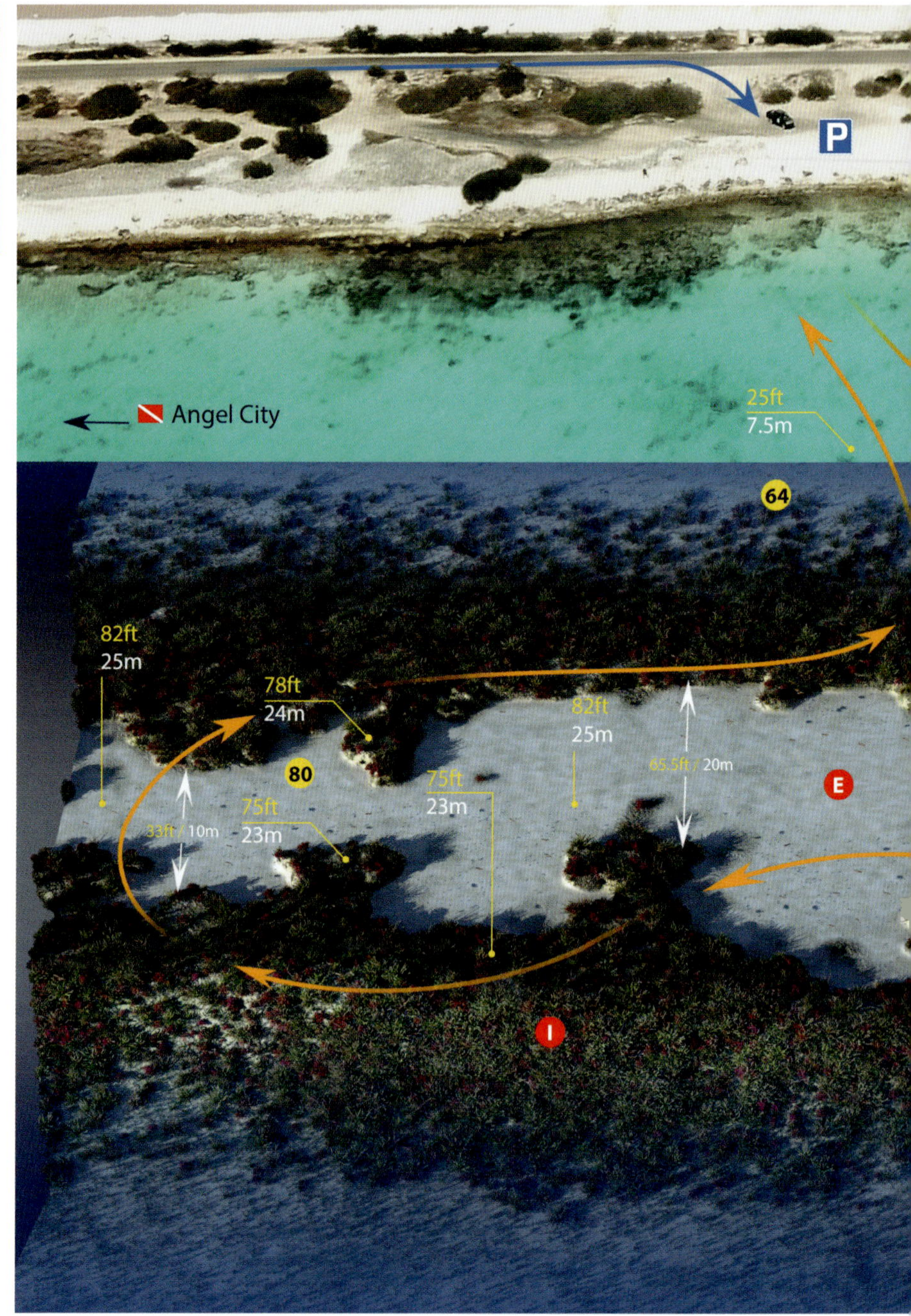

compass if they choose to pass between the two reefs at the southern end of the site, as the sand channel is widest here, and the second reef is not always visible from the first.

Most divers take some time to explore this second reef but they should be sure to return to the first reef with plenty of air and bottom time. Divers typically ascend the first reef slope just south of the buoy where a particularly large coral head exists, before returning to shore.

ALICE IN WONDERLAND

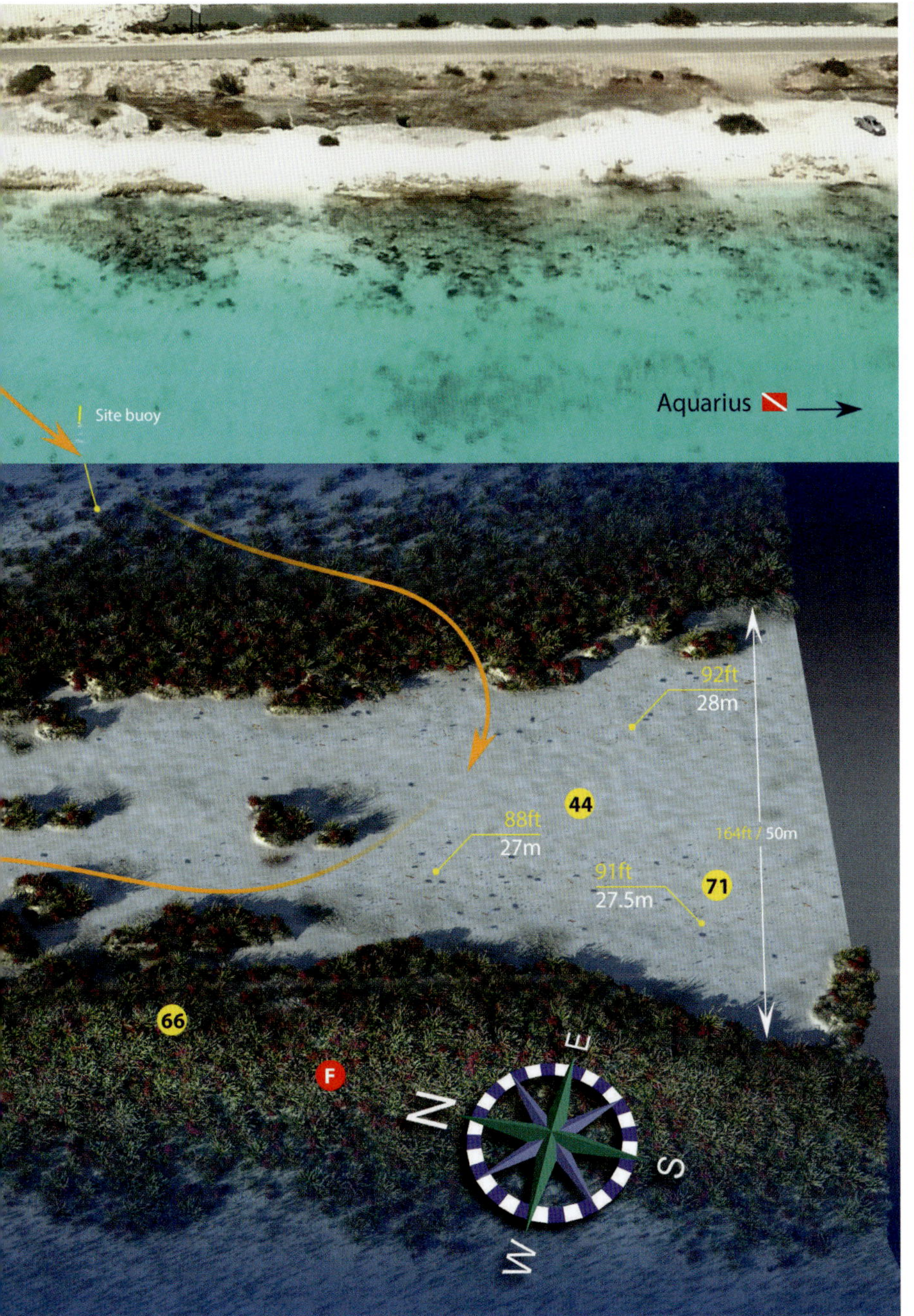

46 BONAIRE

Aquarius

Difficulty ●●○
Current ●●○
Depth ●●●
Reef ★★☆
Fauna ★★☆

Access about 12 mins from Kralendijk (by car)
about 28 mins from Kralendijk (by boat)

Level Open Water

Location
Cargill Salt Works, Bonaire
GPS: 12°05′54.0″N, 68°17′04.1″W

Getting there

Drive south from Kralendijk on Kaya International, which becomes EEG Boulevard as it passes the airport. After Bachelor's Beach, the road bends slightly away from the coastline for about 0.75 miles (1.2 kilometers) before returning to the shore just before The Lake dive site. All the sites between The Lake and Salt Pier are marked with yellow rocks. Pass the *Hilma Hooker*, Angel City and Alice in Wonderland sites before pulling off to the right-hand side of the road and into the parking lot marked with yellow stones. There are two entrances to this parking lot and it has plenty of room for vehicles. Most divers back their cars up to the shoulder that runs between the parking lot and the shore in order to unload their dive gear and enter the water more easily. Aquarius is located about 3.2 miles (5.1 kilometers) from the airport—a drive of about 6 minutes by car.

Access

Divers should gear up and descend the small slope to the water's edge. There are rock piles on the beach that indicate the best entry point. The beach consists mainly of sand with a few scattered rocks. Aquarius is arguably one of the easiest sites to access beyond Bachelor's Beach. Once in the water, most divers surface kick out toward the yellow mooring buoy located about 500 feet (150 meters) to the northwest.

Description

Aquarius is a double reef dive site. The first reef starts 500 feet (150 meters) from shore, so divers should prepare for a long surface swim out to start their dive. They should be careful as they get to the bottom of the first reef slope because the second reef can be hard to spot from the base of the first reef. The sand channel here is wide enough to make navigating to the second reef potentially challenging for less experienced divers, and it generally requires a compass and navigation skills to reach. Divers should watch for stingrays and garden eels in the sand channel.

The second reef is deep—cresting at a depth of around 90 feet (27.5 meters)—so divers should take care to monitor their bottom time. Despite the depth, the second reef is worth a visit, as it is known to have an abundance of snapper, parrotfish, and bar jacks, as well as the occasional sea turtle, eagle ray, and barracuda. The reef is also known for its anemones.

Larry's Lair

Difficulty ●●○
Current ●●○
Depth ●●●
Reef ★★☆
Fauna ★★☆

Access about 13 mins from Kralendijk

Level Open Water

Location
Cargill Salt Works, Bonaire
GPS: 12°05'25.7"N, 68°16'59.2"W

Getting there

Drive south from Kralendijk on Kaya International, which becomes EEG Boulevard as it passes the airport. After Bachelor's Beach, the road bends slightly away from the coastline for about 0.75 miles (1.2 kilometers) before returning to the shore just before The Lake dive site. All the sites between The Lake and Salt Pier are marked with yellow rocks. Once past *Hilma Hooker*, Angel City, Alice in Wonderland and Aquarius, there is a yellow rock on the right-hand side of the road that marks Larry's Lair. Pull off and into the small parking lot. Most divers back their cars up to the shore in order to unload their dive gear and enter the water more easily. Larry's Lair is located about 0.5 miles (0.76 kilometers) north of Salt Pier and about 3.6 miles (5.8 kilometers) from the airport—a drive of about 7 minutes by car.

Access

Access from the parking lot to the shoreline is a little more challenging at Larry's Lair than at nearby sites. The walk is only about 50 feet (15 meters), but there are numerous sharp rocks and a deeply rutted reef ledge at the waterline, so divers should take their time and use their buddy for support if necessary. Corals, including some fire coral, come close to the surface near the shore. Divers should identify a safe path through the reef that avoids these shallow corals and then enter the water and kick out. There is no yellow mooring buoy at this site.

Description

At Larry's Lair, the reef starts more than 500 feet (150 meters) from shore, making this one of the longer swims to reach the reef. This shallow, sand-bottomed plateau, with its plentiful gorgonians and staghorn coral, is one of the key features of this site, however. It makes for a great snorkel or an enjoyable safety stop at the end of a dive.

Visitors to this site regularly spot stingrays, sea turtles and even schools of squid in the back reef, as well as puffers and trumpetfish among the soft corals. The first reef slope descends to a wide sand channel at a depth of around 100 feet (30.5 meters) that runs parallel to shore. Garden eels and sand tilefish are common here. The second reef lies on the seaward side of the channel, cresting at a depth of about 90 feet (27.5 meters). The second reef is not visible from the base of the first slope, and thus requires a compass and navigation skills to reach.

Jeannie's Glory

Access about 14 mins from Kralendijk
about 32 mins from Kralendijk

Level Open Water

Location
Cargill Salt Works, Bonaire
GPS: 12°05'11.1"N, 68°16'56.5"W

Getting there

Drive south from Kralendijk on Kaya International, which becomes EEG Boulevard as it passes the airport. After Bachelor's Beach, the road bends slightly away from the coastline for about 0.75 miles (1.2 kilometers) before returning to the shore just before The Lake dive site. All the sites between The Lake and Salt Pier are marked with yellow rocks. Once past Alice in Wonderland, Aquarius and Larry's Lair, there is a yellow rock marking Jeannie's Glory on the side of the road. Pull off on the right-hand side and park on the shoulder. Jeannie's Glory is located about 0.13 miles (0.2 kilometers) north of Salt Pier and 4 miles (6.4 kilometers) from the airport—a drive of about 8 minutes by car.

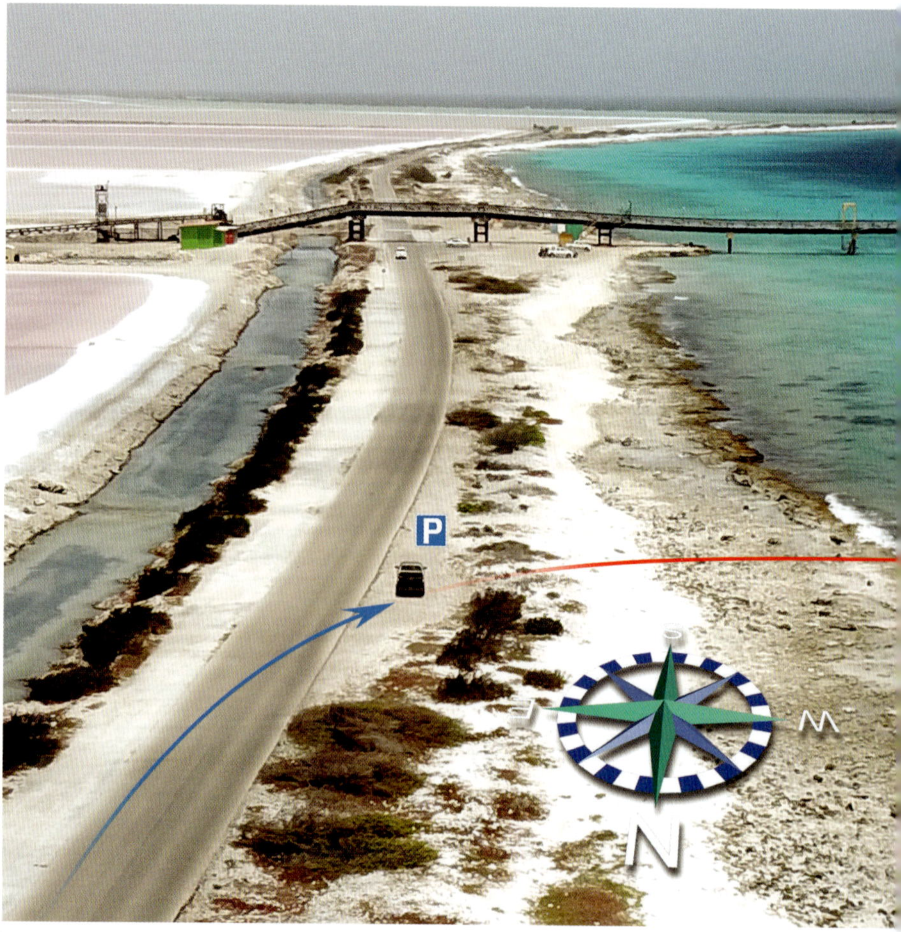

Access

Divers must pick a path through the vegetation, over the sandy area and through the large boulders and rubble to the shoreline. The last step is to pass over the rutted reef ledge and enter the water. This can be challenging, so divers might want to reconsider diving this site during times of high wave action. The yellow mooring buoy is located adjacent to the reef and to the northwest, slightly north of the big red ship mooring.

Description

Jeannie's Glory is a popular double reef dive along the southern coast. The reef at Jeannie's Glory starts nearly 400 feet (120 meters) from shore. The shallow, sand-bottomed plateau offers snorkelers and divers a forest of soft corals to explore, including the opportunity to spot a few rays sheltering in the sand. The sand channel between the two reefs bottoms out at just over 100 feet (30.5 meters), which makes it the deepest sand channel on this stretch of the coast. The reefs on either side of the sand channel are known to support a variety of marine life, including snapper, parrotfish, surgeonfish, and eels. Divers regularly spot barracuda in the water column above the second reef.

DID YOU KNOW?

Near the Jeannie's Glory dive site, between the road and the shore, sits an unmarked grave. The grave holds the skeletal remains of an individual uncovered during excavation in the salt works. The remains are likely to be either a slave who worked in the salt ponds, or perhaps an early settler from the Spanish colonization of the island.

Salt Pier

Difficulty ●●○
Current ●○○
Depth ●●○
Reef ★☆☆
Fauna ★★★

Access about 45 mins from Kralendijk
about 33 mins from Kralendijk

Level Open Water

Location
Cargill Salt Works, Bonaire
GPS: 12°05'00.9"N, 68°16'54.2"W

Getting there

Drive south from Kralendijk on Kaya International, which becomes EEG Boulevard as it passes the airport. After Bachelor's Beach, the road bends slightly away from the coastline for about 0.75 miles (1.2 kilometers) before returning to the shore just before The Lake dive site. Continue all the way down the coast road to the Salt Pier and pull into the parking lot immediately to the north of the pier. Salt Pier is 4.1 miles (6.6 kilometers) from the airport—a drive of about 8 minutes by car.

Access

Salt Pier is a working jetty where ships load and transport salt from the Cargill Salt Works. If there is a ship scheduled to arrive at the pier or if a ship is currently at the pier, diving is not permitted at this site. A representative of the Cargill Salt Works will inform visitors that the site is temporarily closed but when in doubt, ask at the yellow guard shack located on the premises. Most divers gear up in the parking lot and enter the water next to the car park. There is a small step down at the waterline. The seabed can be a little uneven in places, but the access is relatively easy. Divers swim out to the structure on the surface or underwater, using their compass or simply staying relatively close to the central structure as they head west to ensure they hit the seaward platforms that run parallel to shore. It usually takes about five minutes to reach these platforms from shore.

Description

Salt Pier is an iconic Bonaire shore dive. Although the reef is less spectacular than at other sites, marine life has colonized the pillars that support the pier as well as the surrounding waters, and the pillars provide great photo opportunities in the morning and afternoon light. Salt Pier is a must-do dive while in Bonaire. The white sand bottom heading out to the reef is covered in a mix of hard corals and gorgonians and teems with juvenile reef fishes. The reef slope starts at a depth of 32 feet (10 meters) and is covered in low-density hard corals, sponges, and gorgonians. The slope sits just beyond the pier, descending to a depth of 100 feet (30.5 meters). This site is known for its cryptic species, including seahorses, frogfish, octopuses, and moray eels.

While the reef may not be the best of what Bonaire has to offer, the structure of the pier easily makes up for it—the pillars are encrusted with soft corals and sponges, as well as the nests of territorial damselfish. Barracuda and sea turtles are common at this site, as well as schools

DID YOU KNOW?

Bonaire was first recognized for its potential for salt production as far back as the 1600s. It became a major center for salt production in the early 1800s, when under Dutch control. As production of this essential resource increased, the Dutch placed colored pylons along the southern coast of the island next to specific salt production areas to better manage production and distribution—red, blue, orange, and white to match the colors of the Dutch flag and the royal house. These pylons (which are still present today, including the blue one at the Salt Pier site) along with a system of colored flags were used to signal boat captains where to put ashore to pick up their loads of salt. Salt production tapered off with the abolition of slavery in the late 1800s but has since picked up under the management of Cargill, an international salt company that leases the land from the Bonaire government.

FEATURED OPERATOR 

VIP Diving began with a vision to provide a 'VIP diving experience' in Bonaire—combining top-notch equipment, personal attention to detail and service and prime dive spots. When it comes to prime dive spots, Salt Pier is often at the top of the list for both visitors and locals alike. The passionate dive professionals at VIP Diving know every site on Bonaire inside and out and love to provide in-depth knowledge that can help divers and snorkelers find all the hidden treasures that each location has to offer. Their goal is simple - to give you the best experience on Bonaire.

Tel: +599-701-7701
Email: info@vipdiving.com
Visit: **Vipdiving.com**

The pillars at Salt Pier make for an excellent backdrop for underwater photography.

NickPolanszky Photo/Shutterstock ©

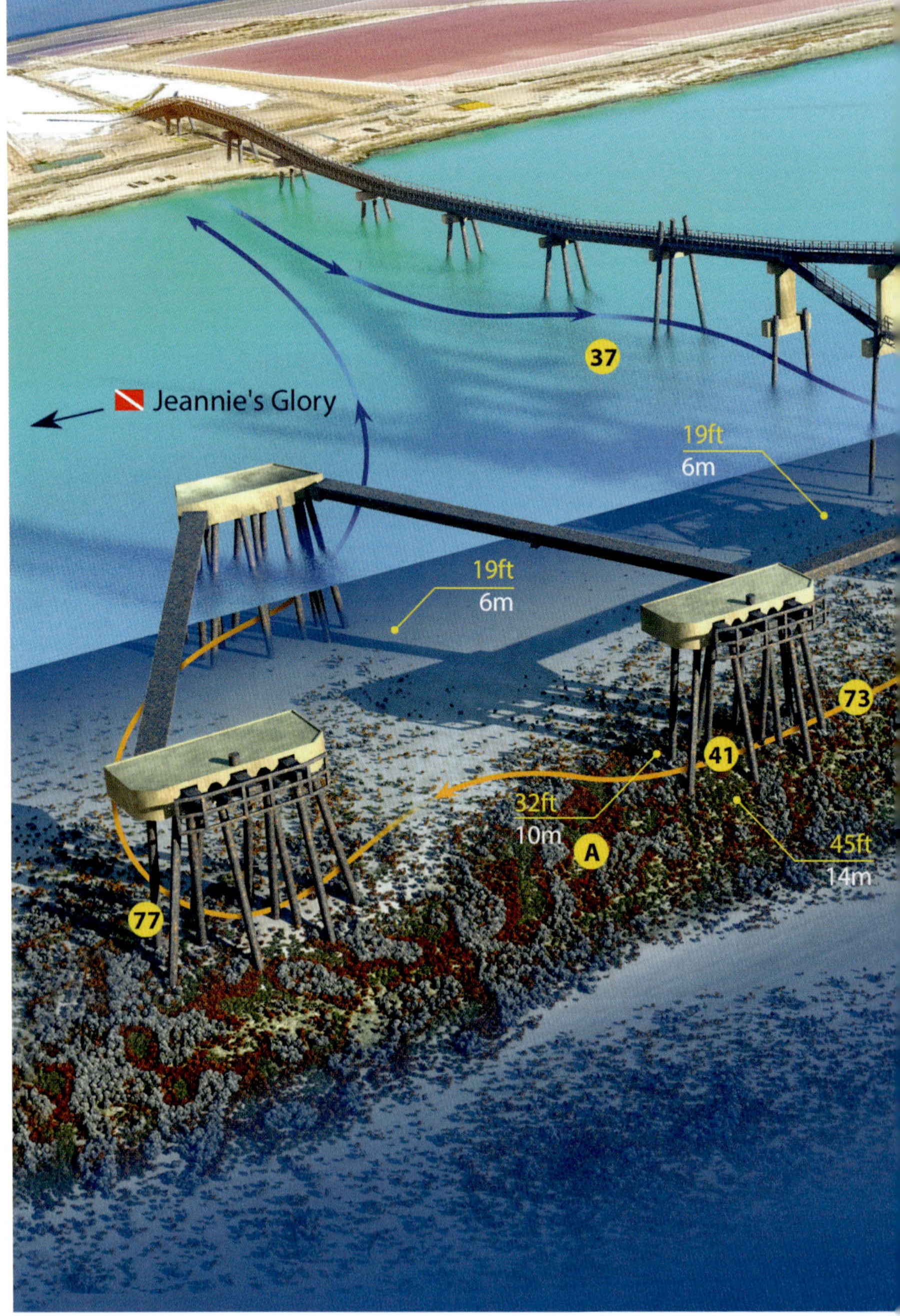

of grunts and snapper, including larger species such as cubera snapper, which can be found weaving through the upper sections of the pillars.

Salt Pier is very popular with divers, so plan on getting there outside of the morning and mid-afternoon rushes. Fortunately, the site is big enough that diving it even during the busy times can still feel like exploring it alone.

Route

Exploring the entire Salt Pier site in a single dive might be a challenge. Most divers begin by heading out along the pier before turning south or north to

weave through the pillars on each of the platforms that run parallel to shore. There are seven platforms in total—one central platform and three separate platforms north and south of the central section.

Divers should watch for tarpon resting at the bottom of the reef slope seaward of the pier and for bar jacks testing their luck on the schools of baitfish that hide among the pillars. Once at the final set of pillars, divers generally head back toward shore, cruising through the back reef where parrotfish are common and redlip blennies cling to the central pillars in the shallower water.

50

BONAIRE

Salt City

Difficulty ●●○
Current ●●○
Depth ●●●
Reef ★★☆
Fauna ★★☆

Access about 15 mins from Kralendijk
about 35 mins from Kralendijk

Level Open Water

Location
Cargill Salt Works, Bonaire
GPS: 12°04′46.9″N, 68°16′50.4″W

Getting there

Drive south from Kralendijk on Kaya International, which becomes EEG Boulevard as it passes the airport. After Bachelor's Beach, the road bends slightly away from the coastline for about 0.75 miles (1.2 kilometers) before returning to the shore just before The Lake dive site. Continue down the coast past Salt Pier and pull over into the sandy parking lot where yellow rocks mark the site on the side of the road. Salt City is just over 0.3 miles (0.45 kilometers) south of Salt Pier and 4.3 miles (6.9 kilometers) from the airport—a drive of about 9 minutes by car.

Access

Large boulders line the shore at Salt City, and the reef ledge at the waterline has numerous sharp rocks, so divers must take care as they enter the water, especially when there is wave action. The step down into the water at the shoreline is also quite steep—about 3 feet (1 meter)—so divers should ensure they have air in their BCDs and that their face masks are on. There is fire coral in the shallows close to shore as well. The yellow mooring buoy is almost directly off shore from the parking lot, and south of the big red ship mooring.

Description

Salt City is one of Bonaire's double reef dive sites, but the distance between the two reefs is much smaller here than to the north of Salt Pier. The site begins in the back reef as patches of hard and soft coral on a largely sandy seabed. The shallow plateau has a depth of 20 feet (6 meters), and supports some stands of staghorn coral. Observant divers may also spot razorfish darting into the sand as well.

As the reef gradually gets deeper, the soft corals increase in abundance until the first reef starts

A stingray cruises through the sandy back reef.

Richard Whitcombe/Shutterstock ©

to slope into deeper water at a depth of 38 feet (11.5 meters). The southern end of this site has a more gradual initial slope than the northern end. The first reef slope ends at a depth of 75 feet (23 meters), disappearing into the flat sand channel that runs parallel to shore. The channel ranges in width from 72 to 92 feet (22 to 28 meters), becoming narrower the farther north it goes.

The second reef crests at a depth of around 65 feet (20 meters) before descending to a depth of over 120 feet (36.5 meters). The slope of this second reef is gentler than that of the first, and consists of plate-form corals and sponges, including large elephant ear sponges. Divers can often find peacock flounders, garden eels, yellow goatfish, stingrays, and schools of palometas in the sand channel between the two reefs. On the reef slopes, divers may see porcupinefish, snapper, parrotfish, and even the occasional sea turtle cruising by along the reef.

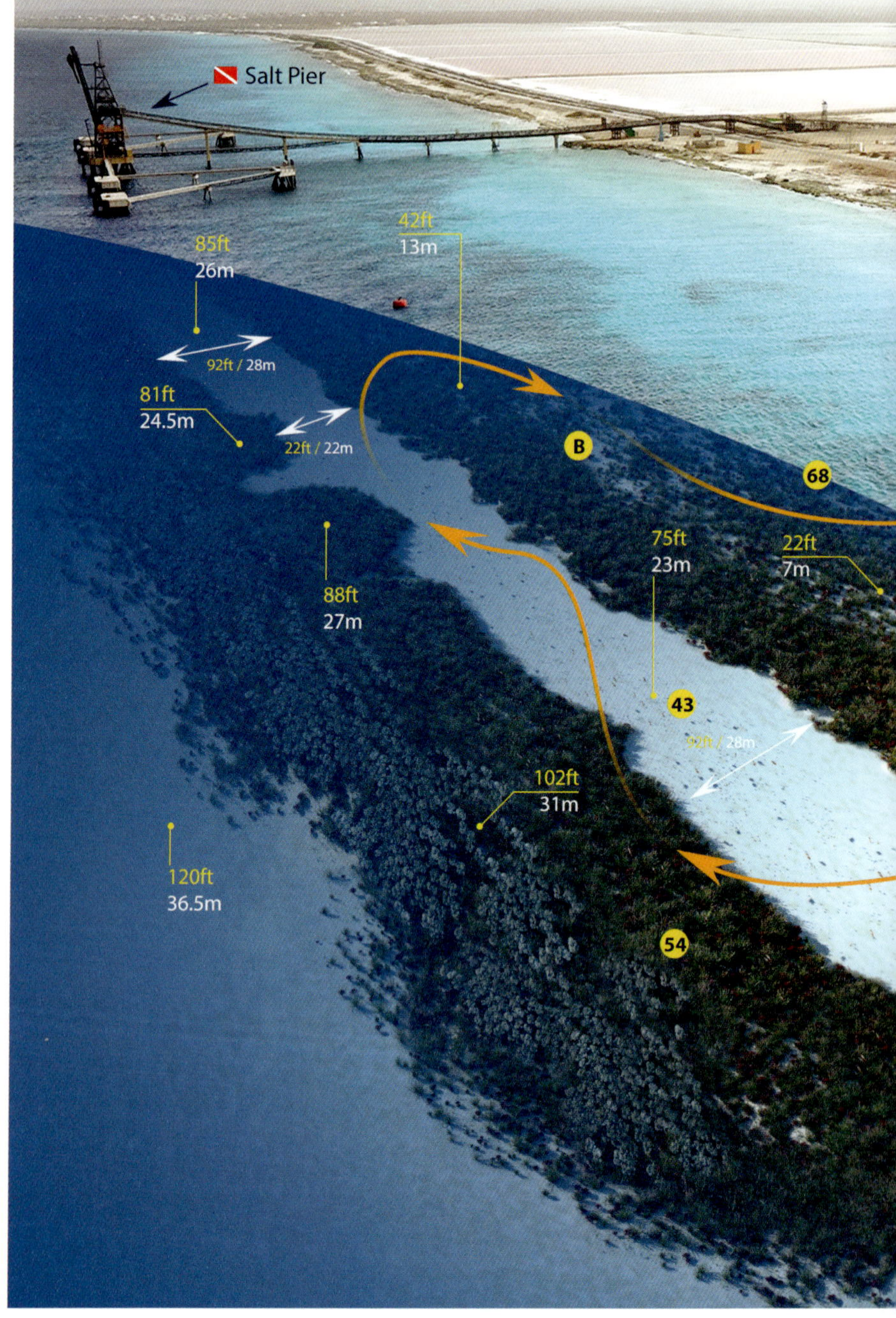

Route

Most divers swim out to the buoy and descend the first reef slope, passing across the sand to explore the second reef, which has better coral cover. The second reef becomes deeper to the north, so divers typically cross back to the first reef as they head toward the Salt Pier. Gradually ascending along the first reef slope, divers might see (and will probably hear) the chains of the large red mooring buoy that marks the northern edge of this site. The buoy is located in a large area of sand and rubble at a depth of 40 feet (12 meters). It is anchored via massive chains attached to concrete blocks.

Invisibles
Site buoy
N
E
W
S
13
38ft
11.5m
38ft
11.5m
32
44
80ft
24m
E

51 BONAIRE

Invisibles

Difficulty ●●○
Current ●●○
Depth ●●○
Reef ★★★
Fauna ★★☆

Access about 15 mins from Kralendijk
about 37 mins from Kralendijk

Level Open Water

Location
Cargill Salt Works, Bonaire
GPS: 12°04'39.1"N, 68°16'47.9"W

Getting there

Drive south from Kralendijk on Kaya International, which becomes EEG Boulevard as it passes the airport. After Bachelor's Beach, the road bends slightly away from the coastline for about 0.75 miles (1.2 kilometers) before returning to the shore just before The Lake dive site. Continue down the coast past the Salt Pier site and pull over into the gravel parking lot next to the yellow rocks that mark the site for Invisibles. The site is nearly 0.4 miles (0.6 kilometers) south of Salt Pier and 4.5 miles (7.2 kilometers) from the airport—a drive of about 8 minutes by car.

Access

Access at the Invisibles dive and snorkel site is relatively easy. Divers generally gear up in the parking lot and head down to the shoreline, avoiding the larger, unstable boulders located around the waterline. The rutted reef ledge has several holes that can result in a twisted ankle and cause a fall, so divers should take care as they enter the water. The yellow mooring buoy is slightly to the north of the parking lot.

Description

Invisibles is one of Bonaire's southernmost double reef dive sites. The reef slope starts nearly 450 feet (137 meters) out from shore, offering divers and snorkelers plenty to explore in the wide, relatively shallow back reef zone. While this area does not have high densities of gorgonians and hard coral heads, many cryptic species still call this sand and coral rubble habitat home, including razorfish and yellowhead jawfish.

Sea turtles are common at many sites in Bonaire.

NaturePicsFilms/Shutterstock ©

DID YOU KNOW? 

Reef Smart produces handheld waterproof guides for a number of sites in Bonaire, including Invisibles, which is one of the more complex sites on the island. These guides can be taken into the water and used to help navigate through the various coral islands that form the deeper second reef.

The slope of the first reef begins at a depth of 20 feet (6 meters) where the mooring buoy is anchored. Hard corals dominate the first slope, along with the occasional sponge and sea fan. At a depth of 85 feet (26 meters), the reef slope gives way to the sand channel that runs parallel to shore, separating the first and second reef slopes. The sand channel harbors garden eels and the occasional eagle ray.

The second reef at Invisibles is not a contiguous reef as it is to the north, but rather it fragments into multiple coral islands. These islands are covered in hard corals and reef sponges at a higher density than divers will see on the first reef. Navigation skills, a compass and one of Reef Smart Guides' waterproof maps will come in handy at this site (see the Did You Know? box above). These coral islands crest at an average depth of 65 feet (19 meters), making them more accessible than the double reefs farther to the north. The seaward side of the second reef drops off to over 120 feet (36.5 meters).

Route

Snorkelers can spend time exploring the rubble and soft corals of the back reef as well as the start of the reef slope that begins near the mooring buoy. Divers will want to make their way directly out to the second reef via the sand channel located immediately beyond the mooring buoy. Most divers follow the narrow channel out to the second reef and before heading south as they explore the coral islands that form the deeper section of the reef. Divers should take time to explore both the reef crest as well as the transition between reef and sand, given that these different habitats typically attract distinct organisms.

Cryptic species such as frogfish and scorpionfish can be found on the reef, as well as butterflyfish, parrotfish, grunts, and snapper. Stingrays, eagle rays, conch, and sand tilefish can be found in the sand, and jacks and black durgons are common in the water column above the second reef. Most divers continue south as they explore the second reef until the sand opens into a wide secondary channel that stretches nearly 165 feet (50 meters) across to the next coral island. At this point, divers typically turn east to head back across the main sand channel to return to the first reef

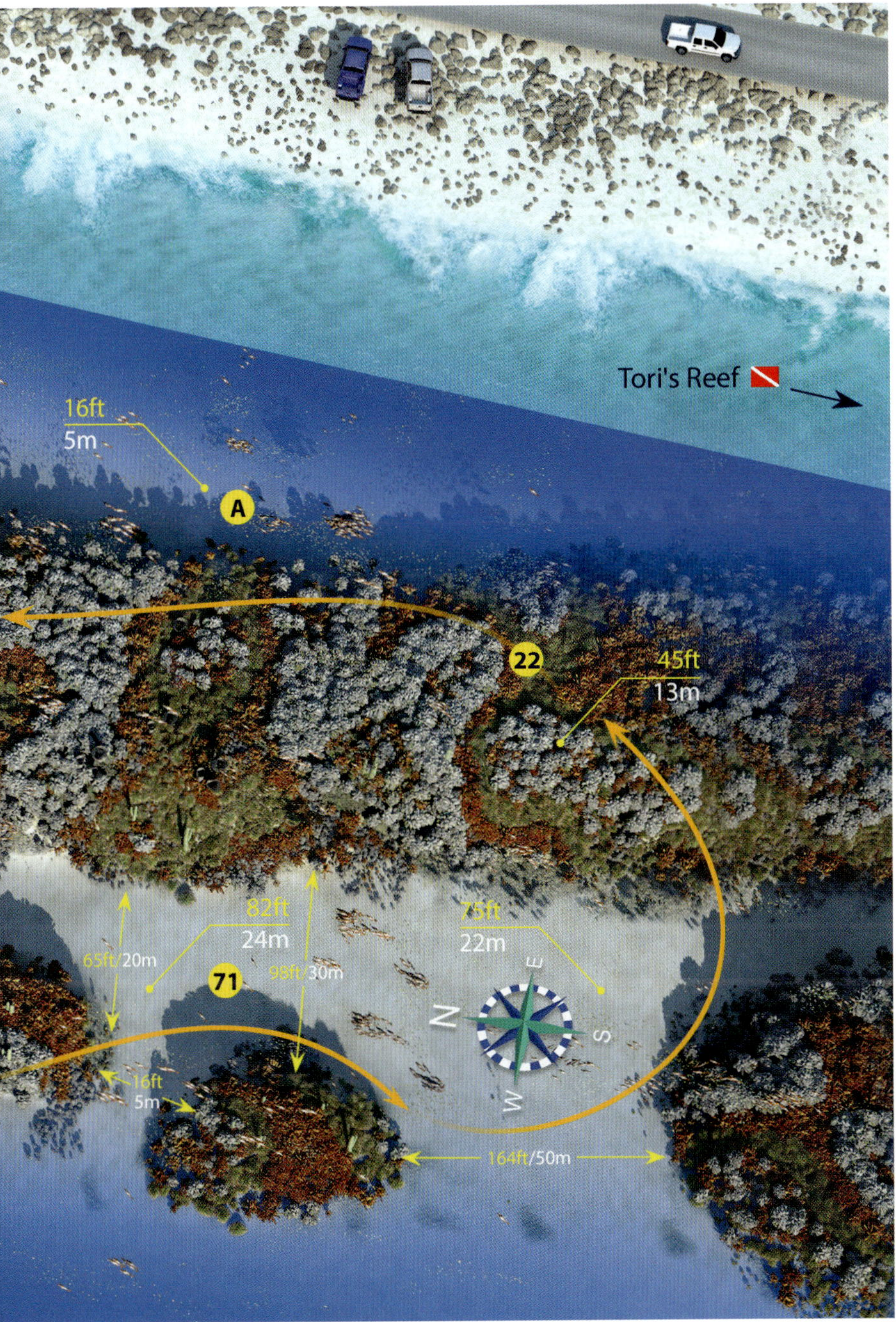

slope. From there divers can ascend to around 45 feet (13 meters) and head back north toward the mooring buoy. There are wrasses, small moray eels and blennies along this path, as well as sea turtles that are often seen cruising along the reef.

Tori's Reef

52

BONAIRE

Difficulty ●●○
Current ●●○
Depth ●●○
Reef ★★☆
Fauna ★★★

Access about 16 mins from Kralendijk
about 38 mins from Kralendijk

Level Open Water

Location
Cargill Salt Works, Bonaire
GPS: 12°04'13.9"N, 68°16'49.2"W

Getting there
Drive south from Kralendijk on Kaya International, which becomes EEG Boulevard as it passes the airport. After Bachelor's Beach, the road bends slightly away from the coastline for about 0.75 miles (1.2 kilometers) before returning to the shore just before The Lake dive site. About 0.8 miles (1.3 km) past the Salt Pier there is the first of two small red and white bridges that span drainage

channels from the salt ponds. Yellow rocks are located on either side of the second, southernmost bridge. Tori's Reef can be best accessed by parking on either side of the second bridge, where there is ample parking between the road and the shoreline. The site is 5 miles (8.1 kilometers) from the airport—a drive of about 9 minutes.

Access

Divers should gear up and walk from either parking lot to the outflow channel. The reef ledge at the waterline is deeply rutted and strewn with sharp boulders, so it is much easier to enter via the channel where there are several large, flat rocks to use as stepping stones. It is a relatively easy swim out to the buoy located to the north, between the two bridges.

Description

Tori's Reef is known as an attractive dive site that offers multiple reefs, although not in the same double-reef structure found at sites to the north. The site alternates between sand channels and reef lines, offering complex habitat that can be difficult to navigate.

The complexity of the habitat helps support a wide variety of species, including eagle rays and stingrays, parrotfish, snapper and barracuda. Stands of staghorn coral grow in the shallower waters of the plateau and this area of the reef is known to support a great abundance of juvenile reef fish, particularly angelfish, grunts, puffers and drums.

Pink Beach (Kabayé)

Difficulty
Current
Depth
Reef
Fauna

Access about 16 mins from Kralendijk
about 41 mins from Kralendijk

Level Open Water

Location
Cargill Salt Works, Bonaire
GPS: 12°03′51.0″N, 68°16′53.8″W

Getting there

Drive south from Kralendijk on Kaya International, which becomes EEG Boulevard as it passes the airport. After Bachelor's Beach, the road bends slightly away from the coastline for about 0.75 miles (1.2 kilometers) before returning to the shore just before The Lake dive site. Continue down the coast past Salt Pier and over the two red and white bridges that mark the drainage channels at the end of the Cargill Salt Works. The distance between the road and the ocean widens slightly near Pink Beach and there are multiple palm trees along the shore. Divers should pull over by the gate next to the yellow rocks that mark this site and the giant boulder that has a plaque attached to it. There is enough room for several cars to park along the road beside the gate. Pink Beach is 5.3 miles (8.5 kilometers) from the airport—a drive of about 9 minutes.

Access

Divers should gear up and walk around the gate, over the embankment and down onto the sand and gravel beach. The best place to enter the water is slightly north of the gate and in front of the two palm trees. There is a small sand channel in the water that makes access much easier. These palms are a good reference point for returning to shore. It is a relatively easy swim out to the buoy, which is located slightly to the south.

Description

Pink Beach gets its name from the pink hue of the sand on the nearby beach; the color is a result of the small, shelled organisms called foraminifera. Pink Beach does not have the same double reef system as the dive sites to the north, but it does offer a wide variety of reef fish, including many cleaning stations. Snorkelers and divers may spot rays in the sandy plateau, along with goatfish, small eels and angelfish.

SCIENTIFIC INSIGHT

Foraminifera are small organisms that build a shell, or test, which is the scientific name for an internal shell. They are the most abundant shelled organism in many marine habitats and they are found everywhere that saltwater exists, from the intertidal down to the deepest depths of the ocean. They are important components of the food chain and are proving to be an early warning system for the impact of ocean acidification. The increasing acidity in marine environments is negatively affecting the ability of many foraminifera to build their carbonate shells, a process that also impacts corals. The loss of this important component of the base of the marine ecological web could have far-reaching impacts on the health of the ocean ecosystem.

Tori's Reef

Entrance

54

BONAIRE

White Slave

Difficulty ●●○
Current ●●○
Depth ●●○
Reef ★☆☆
Fauna ★★☆

Access about 17 mins from Kralendijk
about 44 mins from Kralendijk

Level Open Water

Location
Cargill Salt Works, Bonaire
GPS: 12°03'27.9"N, 68°16'50.7"W

Getting there

Drive south from Kralendijk on Kaya International, which becomes EEG Boulevard as it passes the airport. After Bachelor's Beach, the road bends slightly away from the coastline for about 0.75 miles (1.2 kilometers), before returning to the shore just before The Lake dive site. Continue down the coast past Salt Pier and over the two red and white bridges that mark the drainage channels at the end of the Cargill Salt Works. After Pink Beach, and just before the road starts to bend to the southeast, the road passes several buildings on the right-hand side, followed by multiple white huts. Divers should pull off the road into the parking area adjacent to the huts. White Slave is 5.8 miles (9.4 kilometers) from the airport—a drive of about 11 minutes.

Access

Divers can gear up and walk to the water, which is only steps away from the parking lot over a small rubble beach. The best place to enter the water is in the middle of the huts. The reef is shallow in places and has pockets of elkhorn and fire coral that divers need to avoid on their swim out from the beach.

Description

White Slave gets its name from the historic slave huts that sit between the coastal road and the beach, serving as a reminder of Bonaire's past. The reef at this site starts more than 650 feet (200 meters) from shore, requiring a long swim out before starting the dive. The shallow sand-bottomed plateau that sits between the shore and the reef gradually increases in the density of soft corals the farther out toward the reef it gets. Divers have seen sea turtles and rays on this plateau, as well as schools of surgeonfish and parrotfish. Soft corals are particularly dense at the top of the reef, but also extend down the seaward slope. Soft corals love the moderate to strong currents that exist here, which comes from the reef's position on a slight headland. The reef slope itself consists of a low density of hard and soft corals and sponges, which extends to a depth of more than 120 feet (36.5 meters).

ECO TIP

Bonaire is known for its pink flamingos—they are the island's signature bird. Flamingos enjoy protected status on Bonaire, as the island is one of the few flamingo breeding grounds in the southern Caribbean, not to mention one of just 30 regular breeding grounds in the world. The island's flamingos are often seen standing in the shallow, salty waters of the saliñas that dot Bonaire's coastal areas. They feed on brine shrimp, deriving their pink color from the carotenoids they ingest via the shrimp, who in turn live off the halophilic (salt-loving) bacteria that thrive in the salty waters of the salt ponds and saliñas. Flamingos startle easily, which can endanger their chicks. It is important to maintain a safe distance and respect the "No Entry" signs around the island, including along the southern stretch of the coastal road below the Salt Pier.

Wanda

Difficulty ● ● ○
Current ● ● ○
Depth ● ● ○
Reef ★★☆
Fauna ★★☆

Access about 18 mins from Kralendijk

Level Open Water

Location
Cargill Salt Works, Bonaire

GPS: 12°03'12.2"N, 68°16'25.2"W

Getting there

Drive south from Kralendijk on Kaya International, which becomes EEG Boulevard as it passes the airport. After Bachelor's Beach, the road bends slightly away from the coastline for about 0.75 miles (1.2 kilometers) before returning to the shore just before The Lake dive site. Continue down the coast past Salt Pier and Pink Beach. Just after White Slave, the road takes a bend to the left and heads southeast. Divers should continue down this road for another 0.4 miles (0.6 kilometers) where they will see a signpost indicating that the road will narrow, followed by a post without a sign. About 50 feet (15 meters) after this post, there will be a small lay-by on the right, next to a saliña. Pull over into the lay-by between the bushes. There is no yellow rock marking this site. Wanda is 6.4 miles (10.3 kilometers) from the airport—a drive of about 12 minutes.

Access

Divers should gear up and walk between the bushes into the shallow saliña and across to the other side—a distance of about 55 feet (17 meters). The water depth increases slightly in

Margate Bay

P

the middle of the saliña, but should not be much more than knee high. The access at the waterline is not too challenging, although there is a slight step down into the water, and slightly higher surf here than at other sites, which can unbalance a diver. Divers should use their dive buddy for support. A few stands of fire coral exist close to shore, but there is plenty of room for divers to pass through to the back reef. There is no yellow mooring buoy at this site.

Description

Wanda is one of a half-dozen unmarked dive sites along the southern coast of Bonaire. It is not on the official Marine Park list of sites, but many divers regularly visit these unmarked spots. The reef here is similar to adjacent sites of White Slave to the north and Margate Bay to the south, with slightly stronger currents and a higher abundance of soft corals. The reef starts 330 feet (100 meters) from the shoreline and is known to offer a medium density hard coral cover with plenty of sponges and soft corals. It also has a wide variety of fish life, including moray eels, black durgons, black margates and rays.

ECO TIP

The shore-diving-friendly nature of Bonaire means that divers can essentially strap on a tank and step into the water pretty much anywhere along the coast and have a good chance of exploring fantastic coral reefs. However, by limiting diving to established locations, visitors can help minimize the potentially negative impacts on the remaining reef habitat. We feature a few unmarked sites in this guidebook as they are well-established and well-visited, even though they are not included in the official list of dive sites maintained by the Bonaire National Marine Park. But we strongly encourage divers to stick to established sites. Not only will this improve diver safety, but it will help protect the coral reefs of Bonaire for future generations.

Margate Bay

Difficulty ●●○
Current ●●○
Depth ●●●
Reef ★★★
Fauna ★★☆

Access about 18 mins from Kralendijk
about 48 mins from Kralendijk

Level Open Water

Location
Cargill Salt Works, Bonaire
GPS: 12°03′06.6″N, 68°16′18.2″W

Getting there

Drive south from Kralendijk on Kaya International, which becomes EEG Boulevard as it passes the airport. After Bachelor's Beach, the road bends slightly away from the coastline for about 0.75 miles (1.2 kilometers) before returning to the shore just before The Lake dive site. Continue down the coast past Salt Pier and Pink Beach. Just after White Slave, the road takes a bend to the left and heads southeast. Continue down this road for just over half a mile. After the point where the road narrows, pull over into the obvious lay-by parking lot on the right-hand side between the two yellow rocks that mark the site. There should be enough space for several cars to park here next to the large boulders. Margate Bay is about 6.6 miles (10.6 kilometers) from the airport—a drive of about 12 minutes.

Access

Divers should gear up and walk toward the saliña between the gap in the mangroves. The saliña is only 50 feet (15 meters) across. On the far side of the saliña is a rubble-strewn reef ledge, which provides relatively easy access to the water, albeit with a small step down.

Description

Margate Bay gets its name from the profusion of black margates that are found at this site. The back reef stretches just over 300 feet (91.5 meters) from the shore, sloping gently over a mostly sand and rubble bottom. Fire corals located near the shore give way to stands of staghorn coral, followed by a forest of gorgonians, including sea fans and the occasional coral head and sponge.

At a depth of around 26 feet (8 meters) the plateau starts to transition into the reef and the slope begins to steepen. From here the reef descends at a roughly 45-degree slope before bottoming out at maximum depth of 100 feet (30 meters) and a sandy seafloor below. Although the reef starts at a depth that may be hard for snorkelers to observe smaller creatures, the clarity of the Bonaire water means they will be able to take in plenty of the corals and gorgonians in the first section of this site, along with larger reef fish, such as parrotfish, angelfish, snapper and margates. Those snorkelers able to dive down 20 feet will have no problem seeing plenty of marine life along the upper reef slope area.

Black margates swim over the reef.

The reef at this site does not have quite as many channels as can be found at other sites. There is a single sand channel roughly 16 feet (5 meters) wide to the northwest side of the site. Farther along to the southeast, a second channel extends up from below, and splits to form a "Y" at a depth of around 64 feet (19.5 meters). These channels can help orient divers as they explore the site.

Much like other sites along this stretch of coast, Margate Bay offers plenty to see in terms of corals, sponges, and reef fish, thanks in large part to the complex bottom and the mixing currents. Sea fans and soft corals thrive shoreward of the drop-off zone, while hard corals cover the reef wall, interspersed with sponges and sea whips. Trumpetfish and slender filefish are abundant among the soft corals, along with snapper and mixed schools of grunts. The complex habitat also supports schools of chromis, while patrolling barracuda keep watch in the waters above the reef and small grouper wait below. Eagle rays are also known to frequent this site.

John A. Anderson/Shutterstock ©

Route

Divers should enter the water and swim out toward the mooring buoy, keeping the buoy on their left. Fire corals grow close to shore in the shallow water here, so divers and snorkelers should be cautious as they swim out. Once past the fire coral, divers will enter a forest of gorgonians, sponges, and coral heads. Divers should look for juvenile reef fish among the waving soft corals as this type of habitat acts as a nursery for many species.

Divers will encounter the reef line at around 330 feet (100 meters) from shore. Once there, they should descend along the reef taking time to observe both the corals on the seafloor as well as the marine life in the open ocean beyond the reef. Divers are likely to see black durgons schooling over the reef, along with blue and brown chromis. Once descended to their target depth, divers should turn left and make their way toward the southeast. Moray eels and lobsters are commonly found under the ledges found along the sand channels of the reef.

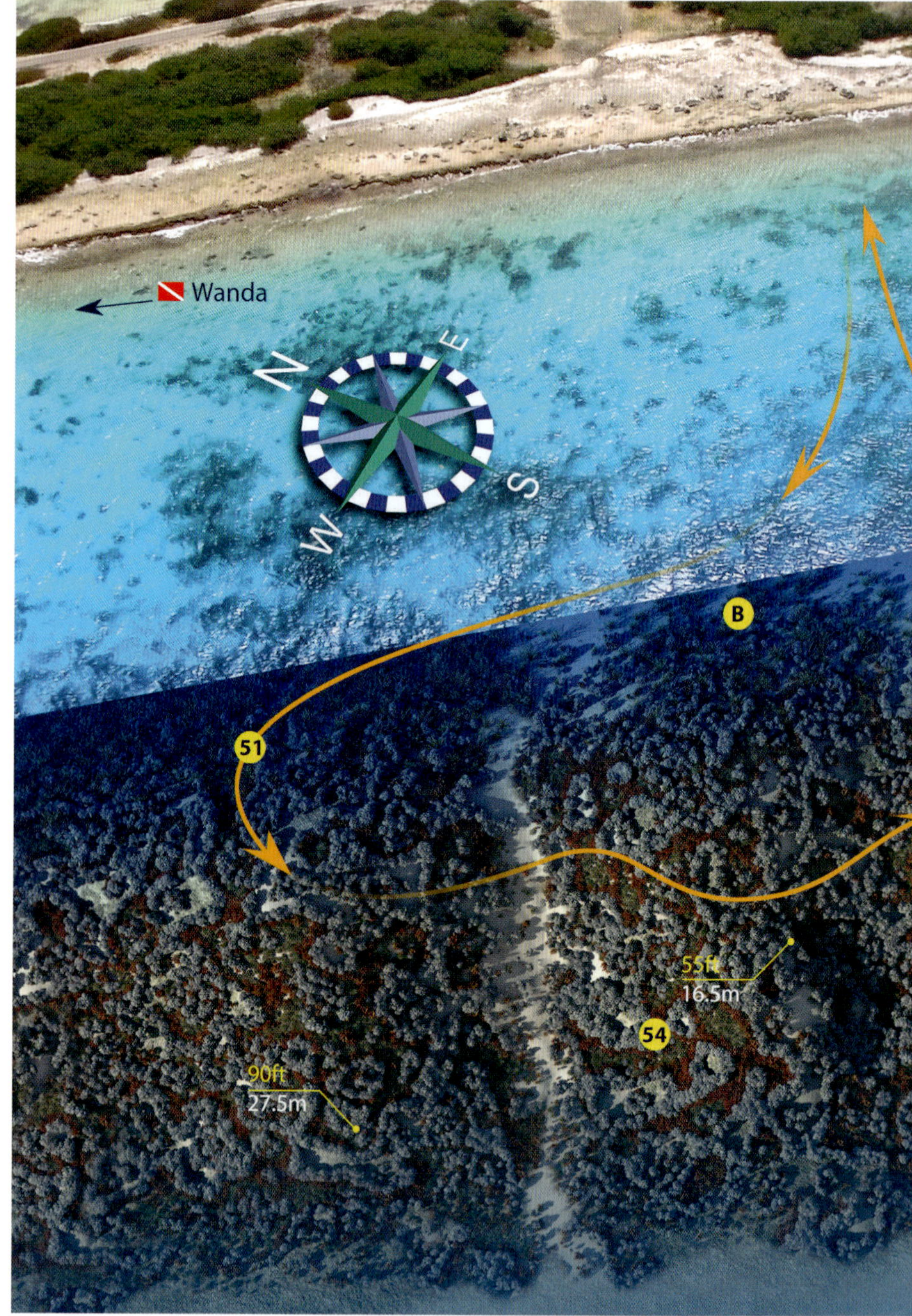

Once divers have passed over the Y-shaped sand channel, they should make their way back up the reef slope toward the shore. Divers can spend what time remains of their dive exploring the forest of soft corals, being sure to make a note of the field of staghorn coral that they will pass through. Divers should be careful of the fire corals as they approach the shore and watch their footing as they exit the water.

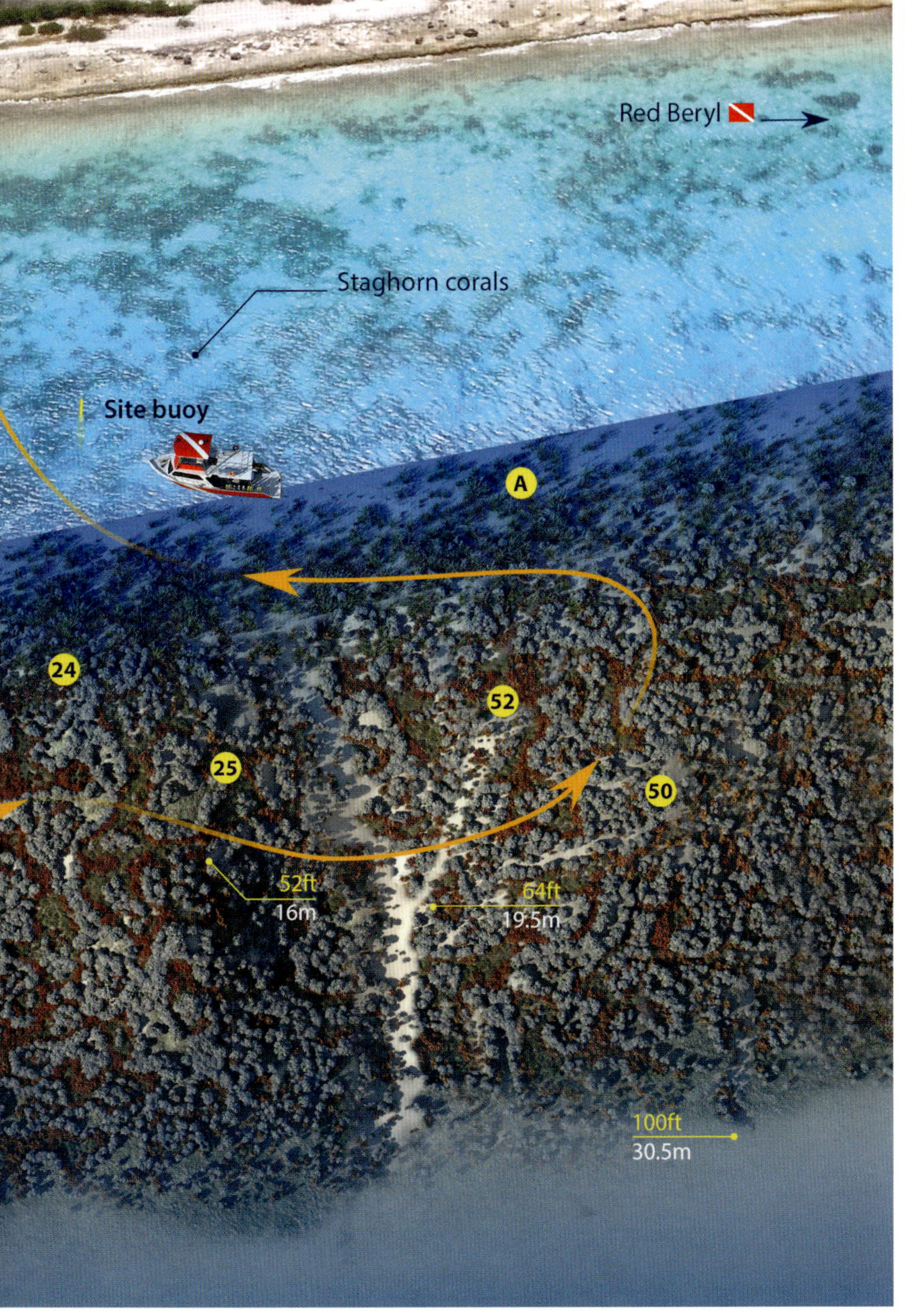
Red Beryl
Staghorn corals
Site buoy
A
24
52
25
50
52ft
16m
64ft
19.5m
100ft
30.5m

Red Beryl

Difficulty ● ● ○
Current ● ● ○
Depth ● ● ○
Reef ★★☆
Fauna ★★☆

Access about 19 mins from Kralendijk

Level Open Water

Location

Cargill Salt Works, Bonaire
GPS: 12°02′49.8″N, 68°16′05.2″W

Getting there

Drive south from Kralendijk on Kaya International, which becomes EEG Boulevard as it passes the airport. After Bachelor's Beach, the road bends slightly away from the coastline for about 0.75 miles (1.2 kilometers), before returning to the shore just before The Lake dive site. Continue down the coast past Salt Pier and Pink Beach. The road bends to the left and heads southeast just after the White Slave site. Continue down the road, past where it narrows and past Margate Bay. The road soon passes another small lay-by, followed by a second lay-by with two yellow rocks that mark the Red Beryl site. A sign is present at the end of the lay-by that indicates there is a sea turtle nesting beach here. There is enough room for several cars to park here. Red Beryl is about 6.6 miles (10.7 kilometers) from the airport—a drive of about 13 minutes.

Access

A small 15-foot (5-meter) path leads from the road toward the shore, passing between several large rocks. A deeply rutted reef ledge provides access to the water. There is no yellow mooring buoy at this site. Red Beryl and several other sites along this stretch of coast are popular with kiteboarders, so divers should try to stay close to the bottom as they head out to the reef and return to shore. This site is best accessed before 10:00am and after 4:00pm, when kiteboarders are less active in the area, particularly if snorkelers plan on exploring Red Beryl.

Description

The reef at Red Beryl begins relatively close to shore, at just 200 feet (60 meters) from the beach. This site is known for a seabed that alternates between reef, sand, and soft corals until the reef slope begins 330 feet (100 meters) from shore. Some of the best exploring can be done between the depths of 33 and 50 feet (10 and 15 meters), where divers will see a mix of hard and soft corals, along with a variety of marine life, including parrotfish and snapper, but also anemones, shrimp, crabs, and octopuses. The reef slope descends to a depth of 105 feet (32 meters), and another, much deeper reef begins at 160 feet (49 meters).

57 BONAIRE

Atlantis

Difficulty ● ● ○
Current ● ○ ○
Depth ● ● ○
Reef ★★☆
Fauna ★★☆

Access about 20 mins from Kralendijk

Level Open Water

Location
Cargill Salt Works, Bonaire

GPS: 12°02'43.8"N, 68°16'01.1"W

Getting there
Drive south from Kralendijk on Kaya International, which becomes EEG Boulevard as it passes the airport. After Bachelor's Beach, the road bends slightly away from the coastline for about 0.75 miles (1.2 kilometers) before returning to the shore next to The Lake dive site. Continue down the coast past Salt Pier and Pink Beach. The road bends to the southeast just past the White Slave site, and the Atlantis dive site is located about 1.25 miles (2 kilometers) past this bend, slightly after the Red Beryl dive site and about 300 feet (91.5 meters) before the kiteboarding camp. The site is marked with a yellow rock on the right-hand side of the road and there is plenty of parking for vehicles. Atlantis is about 7.3 miles (11.7 kilometers) from the airport—a drive of about 13 minutes.

Access
Atlantis is among the easiest sites to access in Bonaire. Divers can make their way through the large boulders that line the parking area, and then walk up and over the slight bank that separates the parking area from the shoreline—a distance of about 100 feet (30 meters). There is a beautiful sandy beach

Atlantis Kite Beach

P

in this location that provides easy access to the water for divers. There is no mooring buoy at this site. This site is best accessed before 10:00am and after 4:00pm, when kiteboarders are less active in the area.

Description

Atlantis Beach is known for sightings of sea turtles and larger pelagic fish such as jacks and mackerel. It is typical of the southern dive sites with a relatively shallow sand-bottomed plateau that gives way to a forest of soft corals, before transitioning to a hard coral and sponge reef. There is plenty for snorkelers to enjoy in the shallows at this site, including schools of surgeonfish and tangs and the occasional eagle ray and stingray among patches of staghorn coral. Snorkelers should make sure they are out of the water before the kiteboarding begins at 10:00am or that they have a clearly visible surface marker buoy (SMB). The reef slope at Atlantis begins over 330 feet (100 meters) from the beach and offers divers an interesting mix of hard and soft corals, as well as large sponges, as it descends to a depth of over 100 feet (30 meters). This site is known for having a high abundance of rock beauties, as well as many filefish and triggerfish species, including black durgons, ocean triggerfish, and sargassum triggerfish in deeper waters.

SAFETY TIP

Surface marker buoys (SMBs) are not necessary on most dive sites on Bonaire since boat activity is low and divers rarely surface in the dark water where vessels are allowed to navigate. However, some of the most southerly dive sites in Bonaire pose a slightly different kind of risk, which might warrant the use of an SMB. Kiteboarding is extremely popular in this area of Bonaire, particularly at Atlantis Beach, also known as Kite Beach. And the activities often extend to Red Beryl to the north and Fish Hut to the south. If divers do not have an SMB with them, they should try to avoid surface swimming as much as possible. Getting as close to shore as possible before surfacing, and then surfacing safely by first lifting an arm out of the water can limit the chance of a collision with a fast-moving kiteboarder.

Fish Hut

Difficulty ●●○
Current ●●○
Depth ●●○
Reef ★★☆
Fauna ★★☆

Access about 20 mins from Kralendijk

Level Open Water

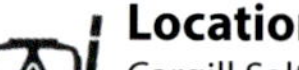

Location
Cargill Salt Works, Bonaire
GPS: 12°2'34.5"N, 68°15'57.4"W

Getting there

Drive south from Kralendijk on Kaya International, which becomes EEG Boulevard as it passes the airport. After Bachelor's Beach, the road bends slightly away from the coastline for about 0.75 miles (1.2 kilometers) before returning to the shore just before The Lake dive site. Continue down the coast past Salt Pier and White Slave, to where the road bends to the southeast. About 1.4 miles (2.3 kilometers) past this corner there will be a kiteboarding camp on the right-hand side of the road. The Fish Hut site is located about 500 feet (152 meters) south of the camp. Turn off the road at the first lay-by and onto a rutted track. There is a large wooden fishing hut visible down by the shore, and the track runs either side of a large bush, just inside the entrance, and then heads across a large, flat rubble area dotted with small bushes toward the hut. This is an unmarked site, so there are no yellow rocks here, nor is there a yellow mooring buoy at the site. There is plenty of parking near the fishing hut. Fish Hut is about 7.4 miles (11.9 kilometers) from the airport—a drive of about 14 minutes.

Access

Divers should walk up and over the slight bank that separates the parking area from the shoreline—a distance of about 100 feet (30 meters). There is a sand and rubble beach at this location, which provides easy access to the water for divers, but divers should watch for holes in the reef ledge as they enter the water. This site is best accessed before 10:00am and after 4:00pm, when kiteboarders are less active in the area.

Description

Fish Hut is another of the unmarked sites along Bonaire's southern coast. It is easily recognizable by the ramshackle building standing near the water. The hut was pieced together by local fishermen using whatever materials they could lay their hands on. Divers may see a few fishermen around the makeshift building—they are generally friendly toward both divers and kiteboarders.

The site is known for its wide plateau featuring swaths of soft and hard corals on a sandy bottom. The reef does not start until over 350 feet (110 meters) from shore. From there it descends to a depth of 115 feet (35 meters), although some of the best sights are above 80 feet (25 meters). The site is known for its large schools of brown and blue chromis. These small damselfish are the favorite prey of small grouper, such as graysbies and coneys, which are also abundant here. Divers frequently see sea turtles at this site, as well as large creole wrasses and yellowhead snapper.

58

BONAIRE

Vista Blue

Difficulty ●●○
Current ●●○
Depth ●●○
Reef ★★☆
Fauna ★★★

Access about 21 mins from Kralendijk
about 55 mins from Kralendijk

Level Open Water

Location
Oranje Pan, Bonaire
GPS: 12°02'20.5493"N, 68°15'51.5829"W

Getting there

Drive south from Kralendijk on Kaya International, which becomes EEG Boulevard as it passes the airport. After Bachelor's Beach, the road bends slightly away from the coastline for about 0.75 miles (1.2 kilometers) before returning to the shore just before The Lake dive site. Continue down the coast past Salt Pier and White Slave, to where the road bends to the southeast. About 1.4 miles (2.3 kilometers) past this corner there is a kiteboarding camp on the right-hand side of the road. Vista Blue is located another 0.4 miles (0.6 kilometers) farther south from this camp. Divers should pull off the road to the right-hand side where the yellow rocks mark the site. They can drive over the flat gravel area toward the shore—a distance of about 250 feet (76 meters). There is plenty of parking for vehicles. Vista Blue is about 7.7 miles (12.4 kilometers) from the airport—a drive of about 15 minutes.

Access

Divers should gear up at their cars and walk to the water's edge. A slight rock ledge is sometimes present at the waterline at this site, but currents and wave action can sometimes cover the ledge with sand and rubble. It is a long swim out to the mooring buoy, and visibility can be poor close to shore depending on the strength and direction of the wind and the surf.

Description

Vista Blue has a similar look and feel to many other sites along the southern coast. A mix of gorgonians and hard corals in the back reef transition into hard corals as the reef drops off to a depth of around 120 feet (36 meters). A few thin sand channels break up the reef slope as it descends to patchy reef and sand. What makes this site different from neighboring sites is the fact that the soft corals extend down the reef slope in high densities, down to a depth of around 50 feet (15 meters). Many of the soft corals are also more than 5 feet (1.5 meters) in height.

It is no coincidence that the best diving on this site is between the depths of 30 and 60 feet (9 and 18 meters). Below that depth, the hard corals become much less dense and are of lower quality. The upper section of the reef slope also boasts finger coral, which is less common on neighboring sites, and can act as nursery habitat for juvenile reef fish.

The quality of the reef and the abundance of large gorgonians contributes to the site's high level of biodiversity. Vista Blue offers divers the chance to see anemones, moray eels, parrotfish, wrasses, snapper, puffers, grunts, butterflyfish, basslets, and barracuda, to name just a few. Even cryptic species are present in high numbers, including slender filefish, arrow crabs, and trumpetfish. Schools of blue tangs, ocean surgeonfish, and doctorfish also frequent the back reef area.

Coralie Mathieu/Shutterstock ©

Trumpetfish like to hide among the soft corals on a reef.

Route

Divers should swim out to the mooring buoy before descending—the reef here is mostly turf and rubble with a scattering of soft corals and the occasional patch of staghorn coral. From there, they can make their way slowly toward the drop-off and head south while exploring the transition between reef and sand. Many species inhabit this dense mix of gorgonians and hard corals. After 10 minutes or so, or once divers reach a narrow crack in the reef slope, they should drop down the wall and start heading back north. There really is

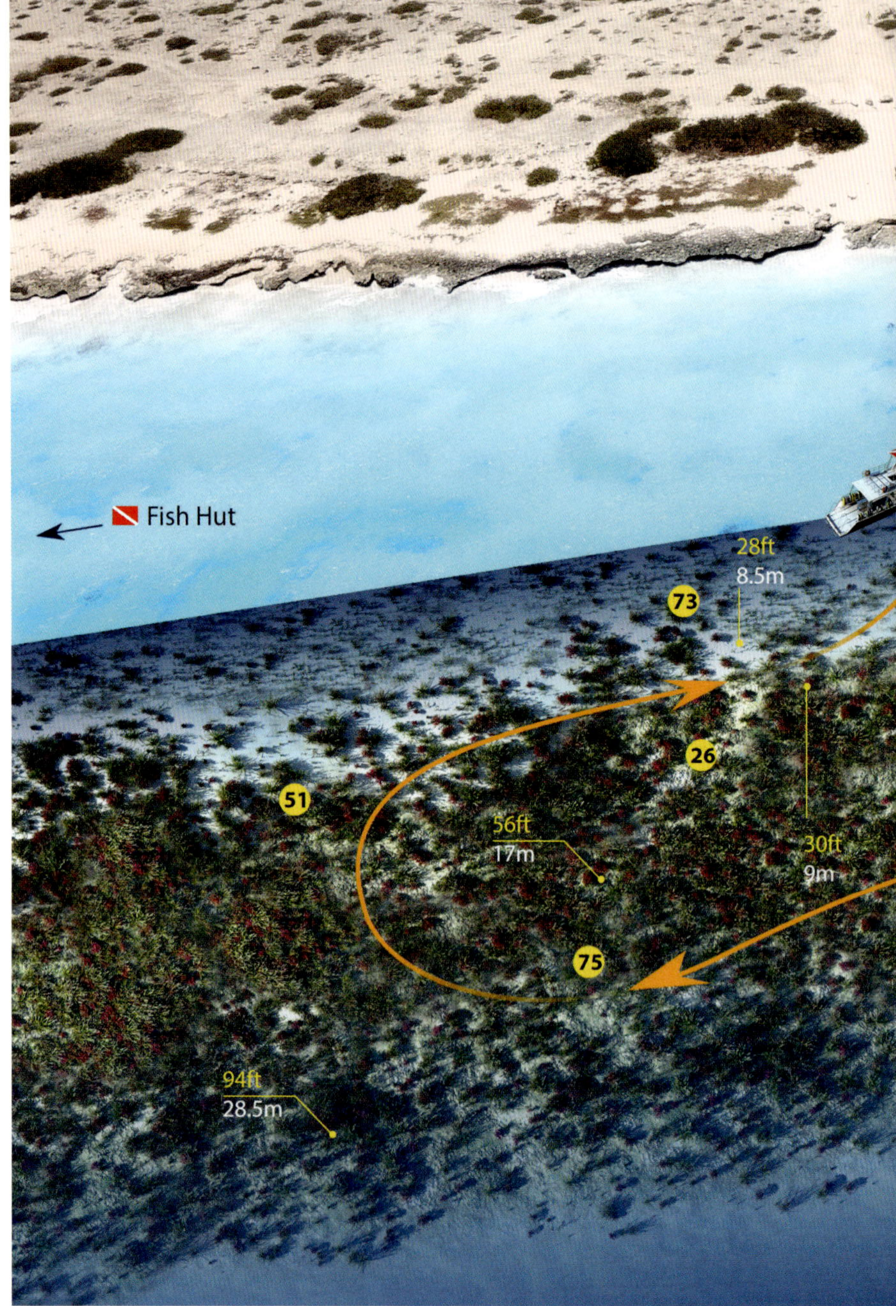

no need to drop too far down on the reef slope; bottom time is best spent above a depth of 75 feet (23 meters) to make the most of the dive.

Divers should continue north along the wall, keeping a look out for giant anemones and their associated cleaning shrimp. Moray eels can be seen snaking their way through the complex terrain, while chromis school above the reef and bar jacks patrol the water. When it is time to turn around, divers can head back toward the buoy along the same transition zone, just at a shallower depth. Once at the buoy they can turn toward shore and exit the water.

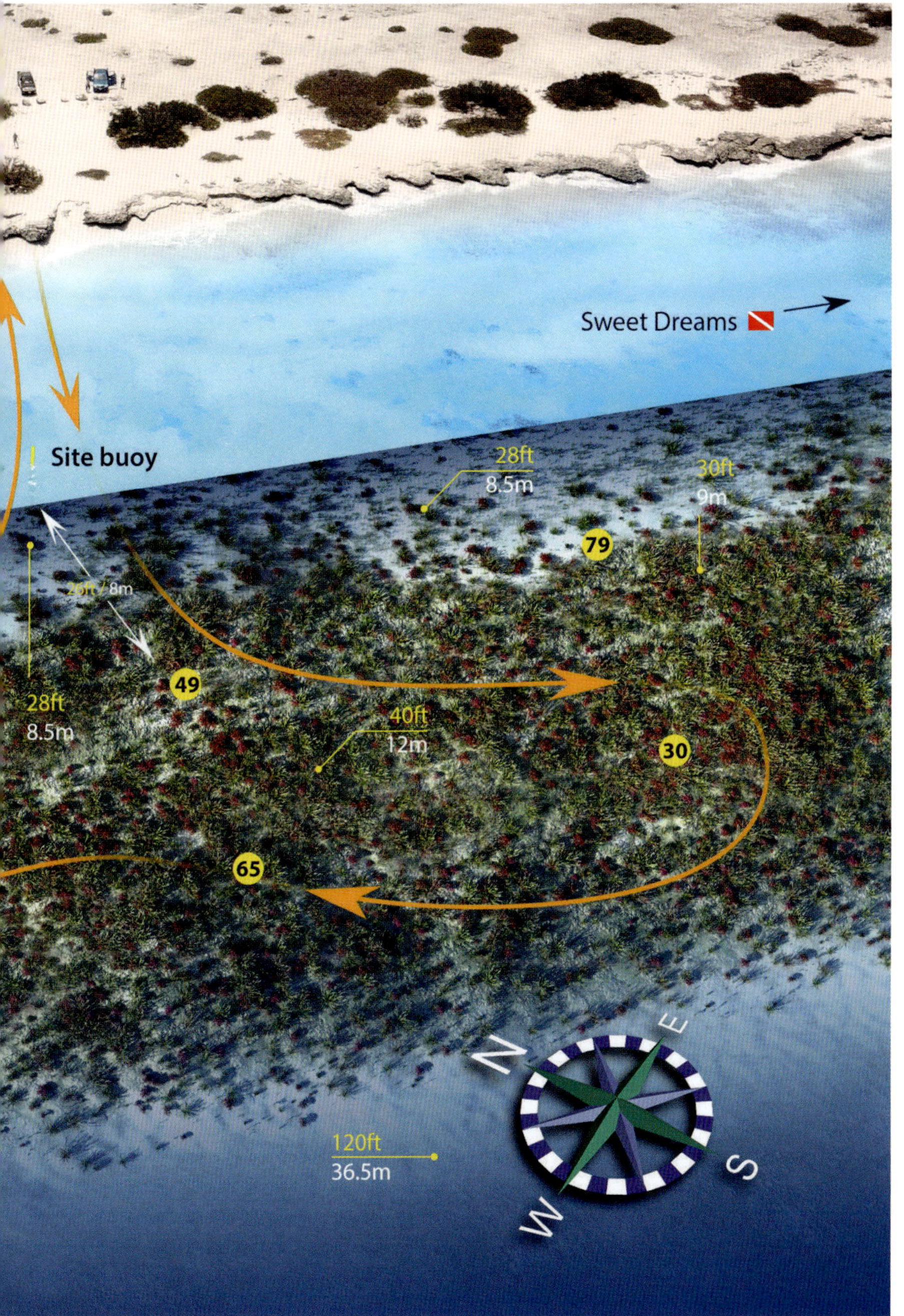
Sweet Dreams
Site buoy
28ft
8.5m
30ft
9m
79
26ft / 8m
49
28ft
8.5m
40ft
12m
30
65
120ft
36.5m
N
E
S
W

Sweet Dreams

Difficulty ●●○
Current ●●●
Depth ●●○
Reef ★★☆
Fauna ★★☆

Access about 22 mins from Kralendijk

Level Advanced Open Water

Location
Oranje Pan, Bonaire
GPS: 12°02'08.0"N, 68°15'44.1"W

Getting there

Drive south from Kralendijk on Kaya International, which becomes EEG Boulevard as it passes the airport. After Bachelor's Beach, the road bends slightly away from the coastline for about 0.75 miles (1.2 kilometers) before returning to the shore just before The Lake dive site. Continue down the coast past Salt Pier and White Slave, to where the road bends to the southeast. About 1.4 miles (2.3 kilometers) past this corner there is a kiteboarding camp on the right-hand side of the road. Sweet Dreams is located another 0.6 miles (1 kilometer) down the road from the camp. Divers should pull off the road to the right-hand side where yellow rocks mark the site next to a small sign. Drive over the flat gravel area toward the shore—a distance of just over 200 feet (61 meters). There is plenty of parking for vehicles down by the shore where some foliage exists and a line of rocks is positioned in the parking area. Sweet Dreams is 7.9 miles (12.7 kilometers) from the airport—a drive of about 15 minutes.

Access

Divers should gear up and walk through the foliage near the shore to the waterline. A yellow rock in the parking area has an arrow with the word "enter" clearly written on it, and there should be another rock on the beach indicating the best area to enter the water. The shoreline consists largely of reef ledge with some rocks that can be slippery in places, so divers should watch their step. Waves tend to break a little more on this stretch of beach than at adjacent sites, which can reduce visibility in the back reef and can make access challenging. Divers should time their entry and use their dive buddy for support if necessary. There is no mooring buoy at this site.

Description

Sweet Dreams is one of a series of adjacent dive sites that offers divers the opportunity to swim along a steeply sloped reef. It has a mix of hard corals and sponges, but soft corals dominate the area as they are most at home in the strong currents often found here. The plateau is known to be narrower here and the seas and the water can get choppy, especially when the winds come from the south.

Divers may see filefish, snapper, and grunts among the soft corals, as well as sea turtles, some of whom may use the beach as a nesting site during the breeding season (for more information, see the turtle ecology section on pages 288-291). For that reason, divers should not park on the beach to avoid damaging any nests that may be present. Divers may also see stingrays, barracuda, and pelagic predators such as rainbow runners and horse-eye jacks, among other species.

Soft Coral Garden

Difficulty ●●○
Current ●●●
Depth ●●○
Reef ★★☆
Fauna ★★☆

Access about 22 mins from Kralendijk

Level Advanced Open Water

Location
Oranje Pan, Bonaire
GPS: 12°02′01.5″N, 68°15′37.2″W

Getting there

Drive south from Kralendijk on Kaya International, which becomes EEG Boulevard as it passes the airport. After Bachelor's Beach, the road bends slightly away from the coastline for about 0.75 miles (1.2 kilometers) before returning to the shore just before The Lake dive site. Continue down the coast past Salt Pier and White Slave, to where the road bends to the southeast. About 1.4 miles (2.3 kilometers) past this corner there is a kiteboarding camp on the right-hand side of the road. Soft Coral Garden is located about another

0.8 miles (1.3 kilometer) farther down the road from the camp. The turn for Soft Coral Garden is on the right-hand side of the road, adjacent to a large bush and between two lay-bys—it can be quite easy to miss, so look for the large rock piles on the shore that mark this site. Divers should pull off the road and drive down the track toward the shore, approximately 150 feet (30.5 meters), between the two saliñas. There is limited parking at this site and only a small area in which to turn around. Soft Coral Garden is 8 miles (13 kilometers) from the airport—a drive of about 15 minutes.

Access

Divers should gear up and walk over the coral rubble ridge to the shore. There are several large boulders near the waterline. The reef ledge here can be a little rutted and slippery in places, and waves tend to break at this location, which can reduce visibility in the back reef and also make access challenging. Divers should time their entry with the waves and use their dive buddy for support if necessary. Since this is an unmarked site, there is no mooring buoy.

Description

Soft Coral Garden is another unmarked site that does not appear on the official list of dive sites in the Marine Park. It gets its name from the profusion of soft corals that cover the back reef area and the upper edges of the reef slope. The back reef also supports stands of both staghorn and elkhorn coral, making it a fun place for snorkelers to explore. Divers have been known to spot relatively rare blue and rainbow parrotfish here, as well as large honeycomb cowfish and porcupinefish. Barracuda are often spotted above the reef and large yellowfin, black, and tiger grouper can be found in the deeper parts of the reef.

59B Hidden Beach

BONAIRE

Difficulty
Current
Depth
Reef
Fauna

Access about 22 mins from Kralendijk

Level Advanced Open Water

Location
Oranje Pan, Bonaire
GPS: 12°01'57.5"N, 68°15'29.3"W

Getting there

Drive south from Kralendijk on Kaya International, which becomes EEG Boulevard as it passes the airport. After Bachelor's Beach, the road bends slightly away from the coastline for about 0.75 miles (1.2 kilometers) before returning to the shore just before The Lake dive site. Continue down the coast past Salt Pier and White Slave, to where the road bends to the southeast. About 1.4 miles (2.3 kilometers) past this corner there is a kiteboarding camp on the right-hand side of the road. Hidden Beach is located 1 mile (1.6 kilometers) farther along and only about 0.15 miles (0.25 kilometers) past Soft Coral Garden. The turn for Hidden Beach can be easy to miss, but it should be possible to spot the 250-foot (76-meter) track that crosses the open area from the main road to the shoreline.

There is plenty of parking at the end of the track. A couple of rock piles, including one that contains a driftwood pole adorned with a flag, help mark this spot. Hidden Beach is 8.2 miles (13.2 kilometers) from the airport—a drive of about 15 minutes.

Access

Divers should gear up and walk over the coral rubble ridge to the shore. There are several large boulders near the waterline. The reef ledge here can be a little rutted and slippery in places, and waves tend to break at this location, which can reduce visibility in the back reef and can make access challenging. Divers should time their entry with the waves and use their dive buddy for support if necessary. As an unmarked site, there is no mooring buoy present here.

Description

Much like the other sites along this section of Bonaire's coast, Hidden Beach has no real beach. It is one of four adjacent unmarked sites that do not appear on the official Marine Park map. The unmarked sites tend to receive fewer visitors than the marked sites, and yet they offer comparable experiences in many cases.

Hidden Beach has a shallow plateau that hosts plenty of soft corals and sea fans. It gives way to the reef slope that descends to a depth of nearly 150 feet (46 meters). At this site, the reef has a lower density of hard corals than some of the other sites in the south, but it has a profusion of soft corals and sponges, which typically attract sea turtles, trumpetfish, and slender filefish. Divers can also see anemones with their associated cleaner shrimp at this site, along with margates, Bermuda chub, spotted drums, and barracuda. Rainbow and blue parrotfish are also fairly common here.

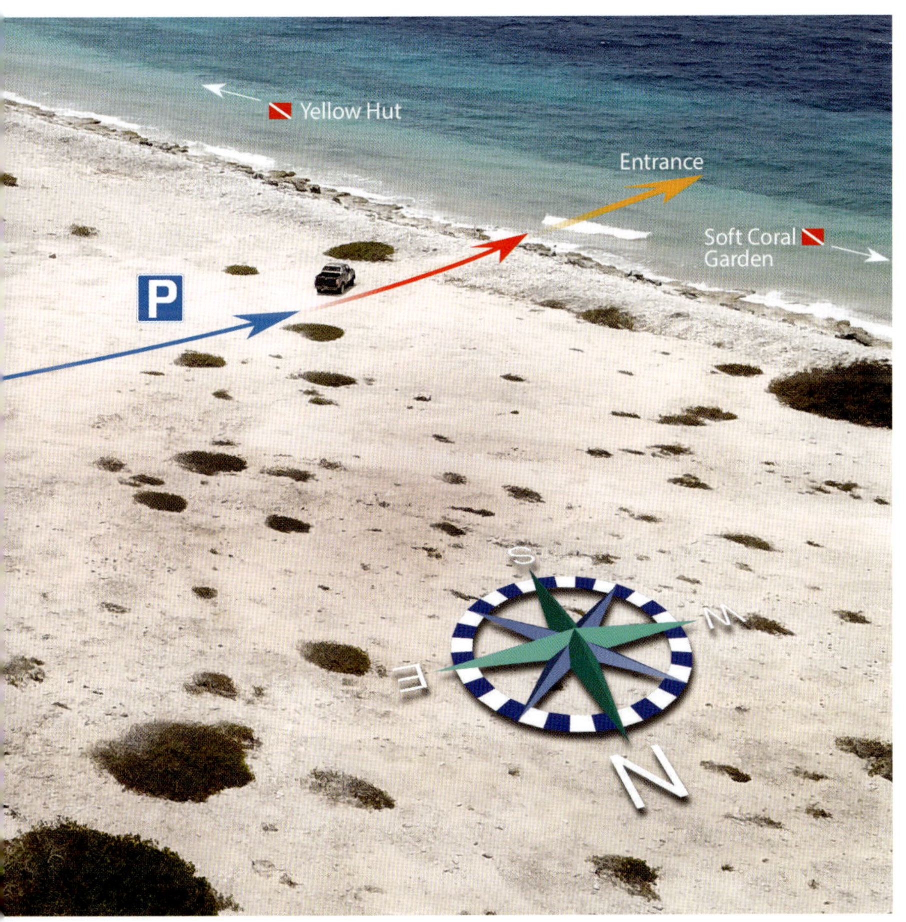

59C

Yellow Hut

BONAIRE

Access about 23 mins from Kralendijk

Level Advanced Open Water

Location
Oranje Pan, Bonaire
GPS: 12°01′52.8″N, 68°15′21.8″W

Getting there

Drive south from Kralendijk on Kaya International, which becomes EEG Boulevard as it passes the airport. After Bachelor's Beach, the road bends slightly away from the coastline for about 0.75 miles (1.2 kilometers) before returning to the shore just before The Lake dive site. Continue down the coast past Salt Pier and White Slave, to where the road bends to the southeast. About 1.4 miles (2.3 kilometers) past this corner there is a kiteboarding camp on the right-hand side of the road. Yellow Hut is located 1.2 miles (1.9 kilometers) farther south from the camp and just less than 0.2 miles (0.3

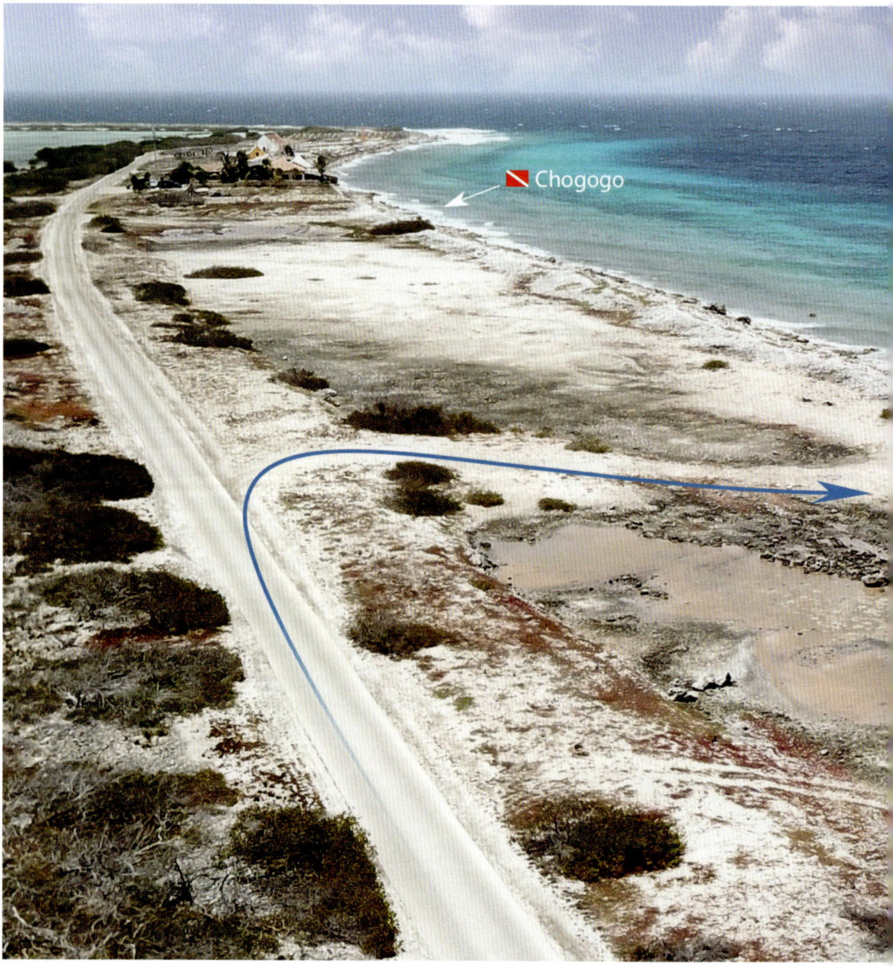

kilometers) past Hidden Beach at the point where the shoreline vegetation ends. The turn for Yellow Hut is on the right-hand side of the road between two large bushes, and it runs slightly back toward the north as it cuts between two saliñas. There is plenty of parking at the end of the track. Rock piles constructed next to the shoreline help mark the site, including one that contains a driftwood pole. Yellow Hut is 8.5 miles (13.6 kilometers) from the airport—a drive of about 16 minutes.

Access

Divers should gear up and walk over the coral rubble ridge to the shore. There are several large boulders near the waterline, but a sand patch located seaward of the rock piles makes entering the water a lot easier than at other sites along this stretch of the coast. Waves tend to break at this location, which can reduce visibility in the back reef and can make access challenging. Divers should time their entry with the waves and use their dive buddy for support if necessary. There is no mooring buoy at this site.

Description

Yellow Hut is one of four adjacent unmarked sites along the southernmost section of Bonaire's coast. The name originates from a small yellow hut that once stood here but has long since disappeared. The reef is still here, however, and it offers divers another chance to explore dense forests of soft corals, along with a gentle reef slope with a mix of hard and soft corals, and sponges. As with other sites around here, divers commonly find sea turtles among the soft corals, as well as trumpetfish and black margates. Snapper are particularly common at this site, namely schoolmaster snapper, but also yellowtail, mahogany, cubera, and grey.

59D

Chogogo

BONAIRE

Difficulty ●●●
Current ●●●
Depth ●●○
Reef ★★☆
Fauna ★★☆

Access about 23 mins from Kralendijk

Level Advanced Open Water

Location
Oranje Pan, Bonaire
GPS: 12°01′47.5″N, 68°15′14.7″W

Getting there

Drive south from Kralendijk on Kaya International, which becomes EEG Boulevard as it passes the airport. After Bachelor's Beach, the road bends slightly away from the coastline for about 0.75 miles (1.2 kilometers) before returning to the shore just before The Lake dive site. Continue down the coast past Salt Pier and White Slave, to where the road bends to the southeast. About 1.4 miles (2.3 kilometers) past this corner there is a kiteboarding camp on the right-hand side of the road. Chogogo is located 1.4 miles (2.2 kilometers) to the south of the

P

Yellow Hut

camp and just 0.17 miles (0.27 kilometers) past Yellow Hut. There is a house with a red roof visible near the shore; the turning for Chogogo is on the right, just north of the house. Divers should head down the track to the shore—a distance of about 150 feet (46 meters). Like many of the sites on this stretch of coast, the site is unmarked on both the road and in the water. However, two large rock piles placed on the rubble shoulder adjacent to the shore help mark the site. Chogogo is 8.7 miles (14 kilometers) from the airport—a drive of about 16 minutes.

Access

Divers should gear up and walk over the coral rubble ridge to the shore, past the rock pile and down onto the reef ledge adjacent to the waterline. The reef ledge is a little rutted and slippery in places, and waves tend to break at this location, which can reduce visibility in the back reef and make access challenging. Divers should time their entry with the waves and use their dive buddy for support if necessary. There are a few shallow reef areas close to shore that divers should be sure to avoid.

Description

Chogogo is the last unmarked dive site along the southern stretch of the Bonaire coastline. The current can be strong so close to the southern tip of the island, so divers should assess the conditions before entering the water and adjust their dive plans accordingly. Chogogo is known for its soft corals, as is characteristic of the dive sites in this area. The hard and soft corals at this site are less dense than at other sites farther up the coast, but there is still plenty to explore. Divers are likely to see black margates, surgeonfish, creole wrasses, spotted drums and even the occasional sea turtle here.

Red Slave

Difficulty ●●○
Current ●●●
Depth ●●●
Reef ★★★
Fauna ★★☆

Access about 24 mins from Kralendijk (by car)
about 60 mins from Kralendijk (by boat)

Level Advanced Open Water

Location
Oranje Pan, Bonaire
GPS: 12°01′35.4″N, 68°15′03.9″W

Getting there

Drive south from Kralendijk on Kaya International, which becomes EEG Boulevard as it passes the airport. Red Slave is just under 9 miles (14.5 kilometers) from the airport—a drive of about 16 minutes. After Bachelor's Beach, the road bends slightly away from the coastline for about 0.75 miles (1.2 kilometers) before returning to the shore just before The Lake dive site. Continue down the coast past Salt Pier and White Slave, to where the road bends to the southeast.

From this corner divers need to continue past the kiteboarding camp until they see the yellow slave huts adjacent to the Red Slave dive site—a distance of another 3 miles (4.8 kilometers) or a drive of about 6 minutes by car. The dive site is located near the southern tip of the island and is easily recognizable by the dozen or so historic huts located on either side of the road. The site is marked with yellow rocks that are visible by the roadside.

Access

The site is accessible by car or by boat, but most divers explore this as a shore dive given the long distance south by boat. There is ample parking in and among the yellow huts, although this site is rarely crowded. A mooring buoy located at the

The iconic slave huts at the Red Slave dive site.

FEATURED OPERATOR

When exploring remote and more extreme sites such as Red Slave, it is worth considering diving with a professional guide. **Xprodiver Bonaire** is a premier family-run scuba center, where passion meets expertise, safety and a love for the underwater world. Xprodiver visits dive sites across Bonaire both from shore and by boat, including Red Slave. They also conduct blackwater night dives, allowing divers to experience the incredible vertical migration that unfolds as a range of deep-sea creatures rise toward the surface at nightfall. It is one of the wildest dive experiences on Earth, and you will receive dedicated and personalized service from Xprodiver that will make your trip to Bonaire unforgettable.

Tel: +599-777-7333
Email: Bonaire@xprodiver.com
Visit: **Xprodiver.com**

southern end of the site can help keep divers oriented as they enter the water. This part of Bonaire's coastline is relatively easy to access, just a short walk from the parking area. With gear on, divers can walk down a slight incline to the left of the last hut in the line along the shore. They should enter the water carefully as the rocks can be quite slippery and swells from the east can wrap around the southern tip of the island, generating sizable surf at times.

Description

Red Slave gets its name from the nearby slave huts. It is a fantastic wall dive with a reef that drops off from a depth of around 30 feet (9 meters) down to a maximum depth of 167 feet (51 meters) and a sandy seafloor below. Because this site is located so close to the southern tip of the island, the rough waters on the east coast often curl around and mix with the calmer waters of the west coast. This southern position means this site sometimes experiences strong currents and large waves, which can deter snorkelers and novice divers. Divers should properly assess the conditions before entering the water.

As it does for much of the sites along the west coast of Bonaire, the reef wall at Red Slave falls like a curtain, with a repeating pattern of vertical channels in the reef wall. Some of those recessed channels have sand at the bottom of them, others have continuous coral coverage from peak to valley. The sections of reef that protrude from the wall vary in width and height, tending to get wider and shallower toward the northern end of the site.

All of this complexity, along with the mixing currents, creates an environment that supports a wide variety of reef fish, sponges, and corals. Sea fans and soft corals thrive shoreward of the drop-off zone, while hard corals cover the reef wall, interspersed with sponges and sea whips. The mixing waters support schools of snapper and chromis, while patrolling barracuda keep watch. Eagle rays are also known to frequent this site.

Route

With currents generally moving from south to north, divers can enter the water and swim out toward the yellow mooring buoy across the turf algae that covers that seafloor in shallower waters. The turf gives way to a forest of soft corals located near the buoy anchor. Divers should

keep an eye open for plenty of juvenile reef fish, including Atlantic trumpetfish and slender filefish, which often frequent these kinds of habitats.

Once at the buoy, divers can descend to the reef and head another 50 feet (15 meters) toward the reef wall. As they drop down the reef slope, divers should watch for larger fish, particularly pelagic species such as jacks and rainbow runners. When they reach their desired depth, divers typically head northeast along the face of the wall where schools of black durgons, snapper, and grunts are common.

To extend their bottom time, divers might consider slowly ascending as they swim along the wall. Halfway through their planned dive time, most divers turn around and head back along the upper section of the wall, checking out the transition between sand and reef. Complete the dive either by returning to the buoy and heading in or simply crossing directly toward shore from the top of the drop-off.

Willemstoren Lighthouse

Difficulty ●●●
Current ●●●
Depth ●●○
Reef ★★☆
Fauna ★★☆

Access about 26 mins from Kralendijk

Level Advanced Open Water

Location
Oranje Pan, Bonaire
GPS: 12°01′41.8″N, 68°14′14.4″W

Getting there

Drive south from Kralendijk on Kaya International, which becomes EEG Boulevard as it passes the airport. After Bachelor's Beach, the road bends slightly away from the coastline for about 0.75 miles (1.2 kilometers) before returning to the shore just before The Lake dive site. Continue down the coast past Salt Pier, Pink Beach, and White Slave, to where the road bends to the southeast. Continue down the last stretch of the southwest coast past Red Slave, and around the bend in the road at the southernmost point of Bonaire. The Willemstoren Lighthouse is just under a mile (less than 1.6 kilometers) past this bend. Divers should pull over beside the lighthouse; there should be plenty of room to park here. Although this is an official site, it is unmarked with no yellow painted rock or yellow mooring buoy. Willemstoren Lighthouse is about 10 miles (16 kilometers) from the airport—a drive of about 19 minutes.

Access

Divers should gear up at their car and walk over the rocky terrain toward the shoreline—a distance of about 150 feet (46 meters). Rock piles that have been constructed on a coral ridge adjacent to the shore help mark the best access points. The ridge slopes down to a reef ledge that provides access to the water. Divers can enter the water on either side of the lighthouse.

Standing on the shoreline at this site can feel quite intimidating. The waves are often large and constant, and the currents here can be particularly strong. It is often best to wait for calm conditions to dive or snorkel this site. Divers should time their entry and exit with the waves, bracing as waves approach and shuffling forward in the water between waves. When starting their dive, divers should descend as quickly as possible.

Description

The Willemstoren Lighthouse dive site is easily identified by the tall lighthouse that stands between the coastal road and the shoreline at the southeastern tip of the island. Because of its location, the waters and currents here are typically very strong, making this dive suitable only for advanced divers. The site is known for its soft corals and sea fans, as well as the opportunity to see large pelagic species, such as horse-eye and crevalle jacks, and cero mackerel, which feed off the large schools of boga. Bar jacks and black durgons are particularly abundant at this site. Large green moray eels and even nurse sharks and the occasional dolphin have also been spotted here.

DID YOU KNOW?

The Willemstoren Lighthouse was built in 1837. It is the first lighthouse built on Bonaire and it remains a fully functioning lighthouse that assists boats in navigating the challenging currents around the southern tip of the island. The lighthouse stands in excellent condition today thanks to government-led renovations completed in 2012. It is one of three lighthouses and two light beacons on the island and is considered by many people to be the most famous.

EAST COAST

The east coast of Bonaire offers a completely unique experience for the more adventurous diver. Characterized by its rugged beauty on land, east coast reefs represent a pristine ecosystem that hosts vibrant marine life. These sites also provide divers with the opportunity to encounter large pelagic species that are rarely seen on the island's more popular west side. Divers who venture to the east coast are often rewarded with sightings of reef sharks, eagle rays, sea turtles, large lobsters and nurse sharks.

RELAX & RECHARGE

There are few better places to relax, unwind and enjoy an awesome meal with stunning views than **Foodies**. This cozy spot on the shores of Lac Bay has rapidly gained a wide following thanks to its delicious food and low-key trendy vibe. The menu is varied, featuring sandwiches, salads, burgers, risottos, pasta and even sashimi from locally caught fish. And if you are looking for a sun-down drink, then you will find plenty of choice in their well-stocked bar. There is also a snack menu, featuring beer battered fish and traditional Dutch Bitterballen.
Visit: **Foodiesbonaire.com**

Lorenzo Mittiga ©

SAFETY TIP

Bonaire's east side has fewer crowds because the diving here tends to be more challenging, often with waves and strong currents. It is therefore better suited to advanced and experienced divers. The sites described in this book can be accessed by boat or from shore. Boat access is possible throughout the year, but shore access tends to be more challenging when conditions are not ideal. The best time to dive the east coast is when the winds drop or change direction, which causes the currents and waves to subside. This happens most frequently during the summer months but can also occur at other times of the year. Excellent navigation skills are essential to explore these dive sites and return to the boat or the correct exit point on shore. As such, diving with an experienced professional guide is essential on Bonaire's east coast. There is a reason this coast is called the "wild side" of Bonaire.

A stingray rests in the sand at White Hole.

63 Cai

Access  about 20 mins from Kralendijk

Difficulty ●●●
Current ●●●
Depth ●●○
Reef ★★☆
Fauna ★★★

Level Advanced

Location

Lac Bay Beach, Bonaire
GPS: 12°06′13.4″N, 68°13′20.3″W

Cai is an advanced dive that is often conducted from shore. Divers enter the water just south of Lac Bay Beach, adjacent to the fishing huts and conch-shell piles located near the boat entrance to the bay. While Cai remains an official STINAPA site with relatively simple access, the currents here can be very strong and unpredictable. Additionally, visibility can change quickly, making navigation challenging. As such, this site should only be visited by extremely experienced divers led by a professional guide.

Cai allows divers to transition between several different habitats on the same dive. The Lac Bay channel hosts large numbers of reef fish and lots of anemones on the seabed. As the channel transitions to the drop-off, divers usually encounter large tarpon. The reef here is steep with numerous undercut ledges where divers can find snapper, grunts and moray eels. Sea turtles and eagle rays are also common visitors to this site.

62A Funchi's Reef

Access about 5 mins from Lac Bay

Difficulty ●●○
Current ●●●
Depth ●●○
Reef ★★☆
Fauna ★★★
Level Open Water

Location
Sorobon, Bonaire
GPS: 12°05'51.1"N, 68°13'30.8"W

Often explored as a drift dive, Funchi's Reef is probably one of the most relaxed dives on the east coast. It provides a wonderful taste of the reefs with less effort. The site is located immediately to the south of the Lac Bay channel. As the current generally flows from south to north at this site, divers are dropped at the southern end of the site, close to White Hole, and drift with the current toward the north at a depth of approximately 50 feet (15 meters).

The site is sometimes referred to as a Sea Turtle Highway by dive guides, as dozens of green sea turtles regularly use this reef to move back and forth between their resting spot at Turtle City and their sea grass feeding grounds inside Lac Bay. Many other species can be seen while drifting through Funchi's Reef, including stingrays, eagle rays and large schools of black margates. The site is usually done as the first dive of the day, which is rush hour for turtle traffic.

62 White Hole

Access about 6 mins from Lac Bay

Difficulty ●●○
Current ●●●
Depth ●○○
Reef ★★☆
Fauna ★★★
Level Open Water

Location
Sorobon, Bonaire
GPS: 12°05'39.4"N, 68°13'41.0"W

White Hole is a boat accessible dive site located adjacent to the barrier reef that separates Lac Bay from the open ocean. The site is technically accessible from shore, but this practice is strongly discouraged because of the damage it could cause both to the reef and to divers who attempt it. The central feature of White Hole is a large, oblong sand patch (or hole) in the reef, measuring close to 500 feet (152 meters) in length and 130 feet (39.5 meters) in width.

The hole is usually visible from the surface, as the sandy seafloor shines white against the surrounding reef. The hole is about 35 feet (10.5 meters) deep and the reef rises in a small wall along the edge at a depth of between 10 and 15 feet (3 to 4.5 meters). Tarpon are almost always found in the hole, while divers may see nurse sharks, eagle rays and barracuda taking advantage of the protection offered by the steep walls. Queen conch and stingrays are often found in the sand. The current can be moderate to strong at this dive site. Visibility can be murky at times because swells can disturb the fine sandy sediment at the bottom of the hole.

61C Turtle City

Access about 7 mins from Lac Bay

Difficulty ●●○
Current ●●●
Depth ●●○
Reef ★★☆
Fauna ★★★
Level Open Water

Location
Sorobon, Bonaire
GPS: 12°05'32.4"N, 68°13'42.8"W

Located about 250 feet (75 meters) south of White Hole, Turtle City has developed an incredible reputation for sea turtles. The reef here extends seaward in a series of plateaus, averaging approximately 40 feet (12 meters) in depth, with lots of crevices and holes in the substrate for sea turtles and other coral reef creatures to hide. Divers may see green moray eels, spiny lobster, stingrays and eagle rays, as well as cubera snapper and large schools of horse-eye jacks, but the stars of the show are the sea turtles.

There are very few sites in the world that dive professionals can guarantee a sea turtle sighting, but this is one of them. It is not uncommon to see as many as 20 to 30 individuals on a single dive—virtually all green sea turtles that feed on the sea grasses in Lac Bay. Loggerheads and hawksbills can sometimes be spotted during the mating season. When conditions allow, White Hole and Turtle City can even be explored in the same dive as they are only about a 15-minute swim apart.

FEATURED OPERATOR

Bonaire East Coast Diving is a specialized boat diving operation that focuses mainly on the famous east side of Bonaire. Divers can expect to see the most exciting creatures Bonaire has to offer, including reef sharks, spotted eagle rays, stingrays, green moray eels and plenty of sea turtles. Bonaire East Coast Diving has two custom-built Zodiacs equipped with all the necessary safety gear to make diving on the windward side of Bonaire a breeze for all levels of divers. Take a deep breath as our passionate and skilled crew guides you beneath the waves.

Tel: +599-701-5211
Email: info@bonaireeastcoastdiving.com
Visit: **Bonaireeastcoastdiving.com**

Sea turtles are incredibly common in the Lac Bay area of Bonaire.

Lorenzo Mittiga and Frederick Bekaert ©

61B Shrimp Factory

Access about 18 mins from Kralendijk
about 7 minutes from Lac Bay

Difficulty ●●●
Current ●●●
Depth ●●○
Reef ★★☆
Fauna ★★★

Level Advanced

Location
Sorobon, Bonaire
GPS: 12°05′05.0″N, 68°14′00.2″W

Shrimp Factory is located just south of Lac Bay. The site gets its name from the abandoned mariculture facility that was established here in the late 1980s. The buildings are still located here, close to the shoreline. The project was intended to serve as a commercial nursery and aquaculture farm for conch and shrimp, as well as several other marine creatures, including tilapia, clams and spiny lobster, but it was shut down in 1994 after years of financial losses. The site is also sometimes known as Marcultura, which was the name of the project.

The walk to the shore from the parking lot adjacent to the abandoned buildings is about 600 feet (183 meters). The shoreline consists of deeply rutted ironshore, which can be difficult to walk over. Booties are essential and divers should take great care while entering and exiting the water. Once in the water, divers must push through about 200 feet (60 meters) of surf before dropping to the bottom and beginning the dive. The reef here is of exceptional quality, and there are plenty of sea turtles to observe. Divers may also encounter sharks and rays.

61A Baby Beach

Access about 19 mins from Kralendijk
about 8 minutes from Lac Bay

Difficulty ●●●
Current ●●●
Depth ●●○
Reef ★★☆
Fauna ★★★

Level Advanced

Location
Sorobon, Bonaire
GPS: 12°04′43.3″N, 68°13′55.0″W

Baby Beach is located about half a mile (0.8 kilometers) south of Shrimp Factory, next to a lay-by in the road close to the shoreline. The site gets its name from the dive totem (a pile of rocks and sticks historically used to mark dive sites in Bonaire), which used to have a child's doll attached to it. The entry point on the shoreline is only about 150 feet from the lay-by, but the ironshore is deeply rutted here and hard to walk across. The surf is also powerful along this stretch of the coast and can easily knock a diver over, so care must be taken when entering and exiting the water. Overcoming the challenging entry and exit point is well worth the effort, however as Baby Beach is a real locals' favorite.

The reef is of amazing quality, but the reason this site is so popular is down to the reef residents. Reef sharks, nurse sharks, stingrays, eagle rays, large hogfish, Queen triggerfish, green moray, midnight parrotfish, lobsters, and sea turtles can all be found here in numbers. To the south, the reef develops into a spectacular spur and groove formation. Several anchors and cannons from the wreck of the *William & Ezra* can be found at the southern edge of this site. She was a North American brig that ran aground at this location in 1825 while en route from New York.

63A Boca Onima

Access about 25 mins from Kralendijk

Difficulty ●●●
Current ●●●
Depth ●●●
Reef ★★☆
Fauna ★★★

Level Advanced

Location
Rincón, Bonaire
GPS: 12°15′14.6″N, 68°18′35.9″W

Boca Onima is located close to Bonaire's iconic Wind Park adjacent to the town of Rincón—much farther north than the other east coast sites described in this book. Boca means "inlet" in Spanish, which describes the access point to the reef. As the inlet itself usually channels large waves that can make surface swimming challenging, the best way to access the site is by leaping off the southern side of the 15-foot (4.5-meter) cliff close to the seaward side of the inlet. The water is approximately 20 feet (6 meters) deep here. Once this "adventurous entry" has been cleared, accessing the dive site is relatively simple. Divers often descend immediately and swim northeast for approximately 500 feet (152 meters) to the reef slope.

As with most east coast dive sites, the current can be strong here, often running in a southerly direction. The reef is about 30 feet (9 meters) deep on top and slopes to over 100 feet on the deep edge. The reef is incredibly pristine, with large corals, particularly gorgonians. Caribbean reef sharks and eagle rays are often encountered at this site, particularly in the deeper parts of the reef. Divers head back to the inlet at the end of the dive, where the wave action within the inlet tends to carry divers to the beach, where they can exit the water.

A diver enters the water from the cliff edge at Boca Onima.

Marijn Bonenkamp©

About Klein Bonaire

Klein Bonaire is a small island just 0.5 miles (0.8 kilometers) off the west coast of Bonaire. The island is shaped like a slightly curved teardrop, roughly 2.5 miles (4 kilometers) long by 1.5 miles (2.5 kilometers) wide, and with a maximum elevation of just 5 feet (1.5 meters) above sea level. (Klein means "small" or "little" in Dutch, and thus Klein Bonaire means "Little Bonaire.")

The island is uninhabited although the remains of several structures, including slave huts, are still visible. In the 1850s, the island was used as a quarantine station to protect Bonaire from cholera. Over the years, the island changed hands numerous times until it was purchased by the government in 1999 and put under the management of the Bonaire National Marine Park. The measures taken to protect the island from future development have paid off, not just in preserving multiple sea turtle nesting beaches but by maintaining the high quality of the coral reefs at the 26 unique dive sites that surround the island.

The dive sites are listed from A through Z in the Marine Park's official list of dive sites, each with a whimsical name chosen by Captain Don Stewart, the patriarch of diving in Bonaire. The reefs start mere steps from shore but are can only be accessed by boat. Many dive centers offer trips out to Klein Bonaire. For those more interested in snorkeling or simply getting away from the mainland, there is a 20-minute water taxi out to the island for as little as $15 USD. The boat ferries visitors out to the island and leaves them there, returning for a pickup later in the day.

There is little to no shade available on the island, so plan accordingly. And remember that visitors must pay the Nature Fee to visit the island. That tag can be bought at most hotels, dive centers, activity centers or at STINAPA headquarters near Oil Slick Leap.

Dive and Snorkel Sites Klein Bonaire

	Name	Access
A	No Name (Playita)	
B	Ebo's Reef	
C	Jerry's Sponges	
D	Just a Nice Dive	
E	Nearest Point	
F	Keepsake	
G	Bonaventure	
H	Monte's Divi	
I	Rock Pile	
J	Joanne's Sunchi	
K	Captain Don's Reef	
L	South Bay	
M	Hands Off	
N	Forest	
O	Southwest Corner	
P	Munk's Haven	
Q	Twixt	
R	Sharon's Serenity	
S	Valerie's Hills	
T	Mi Dushi	
U	Yellow Man	
V	Carl's Hill	
W	Ebo's Special	
X	Leonora's Reef	
Y	Knife	
Z	Sampler	

Andy Troy/Shutterstock©

No Name Beach on Klein Bonaire is a great place to get away from it all.

Landing zone
W
X
Y
Z
A
Westpunt
Reforestation protected area
Pos Kabritu
B
C
KLEIN BONAIRE
J
I
Tanki Kalbas
D
H
E
G
F
No open fires
Do not litter
No pets allowed
No anchoring

A No Name

GPS: 12°10'08.0"N, 68°18'20.6"W

Difficulty ●○○
Current ●○○
Depth ●○○
Reef ★☆☆
Fauna ★☆☆

This site is located directly off the main beach area of Klein Bonaire, which is why it is also known as No Name Beach and Playita, which means "little beach" in Spanish. This spot is more popular for beachgoers than divers, thanks to the frequent water taxi visits that come from the main island. Nevertheless, snorkeling directly off the beach is a popular activity and while the reef is not in the best condition it is still possible to find grouper, parrotfish and angelfish on the reef slope and jawfish, stingrays and sea turtles in the upper areas of the site, which consist mostly of sand and coral rubble.

B Ebo's Reef

GPS: 12°10'00.6"N, 68°17'55.3"W

Difficulty ●●○
Current ●●○
Depth ●●○
Reef ★★☆
Fauna ★★☆

Ebo's Reef is named after Ebo Domacassé, who was one of Bonaire's founding dive industry pioneers. The site may have slightly stronger current and is known for its large elephant ear sponges, tube sponges and vase sponges. There are numerous cleaning stations at this site, which attract fish of all sizes from chromis to grouper, and even the occasional sea turtle. The reef drops relatively quickly from the narrow plateau, which has an average depth of just 10 feet (3 meters). Divers may also spot moray eels, spotlight parrotfish, schoolmaster snapper and Spanish hogfish.

C Jerry's Sponges

See page 258 for full site description and map.

D Just a Nice Dive

GPS: 12°09'28.3"N, 68°17'31.9"W

Difficulty ●○○
Current ●○○
Depth ●●○
Reef ★★☆
Fauna ★★☆

One of just a handful of sites located on Klein Bonaire's east coast, Just a Nice Dive is a steep-sloping reef with relatively mild currents, although they tend to be stronger toward the northeast of the dive site. The buoy is located close to shore but is anchored deep on the reef substrate. There is little back reef area here for snorkelers to explore, which is why this is generally considered a dive-only site. Sea turtles are common here, as are bar jacks, horse-eye jacks, ocean triggerfish and schoolmaster snapper.

E Nearest Point

GPS: 12°09'13.7"N, 68°17'35.1"W

Difficulty ●○○
Current ●○○
Depth ●●○
Reef ★★★
Fauna ★★☆

This dive site was considered the nearest point to the capital Kralendijk, which was where most dive centers were originally located back when the site was named. This site is also sometimes known as Piedra Kolet. Like the adjacent site, Just a Nice Dive, Nearest Point is a relatively steep-sloping reef with little to no back reef, which makes it more suited to divers than snorkelers. Soft corals and sponges abound here, but divers can also find large formations of hard coral. The best time to dive this site is in the morning when the wind is generally lower.

F Keepsake

See page 262 for full site description and map.

G Bonaventure

GPS: 12°08'42.8"N, 68°18'16.4"W

Difficulty ●○○
Current ●●○
Depth ●●○
Reef ★★☆
Fauna ★★☆

Bonaventure dive and snorkel site is located on the south coast of Klein Bonaire, adjacent to the large saliña that stretches along roughly half of the island's southern shoreline. Bonaventure is similar to many of the other southern sites that lie farther toward the west, with a sloping reef that features spurs and sand channels that run from the plateau at the top down to the bottom of the reef. The site is suitable for both divers and snorkelers, who may encounter stoplight and Queen parrotfish, graysbies, schoolmaster snapper and seahorses.

H Monte's Divi

GPS: 12°08'44.2"N, 68°18'29.9"W

Difficulty ●○○
Current ●○○
Depth ●●○
Reef ★★☆
Fauna ★★☆

Monte's Divi is sometimes referred to as Monte's Divi Tree, or sometimes simply Divi Tree. The site got its name from the lone divi tree located in the narrow strip of shoreline between the ocean and the neighboring saliña. The buoy is anchored on the plateau close to the reef slope at a depth of about 33 feet (10 meters). Soft corals dominate the back reef, transitioning to large hard coral mounds and sponges on the reef slope. Rather than being punctuated by spurs, like other sites along the south coast, the reef at Monte's Divi gently undulates. Foureye butterflyfish are particularly common here. Hamlets, honeycomb cowfish and tiger grouper can be found in deeper water.

I Rock Pile

GPS: 12°08'53.7"N, 68°18'42.7"W

Difficulty ●○○
Current ●○○
Depth ●●○
Reef ★★★
Fauna ★★☆

This dive and snorkel site gets its name from the pile of rocks that can be found onshore adjacent to the mooring buoy—the rock pile was a landmark used by boat captains before permanent mooring buoys were installed. The site is sometimes known as Bonheur de Betsy, which is French for Betsy's Joy. Staghorn and elkhorn corals are present in the shallow plateau, which is a great area for snorkelers to explore. Schooling French grunts, mahogany snapper and schoolmaster snapper are common on the

A typical reef in the tranquil water of Klein Bonaire.

NaturePicsFilms/Shutterstock©

reef as well as foureye butterflyfish and spotlight parrotfish. Divers have reported seeing green moray eels in the deeper parts of the reef where plate-form corals can also be found.

 J Joanne's Sunchi

GPS: 12°08′58.7″N, 68°18′54.4″W

Difficulty ●○○
Current ●○○
Depth ●●○
Reef ★★☆
Fauna ★★★

Joanne's Sunchi means Joanne's Kiss in Papiamento. This reef has multiple long spurs with sand channels in between—a common characteristic of the reef along this stretch of Klein Bonaire's southern coast. The reef features numerous hard corals and tube sponges that provide habitat for stoplight parrotfish, yellow goatfish, French angelfish and mahogany snapper. Chromis, black durgon and bar jacks are common in the water column. In the back reef, snorkelers may spot giant anemones, typically with Pederson cleaning shrimp. Sea turtles are often seen at this site as well. A Reef Renewal coral nursery is located between Joanne's Sunchi and the adjacent site of Captain Don's Reef.

K Captain Don's Reef

GPS: 12°08′59.7″N, 68°19′02.5″W

Difficulty ●○○
Current ●●○
Depth ●●○
Reef ★★☆
Fauna ★★☆

Captain Don's Reef is named after the famous Captain Don Stewart, who pioneered diving in Bonaire back in the early 1960s. The resort he founded, Captain Don's Habitat, still exists today on the west coast of Bonaire. Captain Don's Reef received its official name in 1987 and has a plaque dedicated to him on the reef near the mooring. This reef resembles many of the neighboring sites on this stretch of the southern shore, with long spurs and sand channels. A Reef Renewal coral nursery is located between Captain Don's Reef and the adjacent site of Joanne's Sunchi.

DID YOU KNOW? 

Captain Don Stewart is credited with starting the dive industry in Bonaire and is often referred to as the "father of Bonaire diving." When he arrived on the island in 1962 in his sailboat *Valerie Queen*, there were only 4,000 people living on Bonaire, 2,000 annual visitors, no cruise ships and no dive tanks, apart from the six he brought with him from California. Bonaire's main export that year was goats, but Captain Don sensed that the island could become a magnet for tourism and that the new sport of scuba diving could be the perfect tool. Soon after his arrival in Bonaire, Captain Don became the manager of the Flamingo Beach Club (which would eventually become the Divi Flamingo Resort) and opened the island's first dive center there. The early gear they used had no gauges of any kind. Sources say that Captain Don used time to determine air pressure and colored ribbons to determine depth. More recently, Captain Don was responsible for initiating the permanent mooring buoy system in Bonaire and named most of the island's dive and snorkel sites. Sadly, he passed away in 2014.

L South Bay

See page 266 for full site description and map.

M Hands Off

See page 270 for full site description and map.

N Forest

See page 274 for full site description and map.

O Southwest Corner

GPS: 12°09'05.9"N, 68°19'47.8"W

Difficulty	●●○
Current	●●●
Depth	●●○
Reef	★★★
Fauna	★★★

As the name suggests, Southwest Corner is located just offshore of Klein Bonaire's southwestern corner, adjacent to the saliña that occupies that part of the island. The current can be moderate to strong in this exposed location, which makes this site better suited to experienced divers and snorkelers. The back reef plateau stretches about 330 feet (106 meters) from shore to drop-off, which is wider than at any other point on the island. The back reef hosts an abundance of pencil coral, fire coral and soft corals, while the reef slope features a relatively shallow gradient and is remarkably healthy. Divers may encounter sea turtles, barracuda, horse-eye jacks, yellowtail snapper, midnight parrotfish and large schools of boga.

P Munk's Haven

GPS: 12°09'17.9"N, 68°19'44.4"W

Difficulty	●●○
Current	●●●
Depth	●●○
Reef	★★☆
Fauna	★★☆

Munk's Haven is similar in many ways to the neighboring Southwest Corner site. The current is generally stronger here and therefore better suited to experienced divers and snorkelers. Cleaning stations are common throughout the reef, which descends quite quickly initially, before reaching an extended plateau at depth. Hamlet's tiger grouper and green moray eels can be found in the deeper areas of the site. Elkhorn and blade fire coral can be found in the shallows along with yellowhead jawfish, sand tilefish and soapfish.

Q Twixt

GPS: 12°09'22.6"N, 68°19'40.9"W

Difficulty	●●○
Current	●●●
Depth	●●○
Reef	★★☆
Fauna	★★☆

Twixt is the start of a series of dive and snorkel sites that are grouped closely together, often only 500 to 600 feet (152 to 183 meters) apart, along a relatively exposed stretch of coastline on the western edge of Klein Bonaire. As such, divers often end up exploring parts of neighboring sites during their dives. Currents can be moderate to strong here, which makes this site better suited to experienced divers and snorkelers. Twixt consists of a sloping reef that reaches a plateau at depth. Bar jacks are particularly common in the water column above the reef, as are black durgon and blue chromis. Divers often find hamlets, butterflyfish and parrotfish on the reef.

R Sharon's Serenity

GPS: 12°09'28.9"N, 68°19'36.8"W

Difficulty	●●○
Current	●●●
Depth	●●○
Reef	★★☆
Fauna	★★☆

Sharon's Serenity is sandwiched between two other dive and snorkel sites along a relatively exposed part of Klein Bonaire's west coast. As such, divers often end up exploring parts of neighboring sites during their dives. Currents can be moderate to strong here, which makes this site better suited to experienced divers and snorkelers. Divers and snorkelers may encounter foureye butterflyfish, mixed schools of surgeonfish and blue tangs, smooth trunkfish, schoolmaster snapper, and French grunts. Trumpetfish are common in the back reef and chromis school above the reef slope. This site is popular for night dives due to the large numbers of basket stars hidden in the soft corals during the day, which open up at night to feed.

S Valerie's Hills

GPS: 12°09'35.2"N, 68°19'33.2"W

Difficulty ● ● ○
Current ● ● ○
Depth ● ● ○
Reef ★★☆
Fauna ★★☆

Valerie's Hills, sometimes called Valerie's Hill, is a dive and snorkel site named after Captain Don's wife. The site usually has slightly less current than those immediately to the south. Large sponges and dome-shaped hard corals are present across the reef here, which slopes relatively steeply into the depth, ending at about 100 feet (30 meters). Scrawled filefish, creolefish, soapfish and honeycomb cowfish are often seen on this reef.

T Mi Dushi

GPS: 12°09'40.7"N, 68°19'30.0"W

Difficulty ● ● ○
Current ● ● ○
Depth ● ● ○
Reef ★★☆
Fauna ★★★

Mi Dushi, which means "my darling" or "my sweetheart" in Papiamento, is a dive and snorkel site located along the west coast of Klein Bonaire. (The site is sometimes referred to as Joanna's Revenge.) It has developed somewhat of a reputation for being a haven for cryptic critters, with divers and snorkelers often reportedly finding seahorses, octopuses and frogfish on this reef, as well as cleaner shrimp, sailfin blennies and yellowhead jawfish. Lobsters and moray eels can be found in the deeper parts of the reef. There is an outplant site for the Reef Renewal Foundation Bonaire in the shallows here.

U Yellow Man

GPS: 12°09'46.7"N, 68°19'26.1"W

Difficulty ● ○ ○
Current ● ○ ○
Depth ● ● ○
Reef ★★☆
Fauna ★★★

Located just south of Carl's Hill, and often referred to as Carl's Hill Annex, Yellow Man is a relatively sheltered dive and snorkel site on the western coast of Klein Bonaire. It is a great spot for snorkelers, as the back reef is wide and largely protected from the strong currents by the corner of land that juts out from the shore at Carl's Hill. Seahorses are commonly spotted on this reef, as well as rock beauties, trumpetfish, hamlets and trunkfish. A coral outplant site for the Reef Renewal Foundation Bonaire (RRFB) is located in the shallows.

V Carl's Hill

See page 278 for full site description and map.

W Ebo's Special

GPS: 12°09'56.8"N, 68°19'08.9"W

Difficulty ● ○ ○
Current ● ○ ○
Depth ● ● ○
Reef ★★★
Fauna ★★★

Another site named after dive legend Ebo Domacassé, Ebo's Special is also sometimes known as Jerry's Jam, after Ebo's friend and colleague Jerry Schnabel, who wrote Bonaire's first guidebook. The reef slope features multiple distinct ridges and channels, which provides interesting topography for divers. Small caves and undercut areas often provide shelter for lobsters, moray eels and even nurse sharks. While the back reef plateau is quite narrow here, there is plenty of life to see. And snorkelers can also find stands of staghorn and elkhorn, which often shelter yellow goatfish and juvenile grunts. Divers and snorkelers can sometimes find spotted drums, longsnout butterflyfish, Queen angelfish and rare chain moray eels on this reef.

X Leonora's Reef

GPS: 12°10'01.7"N, 68°18'56.0"W

Difficulty ●○○
Current ●○○
Depth ●●○
Reef ★★☆
Fauna ★★☆

Leonora's Reef is located on the north coast of Klein Bonaire, just east of Carl's Hill. This site is known for its light current, which makes it suitable for divers and snorkelers of all experience levels. Small mounds of mustard hill coral and yellow finger coral cover the upper reef area, while large stands of soft coral dominate the back reef, including sea fans with flamingo tongues. Sponges and star corals are more common deeper on the reef, where divers may encounter tiger grouper, cubera snapper and the occasional eagle ray passing through the site.

Y Knife

See page 282 for full site description and map.

Z Sampler

GPS: 12°10'07.7"N, 68°18'36.5"W

Difficulty ●○○
Current ●●○
Depth ●●○
Reef ★★★
Fauna ★★☆

Sampler is one of Klein's Bonaire's most northern sites. It is a popular site for snorkelers as it is adjacent to where they are dropped on the beach by water taxis from the main island. It is also a great spot for divers. There is plenty to see in the shallows, such as sailfin blennies, peacock flounders, sand divers and yellowhead jawfish. The deeper parts of the reef support plenty of angelfish and mixed schools of surgeonfish and blue tangs. The site originally got its name from a flat rock that once contained a diverse array of multiple small coral colonies, much like a tray of samples laid out for divers and snorkelers to observe. Frogfish can also be found on this reef, as well as grouper and moray eels in the deeper parts of the site.

The beach at Klein Bonaire is a great place to relax and unwind.

C

KLEIN BONAIRE

Jerry's Sponges

Difficulty ●○○
Current ●●○
Depth ●○○
Reef ★☆☆
Fauna ★★☆

Access about 5 mins from Kralendijk

Level Open Water

Location
Klein Bonaire
GPS: 12° 9'50.53"N, 68°17'39.04"W

Getting there

Jerry's Sponges is a dive and snorkel site located on the northeastern tip of Klein Bonaire. The only way to reach this site is by boat, which takes around five minutes from Kralendijk. The dive site is adjacent to the narrowest stretch of channel that runs between Bonaire and Klein Bonaire. Most local dive centers visit Klein Bonaire on a regular basis, so divers should call ahead to schedule their trip.

Access

Jerry's Sponges is suitable for divers and snorkelers of all experience levels. There is a permanent mooring buoy at this site, but it is anchored in deeper water due to the shallowness of the sandy plateau, which reaches a maximum depth of just 5 feet (1.5 meters) along the upper edge of the drop-off. This means that divers may need to navigate up to 150 feet (45 meters) across blue water to reach the reef, depending on how currents and winds have oriented the boat relative to the mooring line. Snorkelers will also likely need to surface swim across a similar stretch of deep water in order to reach the relative shelter of the sandy plateau adjacent to the drop-off. Visibility is usually good at this site and currents may be slightly stronger than other sites around Klein Bonaire.

Description

Jerry's Sponges, sometimes referred to as Jerry's Reef, is named after underwater photographer Jerry Schnabel, who helped create one of Bonaire's first dive guides. The name is well-suited for this site, which is dominated more by sponges and soft corals than by the stony corals common at other dive sites on Klein Bonaire. The location of this site in the channel between the two islands means that currents can be quite strong here, which is why the reef is an ideal habitat for large elephant ear sponges, tube sponges and soft corals.

At this site, much of the best reef to explore is located close to the shallow plateau, which is only 5 feet (1.5 meters) deep in places. This area consists of numerous hard coral mounds, often containing stands of

SAFETY TIP 

Divers exploring the top of the wall along Jerry's Sponges should carefully monitor their depth as it is easy to rise shallow enough to break the surface in places. While there are clear rules requiring boats to keep their distance from dive boats displaying a dive flag, the increased boat traffic and Jet Skis in this area mean that divers and snorkelers should remain vigilant at all times when exploring the shallow plateau area of this reef.

ReefSmart ©

The water at Jerry's Sponges is shallow and incredibly clear.

gorgonians and interspersed with sand patches. Goatfish, spotted drums and grunts are common here, as are harlequin bass and sea turtles. Macro-photographers may enjoy shooting the basket stars wrapped up among the soft corals, or the slender filefish and trumpetfish moving within their branches. Many of the gorgonians at this site also host flamingo tongues.

Above the reefs, schools of brown and blue chromis mix with creole wrasses, as well as the occasional barracuda. In the deeper part of the reef, divers may spot creolefish, smooth trunkfish, graysbies, queen and French angelfish and even cubera snapper.

Route

Jerry's Sponges offers divers plenty to explore at a shallower depth profile, which makes this site ideally suited for the second dive of a two-tank trip to Klein Bonaire. The

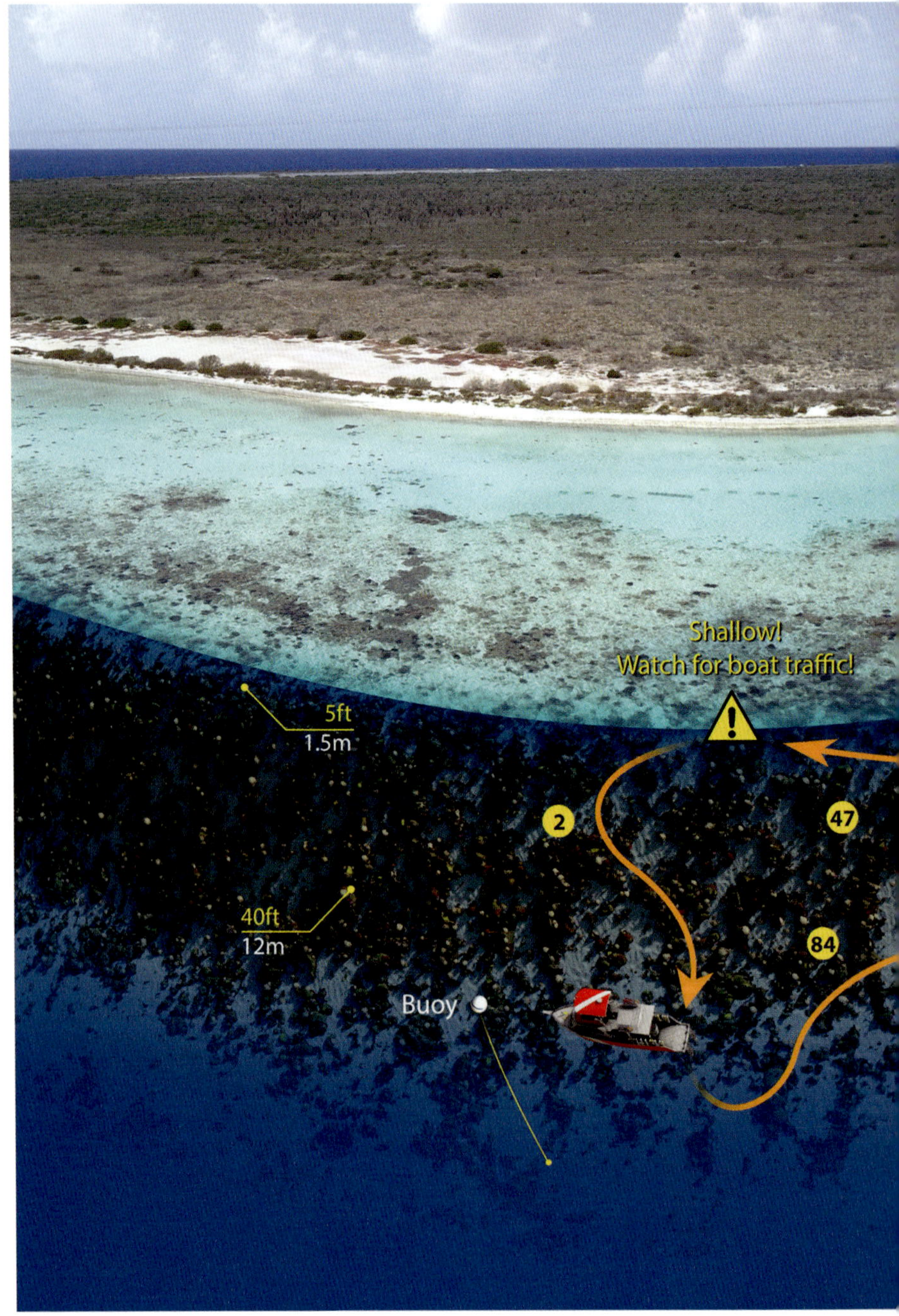

best route for divers to follow is to explore the reef at a depth of around 45 feet (14 meters) while heading into the prevailing current. Once divers have reached their turnaround point, they can retrace their route higher up the wall, at the ideal depth for an extended safety stop. Snorkelers usually move back and forth along the edge of the reef where it connects with the shallow plateau.

JERRY'S SPONGES

F

KLEIN BONAIRE

Keepsake

Difficulty ●○○
Current ●○○
Depth ●●○
Reef ★☆☆
Fauna ★☆☆

Access about 7 mins from Kralendijk

Level Open Water

Location
Klein Bonaire
GPS: 12° 8'48.30"N, 68°17'58.54"W

Getting there

Keepsake is located at the southeastern corner of Klein Bonaire. It is one of the closest sites to the capital Kralendijk, but the only way to reach this site is by boat, which takes around seven minutes from the mainland. Most local dive centers visit Klein Bonaire on a regular basis, so divers should call ahead to schedule their trip.

Access

Keepsake is suitable for divers and snorkelers of all experience levels. There is a permanent buoy anchored in the shallow plateau that extends from the shoreline, where there is a very narrow beach, out to the reef drop-off. The plateau is around 20 feet (6 meters) on average, relatively wide compared to neighboring sites, and sheltered from waves and currents, which makes it an ideal spot for both divers and snorkelers. The visibility is usually excellent at this site.

Description

Keepsake does not offer divers the same level of structure and substrate complexity as some of the other sites on the south coast of Klein Bonaire, but it does still offer enough to make the trip out to Klein Bonaire worthwhile. The site also has a wide variety of reef creatures to observe. As with most of the sites along the southern coast of Klein Bonaire, taking a shallower dive profile will allow divers to experience more marine life than if they were to descend to the lower limits of the wall.

The site is marked by a series of spurs that descend the slope, separated from one another by wide channels. These channels are not as deep or pronounced as they are in the sites farther to the west, but they still provide divers with decent complexity to explore, as well as some help when navigating back to the mooring buoy.

Directly seaward of the buoy, the reef descends as a broad expanse of relatively unbroken slope. This area is bounded to the east and the west by broad flat spurs that extend outward before disappearing into the depths. The western spur branches at a depth of 60 feet (18.5 meters) before splitting into two flat spurs that descend to depth.

The slope is dominated by large orange elephant ear sponges, encrusting corals and small star and mustard hill corals, while the plateau above is covered in stands of gorgonians and other soft corals. Stoplight parrotfish, French angelfish, fairy basslets and rock beauties can be seen throughout the reef. The usual complement of snapper and grunts are also common here, including frequent sightings of schoolmaster and mahogany snapper, along with French and Caesar grunts. Careful observers may even spot a smooth trunkfish or two weaving in

Drew McArthur/Shutterstock ©

Cryptic seahorses can be found on many sites around Klein Bonaire.

and out of the soft corals. Schools of blue and brown chromis dominate the water column above the reef.

Route

Most divers descend from the buoy and head either east or west into the prevailing current, turning around halfway through their dive and returning on a slightly shallower profile to extend their bottom time. Safety stops can be conducted on the back reef plateau, which is the area where most snorkelers explore.

KEEPSAKE

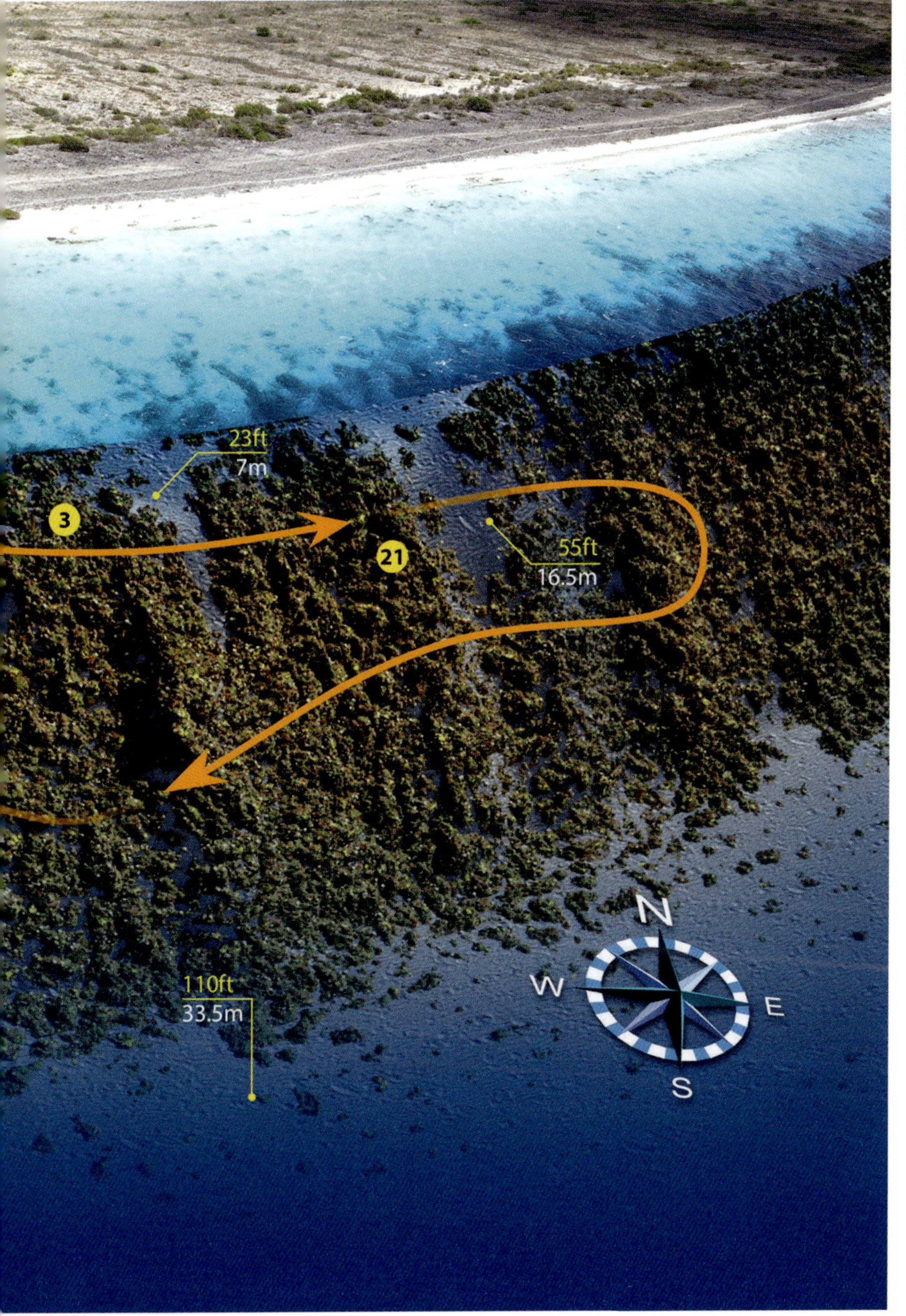
23ft
7m
3
21
55ft
16.5m
110ft
33.5m
N
W
E
S

South Bay

Difficulty
Current
Depth
Reef
Fauna

Access about 20 mins from Kralendijk

Level Open Water

Location
Klein Bonaire
GPS: 12°8′58.3″N, 68°19′13.6″W

Getting there

As the name implies, South Bay is a dive and snorkel site located in a small bay on the southern coast of Klein Bonaire. The only way to reach this site is by boat. This site is relatively close to downtown Kralendijk, and the trip by boat takes approximately 20 minutes. Most local dive centers visit Klein Bonaire on a regular basis, so divers should call ahead to schedule their trip.

Access

South Bay is suitable for divers and snorkelers of all experience levels. The best diving is relatively shallow along the top of the reef wall that drops off to a depth of around 130 feet (40 meters). The shallow plateau leading out from the shore is perfect for snorkeling. The site has a permanent mooring buoy that is quite far off shore, at a depth of 20 feet (6 meters). Snorkelers will want to focus on the area of the site on the shoreward side of the buoy unless they are able to dive down to the bottom or if visibility is very good.

Description

South Bay is an interesting site with plenty to see. Coral rubble and sand dominate the back reef area at depths of less than 17 feet (5 meters). In slightly deeper waters, divers and snorkelers can explore an area that includes mostly gorgonians, yellow pencil coral heads, small brain corals, and soft corals interspersed with sand patches. This back reef area also boasts very high rugosity (a measure of the complexity of the seafloor), which makes it the most interesting part of the site to explore, although divers should still check out the reef wall that begins at a depth of 35 feet (10.5 meters). In several areas on the wall, large coral heads have broken away and toppled over, creating small ledges and exposing holes in the reef wall. There are also a few sand channels wending their way down the steep slope of the drop-off.

A green moray eel hides under the reef.

South Bay offers a chance to see many different species, in part due to the high rugosity that attracts reef fish. Divers will spot many fish cleaning stations throughout the site, both on the wall and in the back reef area. Black durgon and creole wrasses regularly swim through the waters above the reef, and honeycomb cowfish and fairy basslets can be spotted closer to the seafloor. Large green morays are often seen farther down the wall at a depth of around 75 feet (23 meters), while yellow goatfish frequent the sand patches in the back reef. Barracuda regularly patrol the reef drop-off area, and divers have also spotted large grouper on this site.

Route

The current at this site can be moderate, so the route will likely depend on the direction and strength of that current. Drop down at the site of the mooring buoy and divers generally make their way toward the drop-off before turning to head east (into the prevailing current). Divers can choose to descend the reef wall or remain up near the transition between back reef and reef slope where it is most interesting.

Wet Lizard Photography/Shutterstock ©

Most divers continue east until they see the reef wall turning back toward shore, which is just after a 10-foot-wide (3-meter) depression with sand at the bottom. From there, turn around and return toward the buoy along the shallow reef area and through the forest of gorgonians and coral

heads. Once past the buoy, most divers cross back over to the reef line and head west along the top of the wall. Once they reach a 15-foot (4.5-meter) cliff, they generally turn back around and start heading back toward the buoy to end the dive.

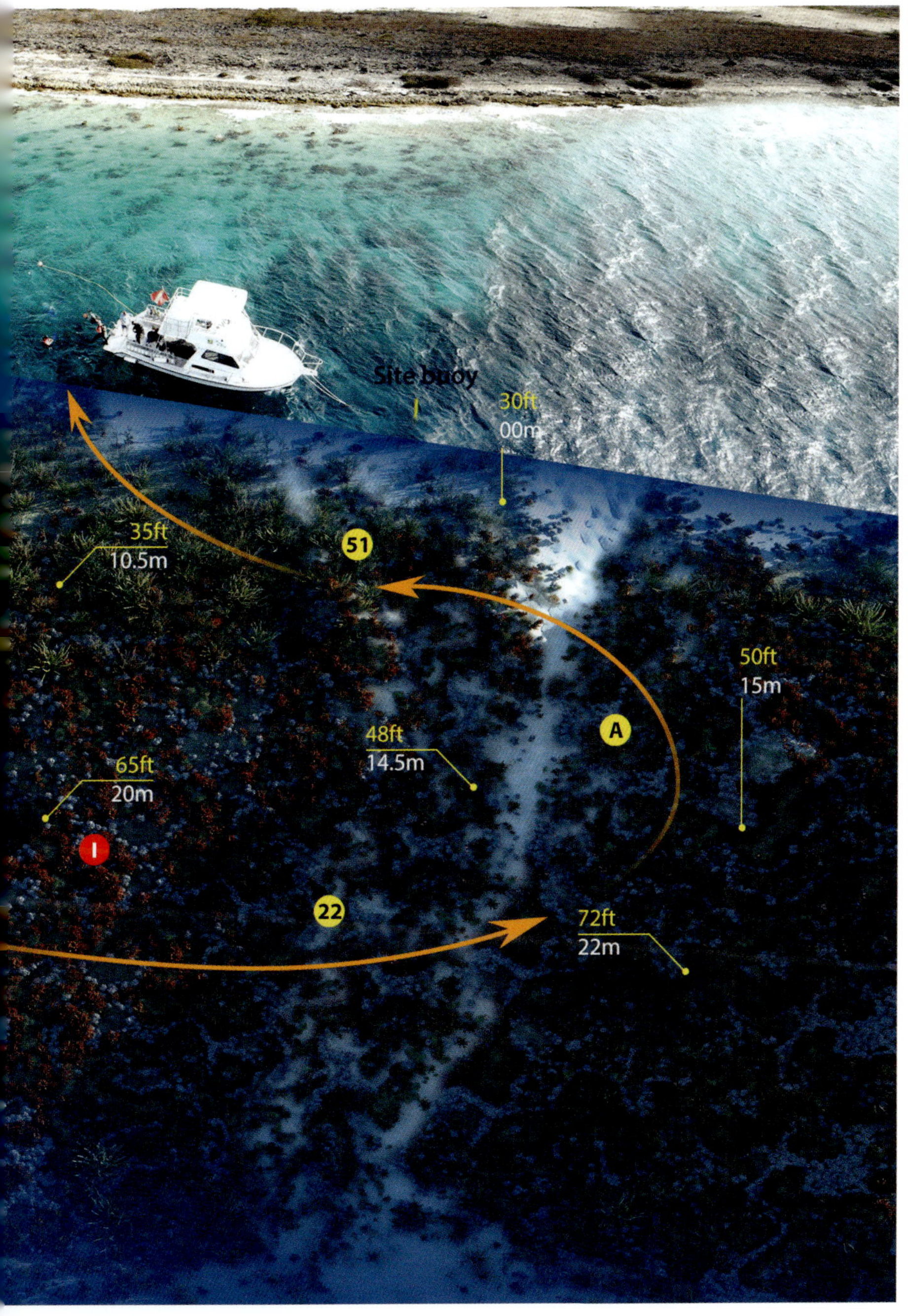
Site buoy
30ft
00m
35ft
10.5m
51
50ft
15m
A
48ft
14.5m
65ft
20m
22
72ft
22m

Hands Off

Difficulty
Current
Depth
Reef
Fauna

Access about 14 mins from Kralendijk

Level Open Water

Location

Klein Bonaire
GPS: 12°9′0.04″N, 68°19′25.50″W

Getting there

Hands Off is a dive site located along the southern coast of Klein Bonaire, close to its western corner and nestled between South Bay and Forest. The only way to reach this site is by boat, which takes around 14 minutes from Kralendijk. Most local dive centers visit Klein Bonaire on a regular basis, so divers should call ahead to schedule their trip.

Access

Hands Off is suitable for divers and snorkelers of all experience levels, although the currents and waves can be strong at times given the site's location near the corner of the island. A permanent mooring buoy is anchored to the plateau at a depth of around 25 feet (7.5

Hands Off was once part of a scientific study to assess the effects of diving.

SCIENTIFIC INSIGHT

Hands Off got its name from a scientific study that was conducted in Bonaire on the impact of underwater photographers and novice divers on the quality of coral reefs. It was hypothesized that these two groups touch the reef more than experienced divers, and that touching the reef causes damage to fragile corals and sponges. Hands Off was used as a control site where photography and dive training were banned, hence "hands off." It has since been documented in numerous studies that these two groups do indeed touch the reef more than experienced divers and that this action can cause damage. The reasons for touching the reef are mainly due to poor buoyancy control and spatial awareness, both of which can be improved by additional dive training.

meters) along the top of the drop-off, which makes it easy for snorkelers and divers alike to access the site. Visibility is usually excellent at this site.

Description

Hands Off contains some of the more dramatic and complex reef structures along the southern coast of Klein Bonaire. The site features sharp spurs that descend at a steep angle from the shallow plateau down into the depths. Along this stretch of the wall, the reef scallops inwards and outwards as massive spurs project out into the water column. Many of the spurs branch out into smaller spurs at depths of around 80 to 90 feet (24.5 to 27.5 meters).

Many of the channels between the spurs contain sand, which varies the habitat and the species that can be found. Some channels are more distinctly sand channels, while others consist of broad stretches of rubble, sand and reef. In many cases the gap between spurs is the widest at the drop-off and narrows as the deeper ends of the spurs approach one another as the depth reaches the limit of recreational scuba.

As with many of the dive sites along Klein Bonaire, the most interesting areas to explore tend to be at shallower depths, typically around the 50-foot (15-meter) level. Here a mix of hard corals, soft corals and abundant marine life can keep divers busy as they swim along the reef slope. Divers may note the dense stand of staghorn coral at the edge of the plateau along the northeastern edge of the dive site. In deeper water, large orange elephant ear sponges dominate the slope.

In addition to the standard complement of blue and brown chromis schooling above the reef, divers are likely to encounter black durgon, schoolmaster and yellowtail snapper. Black grouper are often seen patrolling the reef slope. Divers should be sure to look up in the water column to spot the large barracuda that are often seen here, along with the rare sighting of a reef shark.

Route

Hands Off can be explored in a standard circular route or as a drift dive, if currents allow. The latter route typically involves drifting westward, starting at Hands Off and crossing into the

adjacent site of Forest, to the west. With either strategy, divers typically do not venture too deep during the initial part of the dive, and then conclude their dive by shallowing to the level of the plateau and exploring the complexity there. The plateau tops out at around 25 feet (7.5 meters) at the drop-off, which means divers can safely explore the coral heads and soft coral forests that cover the top of the plateau while they conduct their safety stop. Snorkelers usually explore the shallow plateau.

25ft
7.5m
82
84
F
50ft
15m
90ft
27.5m

Forest

Access about 15 mins from Kralendijk

Level Open Water

Location
Klein Bonaire
GPS: 12°8′57.29″N, 68°19′34.98″W

Getting there

Forest is a dive site located on the southwestern corner of Klein Bonaire, just inside the sharp point made by the island as it extends from the main island of Bonaire. The only way to reach this site is by boat, which takes around 15 minutes from Kralendijk. Most local dive centers visit Klein Bonaire on a regular basis, so divers should call ahead to schedule their trip.

Access

Forest is suitable for divers and snorkelers of all experience levels, although the currents and waves can be strong at times given the site's location close to an area that juts out from the island. The mooring buoy is anchored to the plateau at a depth of around 25 feet (7.5 meters) along the top of the drop-off, which makes it easy for both divers and snorkelers to access the site. Visibility is usually exceptional at this site.

Description

Forest is very similar to the adjacent site of Hands Off, which is located immediately to the northeast. Large spurs extend from the wall, descending from the sand and coral-covered plateau at a depth of 25 feet (7.5 meters) to the bottom edge of the reef. The tops of the spurs are covered in a mix of hard and soft corals and sponges, which eventually give way to hard corals and larger barrel sponges at greater depth.

Forest is known for its dense cover of soft corals.

The reef located directly seaward of the buoy features a dense area of yellow pencil coral and drops quite sharply in the form of a small wall from 28 feet (8.5 meters) to approximately 50 feet (15 meters). Large spurs bracket this small wall, with the spur to the southwest featuring a shoulder plateau at a depth of around 60 feet (18 meters). Similar shoulders can be found on many of the spurs up and down this stretch of reef wall, varying in depth but usually around the 60-foot (18-meter) mark. These plateaus offer divers a useful way to maintain a depth profile that will allow them to see the most interesting features and creatures.

To the southwest, the distinct spurs give way to a more uniform slope as the reef starts to wrap around the corner of Klein Bonaire. Here, the plateau shallows just 15 feet (4.5 meters) featuring a more rubble-dominated slope for the first 10 to 15 feet (3 to 4.5 meters). The transition from spurs to slope offers a useful indication of where to turn and head back to the boat.

The reef slope along the core of the site is dominated by large orange elephant ear sponges, encrusting corals and small star coral heads, along with some tube sponges, soft corals and fire coral. The plateau above is covered in stands of gorgonians and other soft corals as well as pencil coral. Multiple large and well-defined sand patches pepper the plateau, providing interesting habitat for both divers and snorkelers to explore.

John A. Anderson/Shutterstock ©

Large schools of brown chromis can be seen in the water column above this reef, often mixed in with juvenile creole wrasses. Black durgons and bar jacks are also common here, as are mahogany snapper and yellowtail snapper. Large barracuda are often seen patrolling the water, while French angelfish, stoplight parrotfish and foureye butterflyfish swim around the coral heads.

Route

Divers often explore Forest in a circular pattern, beginning and ending at the mooring buoy. Alternatively, Forest can be explored as a drift dive, sometimes starting at the adjacent site of Hands Off, if the current is particularly strong. As with most other dive sites along the southern coast

of Klein Bonaire, the most interesting areas to explore are above a depth of 60 feet (18 meters). Most divers conclude their dive by conducting an extended safety stop on the sandy plateau, making their way back to the buoy. Snorkelers often stick to the shallow plateau at this site, which has plenty to explore and has great visibility.

8
21
50ft
15m
57
87ft
26.5m

Carl's Hill

Difficulty ●○○
Current ●●○
Depth ●●○
Reef ★★☆
Fauna ★★☆

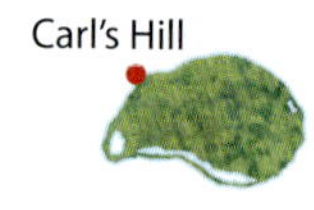

Access about 17 mins from Kralendijk

Level Open Water

Location
Klein Bonaire
GPS: 12°9′51.31″N, 68°19′23.71″W

Getting there

Carl's Hill is located in the northwestern corner of Klein Bonaire, at the point where the island's coastline forms a small point that sticks out into the ocean. The only way to reach this site is by boat, which takes around 17 minutes from Kralendijk. Most local dive centers visit Klein Bonaire on a regular basis, so divers should call ahead to schedule their trip.

Access

Carl's Hill is suitable for divers and snorkelers of all experience levels, although the current can sometimes be strong here as the site juts out in a point from the rest of the island, known as Punt P'Abou, which is an alternate name occasionally used for this dive site. The shallower water is generally better protected, but divers on the wall may benefit from experience when the current is strong. There is a permanent buoy anchored to the reef at a depth of 25 feet (7.5 meters) in the southwestern part of the site, which provides easy access to both the wall and the shallow plateau. As the current generally moves from east to west at this site, divers who enter the water at the mooring are usually swimming into the current and drifting back to the boat at the end of the dive. Visibility is usually good at this site.

Description

Carl's Hill is named after dive travel pioneer and underwater photographer Carl Roessler, who lived and worked in Bonaire and Curacao during the early days of diving in the 1960s. The central feature of Carl's Hill is a shear wall or cliff that rises from the reef slope, directly out from the angled point created by the shoreline and just north of the mooring buoy. At its deepest point, the slightly undercut wall reaches 66 feet (20 meters) and rises to around 28 feet (8.5 meters) at its shallowest point. The current can be strong at this site as it curls around the wall, yet divers might not notice it until they round this feature and are exposed to the full force of the current.

Parts of Carl's Hill are ideal for both divers and snorkelers.

The top of the wall is dominated by soft corals. This area is great for snorkeling but also ideal for divers looking to complete their safety stop while searching for cryptic species hidden within the branches of the corals, such as filefish, trumpetfish and seahorses. The base of the wall meets the top of a narrow groove or sand channel that ends at a small ledge at a depth of 100 feet (30.5 meters). From there, the sand channel continues down the slope into the depths.

Immediately to the south of the wall sits a broad spur that features a second sand channel on its far side. These twin channels can help divers as they navigate from the base of the mooring buoy across to the wall. The reef slope extends to either side of the wall at a relatively steep angle with broad spurs providing some complexity to the terrain. The spurs are broken up by the occasional sand channel, but do not offer the same level of complexity as is found in the vicinity of the cliff.

In the northeast area of the cliff divers can find a pillar coral sitting near the top of the wall, at a depth of about 25 feet (7.5 meters). Divers may also see fairy basslets on the wall, along with schools of creole wrasses, which often feed in the water column adjacent to the cliff, and the occasional barracuda. Porcupinefish are commonly seen here, as are foureye and longsnout butterflyfish.

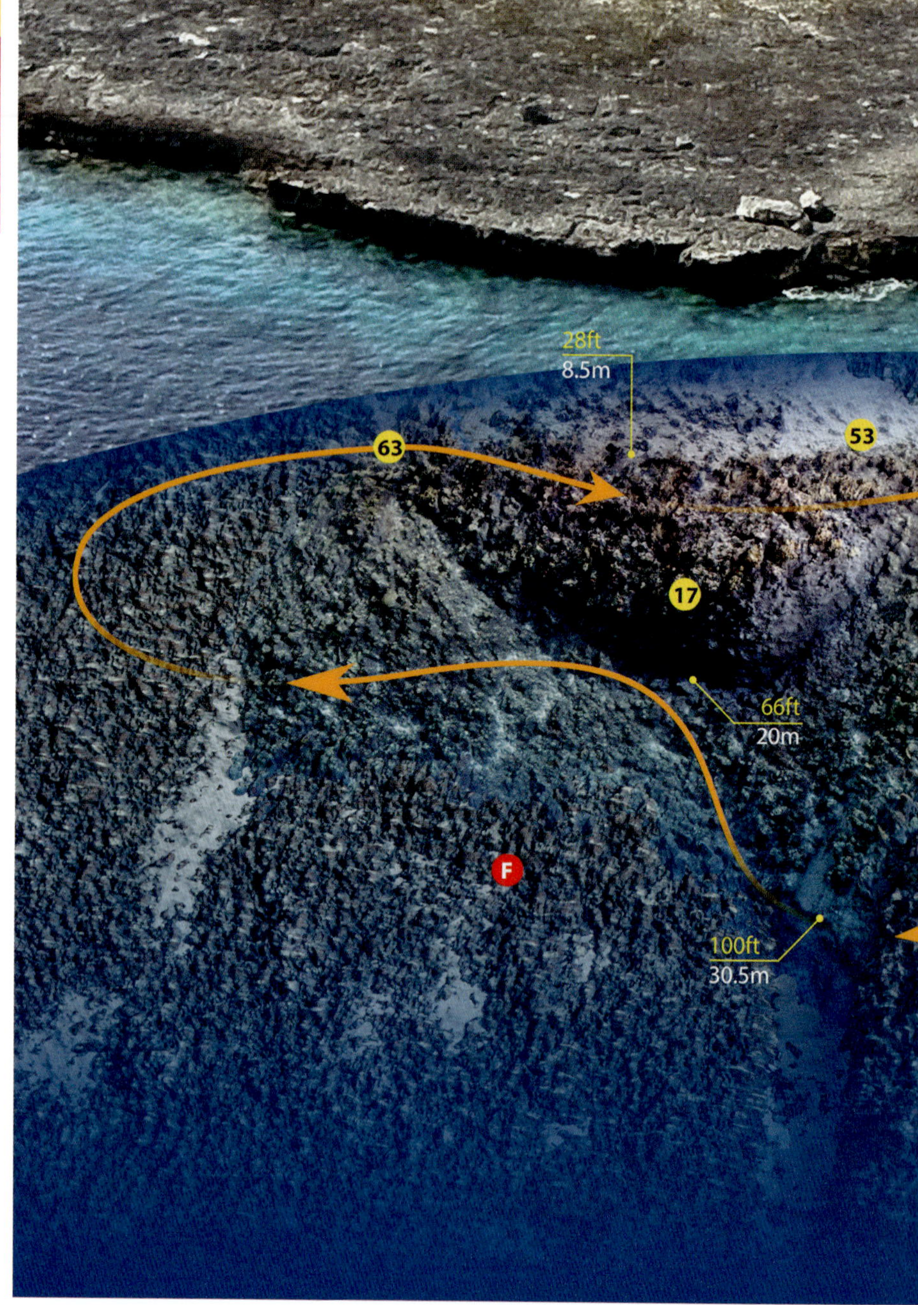

Route

Divers typically begin their dive exploring the wall itself. The structure is large enough to allow numerous divers to inspect the habitat at the same time, including the undercut area at the base. While the focus of Carl's Hill is definitely the striking cliff, divers can also choose to explore the reef slope beyond the wall in either direction, generally heading into the prevailing current to start. Snorkelers often explore the upper area of the cliff and the shallow plateau, which has great visibility.

CARL'S HILL

Knife

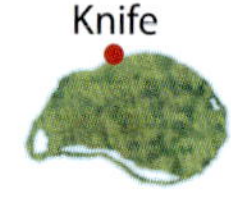

Access about 13 mins from Kralendijk

Level Open Water

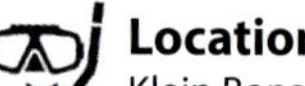

Location
Klein Bonaire
GPS: 12°10'7.20"N, 68°18'48.22"W

Getting there

Knife is located about midway along the north coast of Klein Bonaire. The only way to get there is by boat, which takes around 13 minutes from Kralendijk. Most local dive centers visit Klein Bonaire on a regular basis, so divers should call ahead to schedule their trip.

Access

Knife is suitable for divers and snorkelers of all levels. The plateau at the top of the wall is very wide here and offers snorkelers plenty of reef to explore without needing to venture out into deeper areas of the reef. There is a permanent mooring buoy at a depth of 18 feet (5.5 meters), but most of the plateau is much shallower. There is typically little to no current along this sheltered portion of the island, which makes this site ideal for novice divers and snorkelers. Visibility is usually excellent at this site.

Description

According to some sources, Knife was named by dive legend Captain Don, who was attacked at this site by a "narked" diver wielding a dive knife. Alternatively, the site could be named after the distinct spur that extends from the wall at an angle, resembling a knife, located just east of the mooring buoy. Divers can follow this feature down the reef, before turning west to explore the rest of the site.

The reef at Knife is marked by alternating reef and sand channels. The reef sections are occasionally interrupted by broad spurs that offer some complexity, but nothing quite so dramatic as what is on display at other sites along the southern coast of Klein Bonaire. Even so, there are multiple complex reef structures located along the top of the wall between 20 and 30 feet (6 and 9 meters) that are interesting for divers and snorkelers to explore.

The plateau is also an interesting region for divers and snorkelers to explore. This shallow reef area has a mix of boulder star coral and yellow pencil coral and there are numerous cleaning stations operated by bluehead wrasses and juvenile

Spanish hogfish. The plateau is slightly deeper in the western part of the site where the reef slope features a number of Reef Renewal coral nurseries at a depth of around 30 feet (9 meters). Reef Renewal coral outplant sites are also located at Knife. The slope beyond the coral nurseries becomes gradually steeper and features large orange elephant ear sponges that are scattered across the reef. The reef slope to the east is relatively featureless and is a mix of coral and sand, offering less interesting habitat for divers to explore.

Divers can often find hamlets on the reef, as well as butterflyfish, French angelfish, parrotfish and goatfish. Tiger grouper might occasionally be spotted among the coral heads, while those divers with patience and excellent eyesight may be able to pick out banded coral shrimp and arrow crabs hiding within the reef structure.

The reef at Knife is interrupted by broad spurs containing star coral.

Route

Most divers explore this site following a roughly circular route, heading east initially while descending the central spur, before turning to the west and gradually shallowing. Most of the interesting features to explore at Knife are above 60 feet (18 meters). Most divers leave plenty of air and bottom time to explore along the top of the reef slope and the complex reef plateau with coral mounds and soft corals, which is where snorkelers often focus their attention.

18ft
5.5m
46
33ft
10m
1
58
75ft
23m

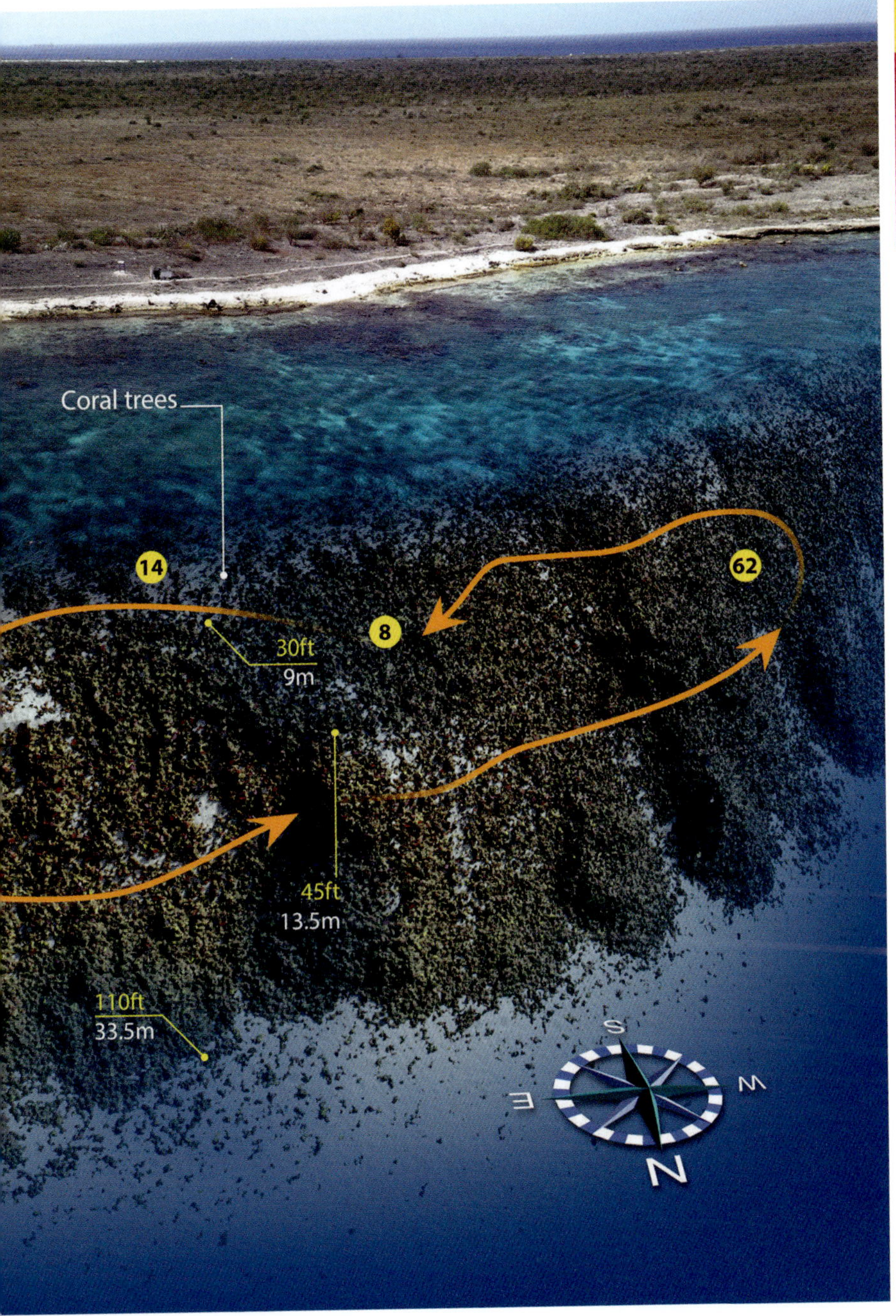
Coral trees
14
8
62
30ft
9m
45ft
13.5m
110ft
33.5m
S
W
E
N

Species

Identifying coral reef organisms is an enjoyable part of any underwater adventure. Not only can divers and snorkelers appreciate the diversity and wonder that surrounds them on a reef, but they will be better able to understand the story that is unfolding right before their eyes.

For example, learn where and when to look for certain species, as well as what they eat, who eats them, how big they get and how long they will live. But more specifically, learn about various behaviors that can be observed on coral reefs, such as why damselfish attack larger creatures, or which creatures form symbiotic relationships and why?

Many times, behavior is an integral part of the identification process. In some cases, understanding how a particular fish behaves,

SAFETY TIP 

The section on dangerous species that follows is intended to provide the information needed to recognize the handful of species that can cause injury. These species should not be considered "active threats," but rather organisms that have the potential to cause harm. Most injuries occur because the organism in question has felt threatened and because a diver or snorkeler has not recognized the warning signs. Engaging in safe and conscientious diving and snorkeling practices, and keeping in mind a few key safety tips, can help avoid having an experience ruined by an unpleasant sting or bite.

Orange elephant ear sponges are found on many of the deeper reefs in Bonaire.

such as whether it is active during the night or day, or whether it is an ambush predator or active forager, can be more useful in determining its identity than its color or shape.

Many reef organisms may appear very similar at first glance, and the wide diversity of species on coral reefs can appear to be a chaotic jumble. But by combining an understanding of animal behavior with some basic identification information, divers and snorkelers can start to tease apart that puzzle and experience the wonder of the coral reef.

John A. Anderson/Shutterstock ©

Horse-eye jacks often school over Bonaire's reefs. Luiz Felipe V. Puntel/Shutterstock ©

The information provided in this guidebook represents the most up-to-date scientific knowledge available at the time of publication. It covers some of the most common reef species observed during diving and snorkeling in Bonaire. However, it should be noted that coral reef ecologists continue to discover new information about species, their behaviors and their interactions. Later editions of this book may contain modifications that reflect new knowledge.

The following pages are divided into three sections, featuring information about sea turtles, which have a rather unique life history; dangerous species, including details on the kind of threat they pose and how to treat injuries caused by them; and finally, a general species section that helps divers and snorkelers identify and learn about the most common species found at the Bonaire sites featured in this guide.

Sea turtle identification

GREEN TURTLE
CHELONIA MYDAS

Maximum size: 4ft (1.4m)
Longevity: Up to 75 years
Habitat: Seagrass beds, reefs
Diet: Jellyfish and crustaceans when young, and algae and seagrass as adults
Sightings: Juveniles and sub-adults common, while adults are present during nesting season
Behavior: Green turtles can be found grazing on vegetation in shallow water or cruising the reef. Most green turtles migrate short distances along the coast to reach nesting beaches, but some may migrate up to 1,300 miles (2,100 kilometers) to reach nesting beaches.
Predators (adults): Tiger sharks, orcas (killer whales)

B

HAWKSBILL SEA TURTLE
ERETMOCHELYS IMBRICATA

Maximum size: 3ft (0.9m)
Longevity: Beyond 20 years
Habitat: Reefs
Diet: Sponges, tunicates, squid, shrimp
Sightings: Juveniles and sub-adults common, while adults are present during nesting season
Behavior: Hawksbills can be found feeding throughout the day or resting with their bodies wedged into reef cracks and crevices. Some hawksbills don't migrate at all, while others migrate over thousands of miles / kilometers.
Predators (adults): Tiger sharks, orcas (killer whales)

LOGGERHEAD SEA TURTLE
CARETTA CARETTA

Maximum size: 3.5ft (1.1m)
Longevity: Up to 60 years
Habitat: Reefs and open ocean
Diet: Crabs, shrimp, jellyfish, vegetation
Sightings: Almost always of adults
Behavior: Loggerheads are occasionally found in the open ocean, but regularly move inshore to feed on reef invertebrates. Loggerhead sea turtles can migrate for thousands of miles / kilometers to reach new feeding grounds and return to the same nesting beaches.
Predators (adults): Tiger sharks, orcas (killer whales)

SEA TURTLE CONSERVATION STATUS: ENDANGERED

All species of sea turtles are endangered and many human activities contribute to their decline:

- Turtles are hunted in many parts of the world, targeting their meat and eggs for food, and their shells to make jewelry, eyeglass frames, and curios. Many others drown in fishing nets intended for shrimp or fish, or are struck and killed by passing boats.
- Turtles eat and choke on plastic and other trash, while pollution increases the frequency of turtle disease.
- Coastal development is rapidly reducing the number of active nesting beaches.

Juvenile sea turtles are a common sight in Bonaire. Tropicdreams/Shutterstock ©

Sea Turtle Conservation Bonaire

All three of the turtle species in Bonaire nest on the island's beaches—with the bulk of nesting activity taking place on the northeast coast of Klein Bonaire. Hawksbills account for nearly half of all nests, but divers and snorkelers will still see plenty of loggerheads and green sea turtles in the water. The STCB started protecting Bonaire's turtles in 1991. In addition to a tagging program, the non-profit organization also leads nesting patrols as part of an outreach effort. For those interested in learning more, supporting the STCB or even joining them for a patrol, visit: **Bonaireturtles.org**

If you see a turtle in trouble, call the STCB hotline: +599-780-0433

ECO TIP

Sea turtles need our help to survive and thrive alongside our coastal communities. Consider the following tips:

LIGHTS OUT
Turn out lights visible from the beach to avoid disorienting nesting turtles and hatchlings.

DON'T LITTER
Plastic cups, bags, and other trash can kill turtles when they mistake them for food.

DON'T DISTURB
Turtles you see on the beach or in the water, whether nesting, feeding or hatching, should be left alone and observed from a distance—without flashlights.

PLEASE DON'T FEED
Human food can make sea turtles sick and can leave them vulnerable to capture.

VOLUNTEER
Support your local turtle conservation programs, including participating in beach cleanups.

Sea turtle ecology

Nesting

Females crawl onto the beach at night (or during the day in the case of Kemp's ridleys) and dig a shallow nest. They lay up to 200 small white eggs before covering the nest and returning to the sea. The eggs incubate for 45 to 70 days, depending on the species.

Mating

Most sea turtles reproduce in the warm summer months except for the leatherback, whose mating season spans fall and winter. Many species migrate great distances to return to their customary nesting beach. Courtship and mating occur in the shallow waters offshore.

Stephan Kerkhofs /Shutterstock ©

Arnunthorn R /Shutterstock ©

4

Adulthood

In adulthood, some sea turtle species return to coastal waters where coral reefs and nearshore waters provide plenty of food and protection from predators.

UWPhotog /Shutterstock ©

David Evison/Shutterstock ©

David Evison/Shutterstock ©

Omaly Darcia/Shutterstock ©

Hatching
When they hatch, hundreds of tiny turtles dig their way out of the nest and head away from the darkness of land, and toward the light reflecting off the sea. As many as 90 percent are eaten by predators as eggs or as hatchlings within the first few hours of their lives.

Juvenile stage
Young turtles drift through the open ocean for years, often associating with floating sargassum (seaweed) mats. They feed on plankton and small jellyfish. Little is known about this stage of their lives.

Laura Dinraths /Shutterstock ©

Dangerous species

MEDICAL DISCLAIMER

The treatment advice contained in this book is meant for informational purposes only and is not intended to be a substitute for professional medical advice, either in terms of diagnosis or treatment. Always seek the advice of your physician or other qualified health provider if you are injured by a marine organism. Never disregard professional medical advice or delay seeking it because of something you have read in this book.

CARIBBEAN REEF SHARK
CARCHARHINUS PEREZII

Maximum size: 10ft (3m)
Longevity: Unknown, but possibly 20 years or more
Typical depth: 3–213ft (1–65m)
Behavior: The Caribbean reef shark is the most common shark species encountered on Caribbean coral reefs. They tend to inhabit drop-offs and the seaward edges of reefs, where they feed on most reef fish species, as well as stingrays and eagle rays.
Predators: Larger shark species, such as bull and tiger sharks

WARNING: Caribbean reef sharks rarely attack humans, but they have been known to cause injury if threatened or cornered. Warning signs of an attack include head swings, exaggerated swimming, back arching and lowered pectoral fins. Attacks usually result in biting or raking with the teeth, which can cause deep lacerations. There have been numerous documented attacks on humans by Caribbean reef sharks but no known fatalities.

TREATMENT: Exit the water as soon as possible. Rinse the bite with soap and water, and apply pressure to control bleeding. Shark attacks often result in shock, so keep the patient warm, calm and shaded. Elevate the feet unless that may cause additional injury. Do not provide anything to eat or drink. Seek medical attention as soon as possible, since even minor bites require cleaning and suturing.

SOUTHERN STINGRAY
DASYATIS AMERICANA

Maximum size: 7ft (2m) disk diameter, 300lbs (136kg)
Longevity: Unknown, but probably over 10 years
Typical depth: 0–170ft (0–53m)
Behavior: Stingrays are most active at night when they hunt for hard-shelled prey such as snails, crabs, lobsters and occasionally fish. During the day, they are often found buried up to their eyes in sand.
Predators: Sharks and large grouper

WARNING: Stingrays have a serrated venomous spine at the base of their tail that they use for defense. The area around a puncture wound from this spine may become red and swollen, and you may experience muscle cramps, nausea, fever, and chills.

TREATMENT: If you are stung, exit the water immediately. Apply pressure above the wound to reduce bleeding, clean the wound and soak the area with hot water, ideally around 113°F (45°C), to reduce the pain. Apply a dressing and seek medical attention. Antibiotics may be needed to reduce the risk of infection. Stingray injuries can be very painful, often reaching a peak around one hour after the injury and lasting up to two days. But they are rarely fatal unless the injury is to the head, neck, or abdomen.

GREAT BARRACUDA

SPHYRAENA BARRACUDA

Maximum size: 6ft (2m), 110lbs (50kg)
Longevity: Around 20 years
Typical depth: 3–330ft (1–100m)
Behavior: Barracuda are most active during the day, feeding on jacks, grunts, grouper, snapper, squid and even other barracuda. They are often solitary in nature, but occasionally school in large numbers. They have even been documented "herding" fish they plan on consuming. Barracuda use their keen eyesight to hunt for food. They are one of the fastest fish in the ocean, capable of bursts of speed up to 30mph (48kph). Along with their two sets of razor sharp teeth, there are few prey capable of escaping a barracuda once it decides to attack.
Predators: Sharks, tuna, and large grouper

WARNING: Barracuda do not usually attack divers or snorkelers unless provoked. However, evidence suggests they are attracted to objects that glint or shine, such as necklaces, watches or regulators, which they may mistake for prey. The bite of the barracuda is not toxic, but their teeth can produce a severe laceration or deep puncture wound.

TREATMENT: Exit the water as soon as possible and apply pressure to reduce bleeding. The wound should be cleaned and dressed. Medical attention may be necessary for severe bites, including sutures to close the wound and antibiotics to reduce the risk of infection.

SPOTTED SCORPIONFISH

SCORPAENA PLUMIERI

Maximum size: 18in (45cm)
Longevity: Around 15 years
Typical depth: 3–197ft (1–60m)
Behavior: Spotted scorpionfish spend much of their time lying motionless on the seabed, using camouflage to ambush fish and crustaceans. They have a large, expandable mouth capable of creating a vacuum to suck in prey, which they swallow whole.
Predators: Large snapper, sharks, rays, and moray eels

WARNING: Scorpionfish have a dozen venomous dorsal spines for self-defense. The spines can penetrate skin (most commonly when stepped on), injecting a toxin that causes severe pain that can last from several hours to several days. The area around the injury may also swell and become red.

TREATMENT: Exit the water quickly and rinse the affected area with seawater. Remove any spines and use pressure to control any bleeding. Apply the hottest water you can stand to reduce pain, ideally around 113°F (45°C). Let the wound heal uncovered, but antibiotics may be required to avoid infection. The toxin can be painful, but it is not usually fatal. However, seek medical attention if concerned or if symptoms are worse than described.

RED LIONFISH
PTEROIS VOLITANS

H

Maximum size: 15in (38cm)
Longevity: Around 10 years
Typical depth: 7–180ft (2–55m)
Behavior: Red lionfish are originally from the Indo-West Pacific, and are considered an invasive species in the Western Atlantic. They are most active at dusk and during the night when they hunt for fish, shrimp, crabs, and other reef creatures. Lionfish can live without food for up to three months.
Predators: Occasional predation by certain sharks and grouper

WARNING: Lionfish have up to 16 venomous dorsal and anal spines that can deliver a powerful neurotoxin when they puncture skin. Lionfish do not generally attack divers and snorkelers, but may sting in self-defense if you get too close. Divers and snorkelers may feel intense pain after being stung, followed by swelling and redness around the wound.

TREATMENT: Exit the water as soon as possible and remove any pieces of the spines that may remain in the wound. Use pressure to control the bleeding and apply the hottest water you can stand, ideally around 113°F (45°C), to reduce the pain. Some people experience shortness of breath, dizziness and nausea. There have been no known fatalities from a lionfish sting, but there is always a risk of complications for vulnerable individuals, including congestive heart failure. Seeking medical attention is advised. The pain may last anywhere from several hours to several days.

GREEN MORAY EEL
GYMNOTHORAX FUNEBRIS

I

Maximum size: 8ft (2.5m), 65lbs (30kg)
Longevity: Unknown
Typical depth: 3–164ft (1–50m)
Behavior: Green morays are solitary animals that hide in reef cracks and crevices during the day. At night, they prey on fish, octopuses, crustaceans, and even other eels, primarily using smell to hunt as their eyesight is poor.
Predators: Unknown

WARNING: Moray eels have sharp teeth that can produce a painful wound, but thankfully they rarely attack unless provoked. There is evidence that the bite of some morays may contain toxins that increase pain and bleeding, but more research is needed. Although all morays can bite, larger species such as the green moray eel can cause more severe injuries than smaller species.

TREATMENT: Exit the water as soon as possible. Treat the wound by immediately cleaning the affected area with soap and water. Apply pressure to reduce the bleeding, then apply a topical antibiotic before dressing the wound to reduce the risk of infection. Sutures may be required in some cases. If in doubt or if the wound becomes infected, seek medical attention.

JELLYFISH & SIPHONOPHORES

HYDROIDOMEDUSAE & SIPHONOPHORAE

Maximum size: 7ft (2m) with tentacles extending much farther
Longevity: From a few hours to several years
Typical depth: 0–66ft (0–20m)
Behavior: Jellyfish and siphonophores are both types of cnidaria. Jellyfish are individual animals, while siphonophores are colonies of specialized cells called zooids, such as the Portuguese man o' war. They both drift in the water and use stinging cells called nematocysts to capture and paralyze prey, including plankton and small fish.
Predators: Salmon, tuna and some sharks and sea turtle species

WARNING: Jellyfish and siphonophores have stinging cells called nematocysts located on their tentacles that can inject a toxin when brushed against bare skin. Depending on the species, jellyfish toxin can cause mild tingling to intense pain, and can be fatal in some rare cases. The contact site may also become red and blistered. Even dead jellyfish on the beach can sting, so avoid touching them.

TREATMENT: Exit the water as quickly as possible, watching out for other jellyfish. Rinse the affected area with seawater to remove any pieces of tentacle on the skin. Do not rinse with fresh water, which can trigger any remaining nematocysts to sting. The best treatment for jellyfish stings may depend on the species, but most can be treated by rinsing the affected area with vinegar or creating a paste using baking soda and seawater. The papain enzyme found in meat tenderizer and papaya can also help. Consider seeking medical attention.

FIRE CORAL

MILLEPORIDAE

Maximum size: 3ft (1m)
Longevity: Unknown, but likely decades
Typical depth: 3–130ft (1–40m)
Behavior: Several fire coral species occur in the Caribbean, attaching to the reef substrate and growing in branching, blade and encrusting forms. Fire corals are hydroids with a hard skeleton, and are more closely related to jellyfish than corals. They get their energy from photosynthetic zooxanthellae in their tissues, but also from feeding on plankton.
Predators: Fireworms, certain nudibranchs, and filefish

WARNING: Microscopic fire coral polyps are located throughout the surface of the hard skeleton. Each polyp has hair-like tentacles that are covered in stinging cells called nematocysts, which they use to paralyze their tiny prey. Fire corals cause a lingering, burning sensation when they contact bare skin. A rash or blistering may occur in some individuals and may last several days, but is not usually dangerous.

TREATMENT: Exit the water as soon as possible and rinse the affected area with vinegar or alcohol to inactivate the fire coral toxin. Do not rinse with fresh water, which can increase the pain by causing untriggered nematocysts to discharge into the skin. Apply hydrocortisone cream to the area once dry. The papain enzyme found in meat tenderizer and papaya can also reduce swelling, pain, and itching.

FRENCH ANGELFISH 1
POMACANTHUS PARU

Maximum size: 24in (60cm)
Longevity: Up to 15 years
Typical depth: 10–330ft (3–100m)
Behavior: French angelfish dine primarily on sponges, but may also feed on gorgonians and algae. Juveniles often act as cleaners, eating the parasites from other reef fish. At dusk, French angelfish find shelter from nocturnal predators in reef cracks and crevices.
Predators: Large grouper and sharks

QUEEN ANGELFISH 2
HOLACANTHUS CILIARIS

Maximum size: 18in (45cm)
Longevity: Up to 15 years
Typical depth: 3–230ft (1–70m)
Behavior: Queen angelfish are often found swimming gracefully between sea fans, sea whips and corals, alone or in pairs. They feed almost exclusively on sponges, but have been known to snack on algae and tunicates as well. Young Queen angelfish also clean parasites off larger fish.
Predators: Large grouper and sharks

ROCK BEAUTY 3
HOLACANTHUS TRICOLOR

Maximum size: 14in (35cm)
Longevity: Up to 20 years (in captivity)
Typical depth: 10–115ft (3–35m)
Behavior: Adult rock beauties are often found on rock jetties, rocky reefs and rich coral areas, while juveniles tend to be found near fire corals. These angelfish are not picky eaters and will feed on tunicates, sponges, zoanthids and algae.
Predators: Grouper, snapper, and sharks

BLUE TANG 4
ACANTHURUS COERULEUS

Maximum size: 16in (40cm)
Longevity: Around 20 years
Typical depth: 3–130ft (1–40m)
Behavior: Blue tangs are often found grazing on algae during the day, either individually or as part of large schools that may also contain surgeonfish, doctorfish, goatfish and parrotfish. At dusk, they settle into a reef crack or crevice to hide for the night.
Predators: Grouper, snapper, jacks, and barracuda

DOCTORFISH 5
ACANTHURUS CHIRURGUS

Maximum size: 15.5in (39cm)
Longevity: Up to 30 years
Typical depth: 6–213ft (2–65m)
Behavior: Doctorfish can be found in shallow, inshore reef habitats and rocky areas. They forage on benthic algae, including the thin algal mat covering sandy bottoms. They generally swim together in loose schools, often with ocean surgeonfish and blue tangs. They have sharp spines near their tail fin that they can use in defense against predators.
Predators: Large carnivorous fish, including tuna

OCEAN SURGEONFISH 6
ACANTHURUS BAHIANUS

Maximum size: 15in (38cm)
Longevity: Up to 32 years
Typical depth: 6–130ft (2–40m)
Behavior: Adult surgeonfish often form large schools to graze on benthic algae and seagrasses in shallow coral reefs and inshore rocky areas. Juveniles rarely school, sheltering instead in the back reef. Researchers have observed spawning aggregations of up to 20,000 individuals in the winter months off of Puerto Rico.
Predators: Sharks, grouper, barracuda, and snapper

BANDED BUTTERFLYFISH 7
CHAETODON STRIATUS

Maximum size: 6in (16cm)
Longevity: Unknown, but probably around 10 years
Typical depth: 10–60ft (3–20m)
Behavior: Banded butterflyfish are most active during the day when they search the reef for food, which includes polychaete worms, zoanthids, anemones and fish eggs. Banded butterflyfish are often found in monogamous pairs and they defend a joint territory together with their mate.
Predators: Moray eels and large carnivorous fish

FOUREYE BUTTERFLYFISH 8
CHAETODON CAPISTRATUS

Maximum size: 6in (15cm)
Longevity: Around 8 years
Typical depth: 6–65ft (2–20m)
Behavior: Foureye butterflyfish are active during the day when they feed on small invertebrates. Their pointed mouth allows them to pull prey from small crevices. They are often found in pairs, and males and females bond early in life and form long-lasting monogamous pairs.
Predators: Barracuda, grouper, snapper, and moray eels

BLUE CHROMIS
CHROMIS CYANEA

Maximum size: 5in (12cm)
Longevity: Unknown, possibly 5 years
Typical depth: 10–70ft (3–20m)
Behavior: Blue chromis gather in schools above the reef to feed on small plankton and jellyfish during the day. They hide in reef crevices at night. Territorial males defend egg nests in the spring and summer.
Predators: Trumpetfish, grouper, and snapper

BROWN CHROMIS
CHROMIS MULTILINEATA

Maximum size: 8in (20cm)
Longevity: Unknown, possibly 5 years
Typical depth: 3–300ft (1–91m)
Behavior: Brown chromis forage in medium-sized schools above the coral reef, feasting on plankton, mainly copepods. They are frequently seen schooling with blue chromis during the day, although their more territorial congeneric tends to chase them out from hiding places in the reef at night.
Predators: Trumpetfish, grouper, and snapper

SERGEANT MAJOR
ABUDEFDUF SAXATILIS

Maximum size: 9in (23cm)
Longevity: Unknown, possibly 5 years
Typical depth: 3–33ft (1–10m)
Behavior: Sergeant majors get their name from their telltale black bars that resemble military stripes. They are usually found in shallow water, typically along the tops of reefs, and often form large feeding schools of up to a few hundred individuals.
Predators: Grouper and jacks

YELLOWHEAD JAWFISH
OPISTOGNATHUS AURIFRONS

Maximum size: 4in (10cm)
Longevity: Unknown, possibly up to 5 years
Typical depth: 10–131ft (3–40m)
Behavior: Jawfish live in burrows in the sediment that they line with stones and bits of crushed shell and coral. Active during the day, they often hover over their burrow and feed on zooplankton. They rarely move far from their burrow and often retreat tail-first when threatened.
Predators: Snapper, grouper, and lionfish

ROSY RAZORFISH 13
XYRICHTYS MARTINICENSIS

Maximum size: 6in (15cm)
Longevity: Around 3 years
Typical depth: 7–69ft (2–21m)
Behavior: Rosy razorfish are commonly found in open sandy areas near coral reefs. They are active during the day as they feed on small sand-dwelling invertebrates such as crabs, shrimp and worms. Large males often defend a harem of females within their territory.
Predators: Grouper, snapper, barracuda, and dolphins

BLUEHEAD WRASSE 14
THALASSOMA BIFASCIATUM

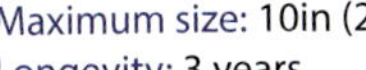

Maximum size: 10in (25cm)
Longevity: 3 years
Typical depth: 0–131ft (0–40m)
Behavior: Bluehead wrasses can be found on reefs, near inshore bays and over seagrass beds feeding on zooplankton, small benthic animals and even parasites on other fish. They start life as female but eventually become males, gaining an unmistakable bright blue head in their terminal phase.
Predators: Grouper, trumpetfish, and soapfish

YELLOWHEAD WRASSE 15
HALICHOERES GARNOTI

Maximum size: 7in (19cm)
Longevity: Unknown, possibly between 3 and 5 years
Typical depth: 3–100ft (1–30m)
Behavior: Yellowhead wrasses are mainly found near coral reefs and rocky ledges. Adults feed on invertebrates while juveniles sometimes clean parasites off larger fish. Yellowhead wrasses are protogynous hermaphrodites, meaning they start life as female but become males at around 3in (7cm) in size.
Predators: Mackerel, grouper, and snapper

PUDDINGWIFE 16
HALICHOERES RADIATUS

Maximum size: 20in (51cm)
Longevity: 10 years or more
Typical depth: 6–180ft (2–55m)
Behavior: Puddingwives are commonly found on reefs, feeding on molluscs, sea urchins, crustaceans and brittle stars. Juveniles typically inhabit shallow coral reefs while adults also frequent deeper reefs. As with other wrasses, adults change color dramatically as they grow and reach terminal phase.
Predators: Reef sharks, greater amberjacks, and snapper

CREOLE WRASSE
CLEPTICUS PARRAE

17

Maximum size: 12in (30cm)
Longevity: Unknown, but probably around 10 years
Typical depth: 26–328ft (8–100m)
Behavior: Creole wrasses are often found schooling in large numbers above bank reefs, wrecks and on the seaward slopes of reefs. They are most active during the day, when feeding on plankton and small jellyfish. At night, they retreat into reef crevices to sleep.
Predators: Moray eels, grouper, and barracuda

SPANISH HOGFISH
BODIANUS RUFUS

18

Maximum size: 16in (40cm)
Longevity: Unknown
Typical depth: 10–230ft (3–70m)
Behavior: Adult Spanish hogfish feed on bottom-dwelling invertebrates, such as brittlestars, crustaceans and sea urchins. Juveniles set up cleaning stations to pick parasites off larger fish. Male hogfish (who start out life as a female) typically manage a harem of three to 12 smaller females.
Predators: Sharks, mackerel, and snapper

PRINCESS PARROTFISH
SCARUS TAENIOPTERUS

19

Max size: 14in (35cm)
Longevity: Unknown, but probably less than 5 years
Typical depth: 3–82ft (1–25m)
Behavior: Princess parrotfish form large schools during the day to feed on plants, algae, sponges and seagrass. Juveniles are more closely associated with seagrass beds. They start out life as female, but can transition to male if no other large breeding males are around.
Predators: Sharks, grouper, jacks, and moray eels

QUEEN PARROTFISH
SCARUS VETULA

20

Maximum size: 24in (61cm)
Longevity: Up to 20 years
Typical depth: 10–80ft (3–25m)
Behavior: During the day, Queen parrotfish feed by scraping algae off rocks and dead coral using their tough, parrot-like beak. At night, Queen parrotfish secrete a membrane of mucus from a gland at the base of the gills which surrounds them like a bubble and masks their scent from nocturnal predators.
Predators: Grouper, eels, and sharks

STOPLIGHT PARROTFISH
SPARISOMA VIRIDE

21

Maximum size: 25in (64cm)
Longevity: Around 9 years
Typical depth: 3–164ft (1–50m)
Behavior: Stoplight parrotfish are only active during the day. Their strong beak-like jaws scrape soft algae off the hard coral. They ingest some coral in the process, grinding it up with the help of specialized teeth in their throats and excreting it as coral sand.
Predators: Sharks, barracuda, grouper, snapper, jacks, and moray eels

BLUE PARROTFISH
SCARUS COERULEUS

Maximum size: 4ft (1.2m)
Longevity: About 10 years
Typical depth: 10–82ft (3–25m)
Behavior: The blue parrotfish is easily identified by its prominent bulging snout and color, as it is the only blue parrotfish. It feeds during the day by biting off pieces of the reef in order to consume plants, algae and small organisms. This species can form large schools, particularly during spawning.
Predators: Large grouper, snapper, moray eels, and barracuda

MIDNIGHT PARROTFISH
SCARUS COELESTINUS

Maximum size: 30in (77cm)
Longevity: Unknown, but possibly up to 10 years
Typical depth: 16–264ft (5–75m)
Behavior: Midnight parrotfish are among the larger parrotfish species in the Caribbean, and are recognizable for their dark blue-black coloration. They can often be spotted schooling with surgeonfish as they munch on algae-encrusted coral. They are typically associated with coral reefs and sport the telltale beak of all parrotfish.
Predators: Sharks, mackerel, and jacks

RAINBOW PARROTFISH
SCARUS GUACAMAIA

Maximum size: 4ft (1.2m)
Longevity: Around 10 years
Typical depth: 10–82ft (3–25m)
Behavior: The rainbow parrotfish is the largest herbivorous reef fish in the Caribbean. During the day, it feeds by biting off pieces of the reef in order to consume the plants, algae and small organisms contained within. Schooling may occur in areas where density is high.
Predators: Large grouper, snapper, moray eels, sharks, and barracuda

BLACK MARGATE

ANISOTREMUS SURINAMENSIS

Maximum size: 30in (76cm), 13lbs (6kg)
Longevity: Unknown
Typical depth: 0–66ft (0–20m)
Behavior: Black margates can be found alone or in small groups. They are nocturnal, feeding on benthic crustaceans, molluscs, smaller fish and long-spined sea urchins at night. During the day, they can often be found under ledges and sheltering in caves or wrecks.
Predators: Sharks

CAESAR GRUNT

HAEMULON CARBONARIUM

26

Max size: 16in (40cm)
Longevity: Unknown, but possibly up to 10 years
Typical depth: 10–82ft (3–25m)
Behavior: Caesar grunts are often found in schools near artificial reefs and over rocky reefs. Like most grunts, they are nocturnal feeders, munching on polychaetes, gastropods and small crustaceans. During the day, they form loose schools under overhangs. Unlike other grunts, however, juveniles settle on shallow reefs and not near mangroves or seagrass beds.
Predators: Sharks, grouper, jacks, and moray eels

FRENCH GRUNT

HAEMULON FLAVOLINEATUM

27

Maximum size: 12in (30cm)
Longevity: Unknown, could be up to 12 years
Typical depth: 3–200ft (1–60m)
Behavior: French grunts form large schools on rocky and coral reefs. During the day, adults can often be found resting under ledges and near elkhorn coral. Juveniles spend the day hiding near the shore. French grunts are nocturnal and typically feed on small crustaceans, polychaetes and molluscs.
Predators: Grouper, snapper, and trumpetfish

GREY SNAPPER

LUTJANUS GRISEUS

Maximum size: 35in (90cm), 44lbs (20kg)
Longevity: Around 20 years
Typical depth: 16–590ft (5–180m)
Behavior: Grey snapper are often found schooling, sometimes in large numbers. They feed mainly at night on a range of organisms, including shrimp, crabs, worms and small fishes, rarely moving far to feed.
Predators: Moray eels, sharks, large grouper, and barracuda

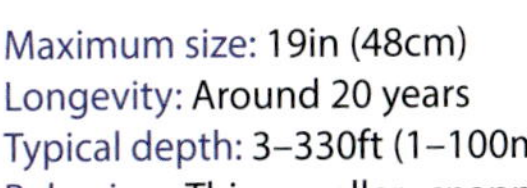

MAHOGANY SNAPPER
LUTJANUS MAHOGONI
29

Maximum size: 19in (48cm)
Longevity: Around 20 years
Typical depth: 3–330ft (1–100m)
Behavior: This smaller snapper forms large schools during the day, typically in shallower waters over coral reefs. At night, mahogany snapper feed on small fish, shrimp, crabs and cephalopods. They frequent warmer waters and only stray into temperate climates during the heat of summer.
Predators: Sharks, mackerel, and other snapper

SCHOOLMASTER SNAPPER
LUTJANUS APODUS
30

Maximum size: 26in (67cm)
Longevity: Up to 42 years
Typical depth: 6–207ft (2–63m)
Behavior: Schoolmaster snapper are found in shallow coastal waters in coral reefs and mangrove habitats—adults are often associated with elkhorn corals while younger individuals sometimes enter brackish waters. They feed on crustaceans and cephalopods, although adults also show a preference for fish once their mouth can open wide enough to catch them.
Predators: Sharks, barracuda, and grouper

CUBERA SNAPPER
LUTJANUS CYANOPTERUS
31

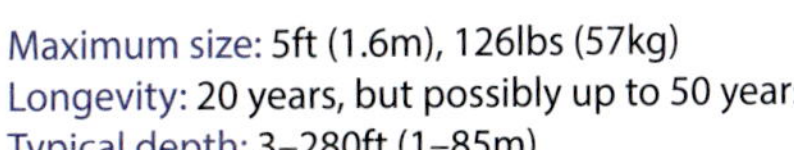

Maximum size: 5ft (1.6m), 126lbs (57kg)
Longevity: 20 years, but possibly up to 50 years
Typical depth: 3–280ft (1–85m)
Behavior: Cubera snapper are the biggest of the Atlantic snapper species. Adults are often seen alone on deeper reefs and wrecks, while juveniles are generally in shallower water near vegetation, including estuaries. Cubera snapper feed on fish as well as crustaceans, such as shrimp, crabs and lobster. Large individuals are rarely removed from the water when caught on fishing lines, due to concerns about ciguatera poisoning.
Predators: Sharks, large grouper, barracuda, and mackerel

YELLOWTAIL SNAPPER
OCYURUS CHRYSURUS
32

Maximum size: 34in (86cm), 9lbs (4kg)
Longevity: Around 13 to 17 years
Typical depth: 3–541ft (1–165m)
Behavior: Yellowtail snapper are typically associated with coral reefs in coastal waters from the U.S. state of Massachusetts, down to the coast of Brazil. They often form schools above reefs and are less commonly seen along the seafloor. They eat plankton and small benthic organisms.
Predators: Sharks, barracuda, mackerel, snapper, and grouper

GLASSEYE SNAPPER

HETEROPRIACANTHUS CRUENTATUS

33

Maximum size: 20in (51cm)
Longevity: Unknown
Typical depth: 10–115ft (3–35m)
Behavior: Glasseye snapper are secretive fish, hiding alone or in small groups in holes and crevices during the day. At night, they exit their shelters to feed on octopuses, pelagic shrimp, crabs, small fishes and polychaete worms. They sometimes form larger schools at dusk.
Predators: Sharks, tuna, grouper, and mahi mahi

GLASSY SWEEPER

PEMPHERIS SCHOMBURGKII

34

Maximum size: 6in (15cm)
Longevity: Unknown
Typical depth: 10–98ft (3–30m)
Behavior: The nocturnal glassy sweeper is a small fish that feeds on zooplankton and small crustaceans in the water above the reef. During the day, it shelters in groups, hiding in reef crevices and caves. Juveniles are nearly transparent—likely the origin of their name.
Predators: Rays and grouper

BLACKBAR SOLDIERFISH

MYRIPRISTIS JACOBUS

35

Maximum size: 10in (25cm)
Longevity: Unknown
Typical depth: 7–115ft (2–35m)
Behavior: Blackbar soldierfish are nocturnal, often hiding in caves and crevices during the day. They congregate around coral and rocky reefs at night to feed on plankton and invertebrates. They most commonly occur on shallow inshore reefs, but can be found at depths of 330ft (100m).
Predators: Snapper, grouper, jacks, and trumpetfish

CLEANING GOBY

ELACATINUS GENIE

36

Maximum size: 2in (4cm)
Longevity: 3 to 5 years
Typical depth: 3–98ft (1–30m)
Behavior: As their name suggests, cleaning gobies clean other reef creatures by removing their parasites. This behavior is a form of symbiosis known as mutualism, where both parties benefit. The client fish get rid of their ectoparasites, while the cleaners get an easy meal.
Predators: Grouper, snapper, and moray eels

REDLIP BLENNY

OPHIOBLENNIUS ATLANTICUS

37

Maximum size: 7in (19cm)
Longevity: Around 2 years
Typical depth: 0–27ft (0–8m)
Behavior: Redlip blennies are common in shallow reef areas with relatively high wave action. Their body shape and modified fins let them "hold on" to the reef. They are herbivorous and territorial, defending a patch of algae during the day and hiding in the reef at night.
Predators: Grouper, snapper, and trumpetfish

SAILFIN BLENNY

EMBLEMARIA PANDIONIS

Maximum size: 2in (6cm)
Longevity: Possibly around 2 years
Typical depth: 3–35ft (1–12m)
Behavior: Sailfin blennies get their name from the large dorsal fin that they can raise over their head like a sail. The fin is larger on males, who use it for territorial and courtship displays. Sailfin blennies live in holes in the reef and coral rubble; they feed on small plankton and invertebrates.
Predators: Many carnivores on the reef, including squid

SPOTTED GOATFISH

PSEUDUPENEUS MACULATUS

Maximum size: 12in (30cm)
Longevity: At least 7 years
Typical depth: 0–115ft (0–35m)
Behavior: Spotted goatfish are most often encountered in shallow water over rocky or sandy habitat near reefs. They feed on bottom-dwelling crabs, shrimp and small fish. Spotted goatfish are easily recognizable by the three dark blotches along their back and the telltale barbels they use to stir up the sand when they hunt.
Predators: Sharks, snapper, and jacks

YELLOW GOATFISH

MULLOIDICHTHYS MARTINICUS

Maximum size: 15in (39cm)
Longevity: Unknown
Typical depth: 0–115ft (0–35m)
Behavior: Yellow goatfish are commonly found swimming in large schools over sandy bottoms. They use their long, sensitive barbels to locate polychaete worms, clams, isopods, amphipods and other crustaceans in the sand. When not feeding, they are often found in groups, sheltering in the reef.
Predators: Sharks, tuna, mahi mahi, grouper, and jacks

LONGLURE FROGFISH

ANTENNARIUS MULTIOCELLATUS

Maximum size: 8in (20cm)
Longevity: Unknown, but probably around 10 years
Typical depth: 0–215ft (0–66m)
Behavior: The longlure frogfish is a bottom-dwelling fish that can change color and texture to blend in with its surroundings. It is an ambush predator, feeding mainly on other fish and crustaceans. Frogfish have one of the fastest attacks in the animal kingdom.
Predators: Moray eels and other frogfish

SAND TILEFISH

MALACANTHUS PLUMIERI

Maximum size: 28in (70cm)
Longevity: Unknown, but potentially as much as 40 years
Typical depth: 33–164ft (10–50m)
Behavior: Sand tilefish build tunnels and mounds in the sand- and rubble-bottomed areas near reefs and seagrass beds. Tunnel entrances can reach 10ft (3m) in diameter and the mounds are built out of the sand, coral rubble and shell fragments found during excavation.
Predators: Sharks and snapper

PEACOCK FLOUNDER

BOTHUS LUNATUS

Maximum size: 18in (46cm)
Longevity: Up to 10 years
Typical depth: 0–66ft (0–20m)
Behavior: Peacock flounders are usually found partially buried in loose sand near coral reefs, mangroves, and seagrass beds. They are the most common flounders around coral reefs, and mainly feed on small fishes, but also crustaceans and small octopuses.
Predators: Sharks and snapper

BROWN GARDEN EEL

HETEROCONGER LONGISSIMUS

Maximum size: 20in (50cm)
Longevity: Unknown
Typical depth: 33–197ft (10–60m)
Behavior: Brown garden eels live in burrows in sandy areas near coral reefs, feeding mainly on plankton that drift by in the current. Individuals rarely leave the safety of their burrows, remaining partially buried with their heads poking out from the sand. They retreat backwards into their burrow when threatened.
Predators: Snake eels and triggerfish

GOLDENTAIL MORAY EEL 45

GYMNOTHORAX MILIARIS

Maximum size: 28in (70cm)
Longevity: Unknown
Typical depth: 0–115ft (0–35m)
Behavior: Goldentail moray eels are common in the Caribbean, living alone in holes and crevices in coral reefs. Unlike other types of morays, goldentails are most active during the day. They feed on fish, molluscs, and crustaceans.
Predators: Grouper

SPOTTED MORAY EEL

GYMNOTHORAX MORINGA

Maximum size: 3.3ft (1m), 6lbs (2.5kg)
Longevity: Around 10 years, but possibly up to 30 years
Typical depth: 0–656ft (0–200m)
Behavior: Spotted moray eels are most active at night, when they hunt for a wide variety of prey, including parrotfish, grunts, trumpetfish, crustaceans, and molluscs. During the day, they are often seen with their head sticking out of a reef hole or crevice.
Predators: Dog snapper and Nassau grouper

SPOTTED DRUM

EQUETUS PUNCTATUS

Maximum size: 11in (27cm)
Longevity: Unknown, but probably around 10 years
Typical depth: 10–98ft (3–30m)
Behavior: Spotted drums are found under ledges, jetties, and near small caves during the day. They are solitary and mostly active at night, when they hunt for crabs, shrimp and worms. Drums can emit a drumming sound when they feel threatened, which is the origin of their name.
Predators: Moray eels, grouper, and barracuda

SCRAWLED FILEFISH

ALUTERUS SCRIPTUS

Maximum size: 43in (110cm), 5.5lbs (2.5kg)
Longevity: Unknown
Typical depth: 10–394ft (3–120m)
Behavior: Scrawled filefish are commonly found on offshore reefs. They are active during the day, feeding on algae, seagrass, hydrozoans, soft corals, and anemones. Juveniles sometimes drift with sargassum mats, which explains how this species is found throughout the tropics, and on many non-tropical reefs.
Predators: Barracuda, mahi mahi, and large tuna

SLENDER FILEFISH

MONACANTHUS TUCKERI

49

Maximum size: 4in (10cm)
Longevity: Unknown
Typical depth: 7–165ft (2–50m)
Behavior: Slender filefish are almost always found hiding among the branches of gorgonians. During the day, they feed on worms, crabs and zooplankton. At night, they wedge themselves into soft coral with their dorsal spine and stomach appendage, sometimes biting down on a coral polyp while sleeping.
Predators: Grouper and barracuda

BLACK DURGON

MELICHTHYS NIGER

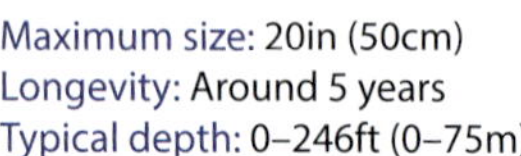

Maximum size: 20in (50cm)
Longevity: Around 5 years
Typical depth: 0–246ft (0–75m)
Behavior: The black durgon is most common on outer bank reef crests, particularly near drop-offs, where they form loose aggregations of as many as 200 individuals. They feed on plant and animal plankton that drift in the water, as well as on reef algae.
Predators: Large grouper, snapper, moray eels, and barracuda

ATLANTIC TRUMPETFISH

AULOSTOMUS MACULATUS

Maximum size: 3ft (1m)
Longevity: Unknown, but likely around 10 years
Typical depth: 6–82ft (2–25m)
Behavior: Trumpetfish are often found camouflaged within the branches of gorgonian corals. They are generally ambush predators that consume small or juvenile reef fish and crustaceans. As known shadow-feeders, they sometimes stalk their prey while swimming alongside other reef fish, using them as cover.
Predators: Grouper, snapper, and moray eels

HONEYCOMB COWFISH

ACANTHOSTRACION POLYGONIUS

Maximum size: 20in (50cm)
Longevity: Unknown
Typical depth: 7–262ft (2–80m)
Behavior: Honeycomb cowfish are protected by hexagon scales that form a rigid carapace over much of their bodies. They are relatively slow and wary, which makes their external armor an essential defense against potential predators. They usually forage alone, feeding on sponges, tunicates, and shrimp.
Predators: Sharks

SMOOTH TRUNKFISH 53
LACTOPHRYS TRIQUETER

Maximum size: 18.5in (47cm)
Longevity: Unknown
Typical depth: 0–164ft (0–50m)
Behavior: Smooth trunkfish are easily recognized by their black mouth and white-spotted, triangular, shape. They are slow, relying on their armor and toxins for protection. They are easily approached and are often seen hunting bottom invertebrates by jetting water from their mouths to shift sand and locate their prey.
Predators: Mahi mahi, cobia, and large carnivorous fish

PORCUPINEFISH 54
DIODON HYSTRIX

Maximum size: 35in (90cm)
Longevity: Up to 10 years
Typical depth: 7–164ft (2–50m)
Behavior: Porcupinefish are solitary nocturnal predators that feed on snails, crabs and sea urchins. During the day, they are often found sheltering in reef caves or crevices. They can inflate their bodies up to twice their normal size by drawing in water or air.
Predators: Dolphins, and large pelagic fish such as sharks and tuna

CARIBBEAN SHARPNOSE PUFFER 55

CANTHIGASTER ROSTRATA

Maximum size: 5in (12cm)
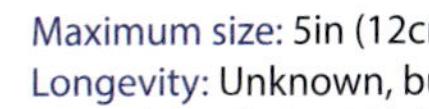
Longevity: Unknown, but possibly up to 10 years
Typical depth: 3–130ft (1–40m)
Behavior: Sharpnose puffers prefer reefs where gorgonian corals are common. They are most active during the day as they search for small reef invertebrates such as crabs, shrimp, worms and snails. They are territorial, so if two individuals happen to be near one another, they may be engaged in defensive displays.
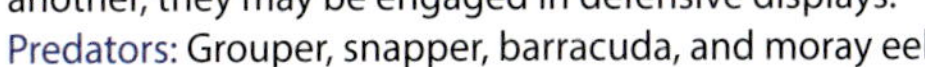
Predators: Grouper, snapper, barracuda, and moray eels

CONEY 56

CEPHALOPHOLIS FULVA

Maximum size: 17in (43cm)
Longevity: 11 years, possibly as much as 19 years
Typical depth: 3–148ft (1–45m)
Behavior: Coneys hide in caves and crevices in the reef during the day, venturing out at night to forage for small reef fish and crustaceans. They are approachable but wary, and the males are territorial. They start out as female, becoming male at around 8in (20cm).
Predators: Sharks, grouper, and snapper

GRAYSBY 57
CEPHALOPHOLIS CRUENTATA

Maximum size: 16in (40cm)
Longevity: Approximately 12 years
Typical depth: 7–561ft (2–170m)
Behavior: Graysbies are found in reef areas that contain caves, crevices or hollow sponges where they hide during the day. At night, they hunt for reef fish, such as chromis, squirrelfish, gobies, and crustaceans. Some individuals hunt alongside moray eels at night.
Predators: Barracuda, sharks, and larger grouper

TIGER GROUPER

MYCTEROPERCA TIGRIS

Maximum size: 3ft (1m)
Longevity: Up to 40 years
Typical depth: 33–130ft (10–40m)
Behavior: A solitary ambush predator, tiger grouper are easily identified by the tiger stripes that run from the dorsal fin down either side of the fish. They vary in color from black, red, tan, and yellow. They feed on a variety of fish, including grunts, parrotfish, croakers, angelfish, and damselfish. A hermaphroditic species, smaller individuals are females while larger fish are males.
Predators: Sharks, large grouper, and mackerel

BLACK GROUPER

MYCTEROPERCA BONACI

Maximum size: 5ft (1.5m), 220lbs (100kg)
Longevity: More than 30 years
Typical depth: 19–246ft (6–75m)
Behavior: Black grouper are relatively common in Bonaire but rarely seen. They tend to shy away from swimmers. Commercially fished in many places, their populations are generally declining as a result. They are solitary except when they congregate to spawn. Adults feed on smaller reef fish such as grunts and snapper.
Predators: Sharks

GREATER SOAPFISH

RYPTICUS SAPONACEUS

Maximum size: 14in (35cm)
Longevity: Up to 6 years
Typical depth: 6–115ft (2–35m)
Behavior: Soapfish are solitary, nocturnal fish that feed on crustaceans and small fish. They are often seen hiding at the base of corals and in crevices in the reef. They secrete a toxic mucus as a deterrent to predators. The mucus covers their bodies and lathers up to a soapy foam when the fish is disturbed, hence the name soapfish.
Predators: Sharks and eagle rays

CREOLE-FISH 61
PARANTHIAS FURCIFER

Maximum size: 12in (30cm)
Longevity: Around 5 years
Typical depth: 26–330ft (8–100m)
Behavior: Creole-fish are typically found on deeper reefs. They can be solitary or form schools above coral reefs and other rocky areas where they feed on zooplankton and crustaceans. Their schools sometimes include damselfish, and they are often skittish, retreating quickly into the reef when startled. Adults vary in color, sometimes appearing bright red, but most often they are grey.
Predators: Sharks, snapper, porgy, and larger grouper

BARRED HAMLET 62
HYPOPLECTRUS PUELLA

Maximum size: 6in (15cm)
Longevity: Unknown
Typical depth: 10–75ft (3–23m)
Behavior: Hamlets are often found on the seaward side of reefs. They feed during the day on crustaceans, particularly shrimp and crabs, and occasionally small fish. Hamlets are fiercely territorial, and are often observed fighting with members of their own species.
Predators: Grouper, snapper, jacks, and barracuda

FAIRY BASSLET

GRAMMA LORETO

Maximum size: 3in (8cm)
Longevity: Around 6 years, but up to 12 years
Typical depth: 3–180ft (1–60m)
Behavior: Fairy basslets are often found on reef walls that are full of caves and ledges. They are most active during the day, feeding mainly on crustaceans—although they occasionally act as a cleaner fish. At night, they retreat into the safety of a familiar reef shelter.
Predators: Snapper, grouper, and moray eels

BERMUDA CHUB

KYPHOSUS SECTATRIX

Maximum size: 30in (76cm), 13lbs (6kg)
Longevity: Unknown
Typical depth: 3–330ft (1–10m)
Behavior: Bermuda chub are a schooling fish found in shallow waters above sandy areas, seagrass beds, and near coral reefs. They feed on benthic algae, but also on small crabs and molluscs. Juveniles often associate with floating sargassum mats, letting them disperse across great distances.
Predators: Sharks, barracuda, snapper, moray eels, and scorpionfish

BAR JACK
CARANX RUBER

65

Maximum size: 23in (59cm)
Longevity: Unknown, possibly up to 30 years
Typical depth: 3–330ft (1–100m)
Behavior: Bar jacks sometimes swim alone, but are usually found schooling in shallow, clear water near coral reefs. They feed on fish, shrimp, and other invertebrates. They are the most abundant species of jack in the Caribbean, and are easily approached by divers.
Predators: Grouper, mackerel, mahi mahi, and large jacks

HORSE-EYE JACK
CARANX LATUS

Maximum size: 3ft (1m), 29lbs (13kg)
Longevity: Unknown
Typical depth: 3–66ft (0–20m)
Behavior: Horse-eye jacks are schooling pelagic fish that frequent the waters above offshore reefs, although juveniles are often seen inshore along sandy beaches. Adults feed on fish, shrimp, and other invertebrates. They often approach divers boldly, but without posing much of a threat.
Predators: Sharks, barracuda, and mahi mahi

RAINBOW RUNNER
ELAGATIS BIPINNULATA

Maximum size: 6ft (1.8m), 102lbs (56kg)
Longevity: Up to 6 years
Typical depth: 6–33ft (2–10m)
Behavior: Rainbow runners are one of the larger members of the jack family, and they are found near the surface of the water over reefs. Though they can get quite large, individuals measuring 2–3ft (60–90cm) are more common. Rainbow runners can form large schools, where they feed on invertebrates and small fish.
Predators: Sharks and tuna

PALOMETA / GREAT POMPANO
TRACHINOTUS GOODEI

Maximum size: 20in (50cm)
Longevity: Unknown
Typical depth: 0–40ft (0–12m)
Behavior: Adult palometa tend to form schools over shallow coral reefs. Juveniles, meanwhile, are more common over sand and rubble habitat. They are most active during the day, feeding on crustaceans, worms, molluscs, and fish.
Predators: Sharks and barracuda

CERO
SCOMBEROMORUS REGALIS

69

Maximum size: 6ft (1.8m)
Longevity: Unknown
Typical depth: 3–66ft (1–20m)
Behavior: A member of the mackerel family, the cero is typically found swimming in open water near coral reefs, occasionally in schools. Ceros eat smaller fish, including herring, anchovies, and silversides, along with squid and shrimp. They are considered a good game fish.
Predators: Sharks, tuna, marlin, king mackerel, and wahoo

TARPON
MEGALOPS ATLANTICUS

70

Maximum size: 8ft (2.5m), 330lbs (150kg)
Longevity: Around 50 years
Typical depth: 3–330ft (0–100m)
Behavior: Tarpon frequent both marine and freshwater ecosystems, from Canada in the north to Brazil in the south. They can feed during both the day and the night on a range of fish and crustaceans. Tarpon have relatively small teeth and tend to swallow their prey whole.
Predators: Sharks and dolphins

SPOTTED EAGLE RAY
AETOBATUS NARINARI

71

Maximum size: 10ft (3m) disc width, 500lbs (230kg)
Longevity: Up to 20 years
Typical depth: 3–260ft (1–80m)
Behavior: Spotted eagle rays are carnivores that specialize in eating hard-shelled prey such as conch, clams, crabs, and lobsters. They sometimes eat octopuses and fish as well, and are often found over sand habitat. They have electro-receptors in their snout to help search for buried prey.
Predators: Tiger, bull, lemon, and hammerhead sharks

NURSE SHARK
GINGLYMOSTOMA CIRRATUM

72

Maximum size: 14ft (4.3m), 242lbs (110kg)
Longevity: Up to 25 years
Typical depth: 0–430ft (0–130m)
Behavior: Nurse sharks are large nocturnal reef predators. At night, they search for hard-shelled prey, such as lobsters, crabs, and conch, which they consume with their specially designed jaws. During the day, they are often found resting in caves or beneath coral overhangs.
Predators: Larger shark species

LONGSNOUT SEAHORSE 73

HIPPOCAMPUS REIDI

Maximum size: 7in (18cm) with tail outstretched
Longevity: Unknown, but probably at least 4 to 5 years
Typical depth: 10–180ft (3–55m)
Behavior: Seahorses are rare throughout the Caribbean. They prefer shallow reef areas. They are often seen clinging to seagrass, macroalgae, gorgonians and sponges with their prehensile tails, while they feed on zooplankton, mysid shrimp, and small crustaceans.
Predators: Rays, turtles, and crabs

PEDERSON CLEANER SHRIMP 74

ANCYLOMENES PEDERSONI

Maximum size: 1in (3cm)
Longevity: Unknown
Typical depth: 3–115ft (1–35m)
Behavior: Pederson cleaner shrimp pick parasites off reef fish. They are found in close association with sea anemones, which help advertise the shrimp's cleaning services and provide shelter. The anemone's stinging tentacles ward off predators but do not sting its resident cleaner shrimp, which can number up to a dozen.
Predators: Unknown

YELLOWLINE ARROW CRAB

STENORHYNCHUS SETICORNIS

Maximum size: 2in (6cm)
Longevity: Around 5 years
Typical depth: 10–130ft (3–40m)
Behavior: Yellowline arrow crabs are small spider-like creatures with triangular bodies and small purple claws. They are often found inside tube sponges, and among the tentacles of anemones and spines of sea urchins. At night, they forage for algae, detritus, tube worms, and bristleworms.
Predators: Grouper, puffers, triggerfish, wrasses, and grunts

CARIBBEAN SPINY LOBSTER

PANULIRUS ARGUS

Maximum size: 18in (45cm)
Longevity: Around 20 years
Typical depth: 0–295ft (0–90m)
Behavior: Caribbean spiny lobsters like to hide in reef caves and crevices during the day. At night, they roam the reef searching for snails, clams, crabs, and dead and decaying organisms to eat. They undergo seasonal mass migrations in the fall, marching in single file toward deeper water.
Predators: Sharks, stingrays, grouper, triggerfish, and moray eels

CARIBBEAN REEF OCTOPUS 77
OCTOPUS BRIAREUS

Maximum size: 39in (1m) with arms spread, 3 lbs (1.5kg)
Longevity: Less than 2 years
Typical depth: 13–82ft (4–25m)
Behavior: Caribbean reef octopuses like to hide in reef caves and crevices during the day. They are masters of camouflage and incredibly hard to spot, since they can change their color, texture, and shape. They are most active at night, hunting for crustaceans, clams, snails, and small fish.
Predators: Grouper, snapper, nurse sharks, and moray eels

CARIBBEAN REEF SQUID 78
SEPIOTEUTHIS SEPIOIDEA

Maximum size: 8in (20cm)
Longevity: Around 1 year
Typical depth: 0–98ft (0–30m)
Behavior: Caribbean reef squid are often found in small schools. They capture food in their 10 arms, feeding mainly on small fishes, as well as crustaceans and other molluscs. They have the largest eyes relative to body size of any animal, and they track their food by sight.
Predators: Grouper, snapper, and barracuda

FLAMINGO TONGUE
CYPHOMA GIBBOSUM

Maximum size: 2in (4cm)
Longevity: Unknown, but likely 2 years
Typical depth: 6–45ft (2–14m)
Behavior: Flamingo tongues are a reef gastropod (marine snail) almost always found feeding on sea fans, sea whips, and other gorgonians. The flesh of the gorgonians they eat contains toxic chemicals that the flamingo tongue converts into its own predator-deterring toxins.
Predators: Hogfish

QUEEN CONCH
STROMBUS GIGAS

Maximum size: 12in (30cm)
Longevity: Up to 30 years
Typical depth: 3–98ft (1–30m)
Behavior: Queen conch are the world's largest marine snail. They are found mainly on sandy reef areas and seagrass beds, where they graze on algae and detritus. They are most active at night, and when threatened, can retreat into their shells for protection.
Predators: Nurse sharks, spotted eagle rays, and sting-rays

GIANT ANEMONE 81
CONDYLACTIS GIGANTEA

Maximum size: 12in (30cm)
Longevity: Around 75 years
Typical depth: 3–82ft (1–25m)
Behavior: Giant anemones come in a variety of colors, from white to dark brown, sometimes with pink or purple-tipped tentacles. Some individuals have stinging tentacles that they use to paralyze and capture fish, shrimp, and worms. Anemones typically attach to the reef, but are also capable of crawling.
Predators: Hermit crabs, snails, and sea slugs

STAGHORN CORAL 82
ACROPORA CERVICORNIS

Maximum size: 8ft (2.5m)
Longevity: Individual polyps live 2–3 yrs but colonies can live for centuries
Typical depth: 3–164ft (1–50m)
Behavior: Staghorn corals are usually found in calm back reef areas with clear water. They provide important habitat for a range of different coral reef organisms. The coral polyps feed at night while the zooxanthellae in their tissue photosynthesize during the day. Staghorn coral is the fastest growing coral species in the Western Atlantic.
Predators: Some worm and snail species. The biggest threat is from disease.

ELKHORN CORAL 83
ACROPORA PALMATA

Maximum size: 12ft (3.5m)
Longevity: Individual polyps live 2–3yrs but colonies can live for centuries
Typical depth: 3–65ft (1–20m)
Behavior: Elkhorn corals are an important reef-building coral species, producing many large branches that coral reef organisms use as habitat. Elkhorn coral is often found in areas of moderate to high current and wave action. The coral polyps feed at night while the zooxanthellae in their tissue photosynthesize during the day.
Predators: Some worm and snail species. The biggest threat is from disease.

ORANGE ELEPHANT EAR SPONGE 84
AGELAS CLATHRODES

Maximum size: 6ft (1.8m)
Longevity: 2,000 years or more
Typical depth: 35–130ft (12–40m)
Behavior: Named for their resemblance to the ear of an elephant, these large sponges are easily spotted in deeper waters on the reef thanks to their bright coloration and large size. It can take different forms, including a thick encrusting form, or lobed and/or ridged forms. Like other sponges, they feed by filtering food particles from the surrounding water.
Predators: Sea turtles, crabs, parrotfish, slugs, and many other sea creatures

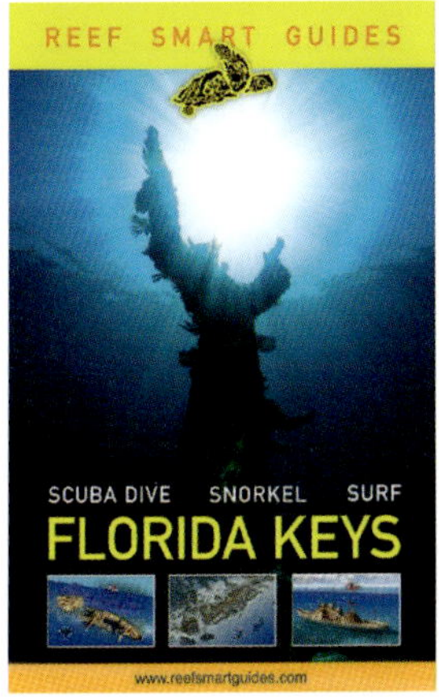

Check out Reef Smart Guides' growing line of regional dive and snorkel guidebooks. For an up-to-date list of locations, visit **Reefsmartguides.com**

Index of Sites

18th Palm 148
1000 Steps 86

A

Alice in Wonderland 184
Andrea I 106
Andrea II 104
Angel City 180
Aquarius 188
Atlantis 220

B

Baby Beach 248
Bachelor's Beach 158
Baka di Laman II 137
Barcadera 102
Barge 101 114
Bari 132
Bari Reef 132
Barkadera 102
Bisé Morto 46
Bloodlet 76
Boca Onima 248
Boka Bartól 38
Boka di Tota 75
Boka Katuna 40
Boka Slagbaai 50
Bon Bini Na Kas 84
Buddy's Reef 128

C

Cai 245
Calabas Reef 146
Candyland 64
Carel's Vision 58
Chez Hines 162
Chogogo 236
The Cliff 120
Coopers Barge 114
Corporal Meiss 156
Country Garden 82
Country Gardens 83

D

Delfins 164
Doblet 56

E

Eden's Rubble 136

F

Fish Hut 222
Fondu di Kalki 159
Front Porch 136
Funchi's Reef 246

H

Hidden Beach 232
Hilma Hooker 174

I

Invisibles 202

J

Jeannie's Glory 192
Jeff Davis Memorial 92

K

Kabayé 208
Kalabas Reef 147
Kalli's Reef 96
Karpata 68

L

La Dania's Leap 72
La Machaca 124
Larry's Lair 190
Lighthouse Point 164

M

Marcultura 248
Margate Bay 214
Mushroom City 83

N

New York 137
North Belnem 157
Nukove 56

O

Oil Slick Leap 98
Ol' Blue 78
Onima 248

P

Pali Grande 142
Petrie's Pillar 108
Pink Beach 208
Playa Bengé 42
Playa Frans 54
Playa Funchi 44
Punt P'Abou 278
Punt Vierkant 168

R

Rappel 74
Red Beryl 218
Red Slave 238
Reef Scientifico 128

Salt City 198
Salt Pier 194
Sea Cow 137
Sea Turtle Highway 246
Sebastians Reef 146
Shrimp Factory 248
Small Wall 110
Soft Coral Garden 230
Something Special 142
South Belnem 163
Sweet Dreams 228

T

Tailor Made 60
The Lake 170
Tolo 78
Tori's Reef 206
Town Pier 31
Turtle City 246

V

Vista Blue 224

W

Wanda 212
Wayaká II 48
Weber's Joy 90
White Hole 246
White Slave 210
Willemstoren Lighthouse 242
Willy Bakanal 137
Windjammer 66
Windsock 152
Witches Hut 91

Y

Yellow Hut 234

Klein Bonaire

Bonaventure 253
Bonheur de Betsy 253
Captain Don's Reef 254
Carl's Hill 278
Carl's Hill Annex 256
Divi Tree 253
Ebo's Reef 252
Ebo's Special 256
Forest 274
Hands Off 270
Jerry's Jam 256
Jerry's Reef 258
Jerry's Sponges 258
Joanna's Revenge 256
Joanne's Sunchi 254
Just a Nice Dive 252
Keepsake 262
Knife 282
Leonora's Reef 257
Mi Dushi 256
Monte's Divi 253
Monte's Divi Tree 253
Munk's Haven 255
Nearest Point 252
No Name 252
No Name Beach 252
Piedra Kolet 252
Playita 252
Rock Pile 253
Sampler 257
South Bay 266
Southwest Corner 255
Twixt 255
Valerie's Hill 256
Valerie's Hills 256
Yellow Man 256

Ian POPPLE

ian@reefsmartguides.com

Born and raised in the U.K., Ian earned his undergraduate degree in oceanography from the University of Plymouth in 1994. He worked for five years at Bellairs Research Institute in Barbados, supporting research projects across the region, before completing his master's in marine biology at McGill University in 2004. He co-founded a marine biology education company, Beautiful Oceans, before founding Reef Smart in 201 raise awareness and encourage people to explo the underwater world. Ian has published in bot the scientific and mainstream media, includin *National Geographic, Scuba Diver Magazine* ar *The Globe and Mail*. He is a PADI Dive Master wi over 3,000 dives in 30 years of diving experien

Otto WAGNER

otto@reefsmartguides.com

Born and raised in Romania, Otto graduated from the University of Art and Design in Cluj, Romania, in 1991. He moved to Canada in 1999, where he studied film animation at Concordia University in Montreal. In 2006, Otto turned to underwater cartography and pioneered new techniques in 3D visual mapping. He co-founded Art to Media and began mapping underwater habitats around the world. Throughout his 25-year career, Otto has received numerous awards and international recognition for his work, including the Prize of Excellence in Design from the Salon International du Design de Montréal. He has also illustrated seven books. Otto is a PADI Advanced Diver with over 500 dives in 20 years of diving experience.

Peter McDOUGALL

peter@reefsmartguides.com

Born and raised in Canada, Peter received his undergraduate and master's degrees from McGill University. His focus on behavioral ecology and coral reef ecology led him to two field seasons at Bellairs Research Institute in Barbados, in 1999 and again in 2002. After graduating in 2003, Peter moved to the United States and began a career in science communication and writing, publishing in both peer-reviewed academic journals and the popular press. He has written on a variety of coastal ecosystem issues, including extensive work surrounding the science of ocean acidification. He is a PADI Rescue Diver with over 500 dives in 25 years of experience.